An
End to Silence

THE SAN FRANCISCO STATE COLLEGE

STUDENT MOVEMENT IN THE '60s

BY WILLIAM BARLOW

AND PETER SHAPIRO

PEGASUS

NEW YORK

A Division of The Bobbs-Merrill Company, Inc., Publishers

Library of Congress Catalog Card Number 79-124675
First Printing

Dedicated to the "S. F. State 700,"
all of whom were arrested and prosecuted
for their participation in the student strike.

Contents

Acknowledgments

Foremost among those who helped this manuscript along its way were the people who lived it; many of them spoke with us at length, and we have tried, in the list of sources at the back of the book, to give their names in the appropriate places. We would like to reserve special mention for Robert Smith of the San Francisco State School of Education, who was gracious enough to submit to an interview and speak with candor. For reading over our work and offering extensive criticisms, we are grateful to Claire Salop, Elmer Cooper, Donna Mikkleson, Fred Thalheimer, Eric Solomon, Del Sonsten, and especially Jim Nixon.

Thanks of a different order go to Robert Quagliata, Nancy Conzett, Phil and Fran Shapiro, Larry Davis, Joe Barndt, and Nick and Marilyn Nicholsen.

Our special thanks to Lucille Birnbaum and Anatole Anton. The former's generosity and kindness in a time of crisis was as helpful to us as her trenchant criticisms of our work; the latter is, more than any other single individual, responsible for the ideological direction this book has taken. In making us and thousands of other San Francisco State students aware of the economic issues of the strike, Anatole Anton added a new dimension to our conception of the struggle.

The authors and the publisher wish to thank the following for permission to reprint:

From "A Conceptual Proposal for Black Studies" and "Reply to John Bunzel" by Nathan Hare; reprinted with permission of Nathan Hare.

From C.I.P. and Tutorial Program files, Associated Students of San Francisco State College; reprinted with permission of Connell J. Persico.

From back issues, 1961–1968, of *The Daily Gater*, reprinted with the permission of Peter Shapiro for *The Daily Gater*; copyright © 1970 by *The Daily Gater*.

From a statement to the U.S. Commission of Causes and Prevention of Violence: "Central to the Problem of Violence on Campus," and the press conference of November 30, 1968; reprinted with permission of S. I. Hayakawa.

From "Engineer Education in California," published by the Coordinating Council for Higher Education in March 1968; reprinted with permission of Horace F. Crandell.

Introduction

San Francisco State College is a domestic Vietnam"—so said Ronald Reagan, the Governor of California, at the height of the bitter student strike which was to paralyze that institution for five months. The Governor's penchant for overstatement is well-known even outside his home state, but there is, in this case, a germ of truth to his words. Of course, the parallel cannot be taken literally; even when it is under continual police occupation for weeks on end, a college campus is not a theater of war. Police used their guns at S.F. State, but no one was actually shot; bombs were planted, but for purposes of destroying property rather than inflicting casualties; hundreds were arrested and there were countless injuries, but no one died of his wounds—though a few came perilously close. Striking students spoke of a "protracted struggle," and their struggle outlasted any previous uprising on an American campus; but the Vietnamese people have been fighting American intervention since 1956, and the modern phase of their national liberation struggle goes back before the end of the last century.

It is only when we begin to think in historical terms that the cogency of the Governor's parallel becomes clear. Barely ten years old, the American student movement has reached a critical turning point: no longer the half-articulated expression of vague generational discontents, endlessly pontificated upon by academic pundits, it has located its target and attacked it head-on. Launched on November 6, 1968 by the Third World Liberation

Front on the campus, the San Francisco State Strike began as a series of demands which projected the educational needs of the various non-white communities of the Bay Area. Each aspect of the institutionalized violence those communities had suffered at the hands of the college was touched upon: its willful distortion of their culture and history; its having closed its doors to all but a handful of their youth; its attempts to turn that handful into apologists while channeling the rest towards lives of unemployment and menial employment. As the strike progressed, it inevitably developed into an attack on the whole direction which mass higher education in California had taken in the past ten years, because it became increasingly clear that the TWLF was not simply taking San Francisco State to task for its various sins, general or specific; it was proposing an alternative philosophy of education.

Mass public higher education in California had come of age in 1960 with the adoption of the Master Plan for Higher Education, a document whose national significance can be gauged by the number of states (most notably New York) which imitated it. The Master Plan was the first systematic attempt to define the relationship between the state's public colleges and the vocational needs of private industry. As such, it took on the burden of keeping the college-educated labor supply closely attuned to the demands of industry, of regulating the flow of high school graduates into the job market, of assuring that the appropriate number of students was channeled towards each of the various levels of the employment pyramid. Private industry would thus enjoy a taxpayers' subsidy of its job training costs; meanwhile the public colleges and universities, manipulating the lives and future opportunities of thousands of young people, would evolve more and more into institutions of social control, their increased stratification giving lie to the egalitarian ethic which was supposedly the basis for mass public education.

All this has had a profoundly disillusioning and dehumanizing effect on the lot of the individual student caught up within the system. The central feature of his education consists of seeing himself reduced to a commodity; the final direction his education takes is determined ultimately by its degree of profitability to

those to whom he will eventually sell his labor. Once the very
elitism of the higher education system made it irrelevant to the
mainstream of American life: while providing evidence of the
existence of class barriers, it did not actually aid in perpetuating
those barriers. Today, though it has technically "opened its
doors" to a fairly broad spectrum of the population, the university is more than ever devoted to what Nathan Hare calls "the
principle of exclusion"—no longer as a simple exercise in snobbery, but as a requisite of its commitment to corporate capitalism. An elaborate system of hierarchies governs the professorial
job market, the institutional standards for selection and retention
of students, the very "learning process" which goes on inside a
classroom, where a professor's authority is derived more from his
power to parcel out grades than from his knowledge of subject
matter. Competition and privilege are cornerstones of the system,
and each is used to reinforce the other: for each student who is
awarded a "A," there is another who is expected to fail, and students who are at a disadvantage, academically or economically,
are inevitably shunted off to institutions where budgetary resources are scanty, classes are overcrowded, and the atmosphere
is brutally mechanized and degrading. Even the privileged student, however, is likely to find his education to be an essentially
take-it-or-leave-it proposition. Everything has been decided in
advance: curriculum, methods of teaching and learning, the ethi-
cal and ideological assumptions implicit in the course material.
He is expected to absorb passively a body of information which is
deliberately presented in such an arbitrary, rigid, compartmentalized fashion as to destroy any meaningful relationship it may
have to his own life or his own experience. He accepts the institution on its own terms, or pays the price by flunking out or
dropping out.

The total failure of the established curricula to deal with the
experience of black people in this country is the logical outgrowth of this process, and is more than a little responsible for
the difficulty black students often have in meeting the standards
of "academic excellence" which the institution sets for itself. The
more stringent these standards, the fewer concessions are made
to the student's humanity: he is, like the worker on the assembly

line, engaged in alienated labor, with nothing to say about the orientation or purpose of his work and, consequently, no real stake in its outcome. In recompense for his having performed tasks that are not intrinsically in his own interest, he is given grades and diplomas instead of wages, but the distinction is a fine one—as everyone knows, academic capital is quite literally money in the bank. The "learning process" which operates according to the capitalist mode of production simply underlines the university's basic commitment to the capitalist ideology, all claims to academic neutrality notwithstanding. In the face of that commitment, the student is left with very little room in which to function, either in terms of personal growth or of developing that faculty of independent critical judgement, towards himself and his environment, which academics purport to hold in such high regard. Meticulously programmed through the initial stages of the educational process, he comes to academia well conditioned to continue in his role as adolescent, sycophant, and chump. He can act out his social prowess in a fraternity or his social conscience in a student government sandbox, but nowhere is he allowed to establish a maturity based on equality and independence—except in revolt. For maturity in America means authority over others.

It is because we see the S.F. State strike as part and parcel of a much longer struggle against conditions such as these that we have chosen to begin our account of it in 1960 rather than 1968. There are, in this book, two sets of dynamics at work—one operates from the top down, the other from the bottom up. The first traces the deterioration of California's public colleges under the Master Plan; the second attempts to show how students on one campus, undergoing a highly representative experience, reacted to the brand of education the Master Plan had instituted, worked towards an educational alternative, and experimented with political forms that were emulated by activists at other schools. Where the two processes intersected, an open conflict could no longer be averted; the college authorities could no longer pretend that the established priorities of the system were compatible with the programs and philosophies of the students. Our understanding of the relationship between these two processes is far from complete, and we hope the reader will bear with us if it occasionally seems as if we have written two separate books and grafted one onto the other. We are convinced that a relationship does exist, and would cite as evidence of its existence the strike and the conditions which provoked it. We are equally convinced that a serious effort must be made to define that relationship, to analyze it, to comprehend it as fully as possible before an understanding of the phenomenon of "campus unrest" can be reached.

Finally, lest there be any questions about our "objectivity": both of us were deeply involved in the strike; the latter two-thirds of this book are drawn heavily from personal experience. It was while we were writing strike propaganda for the student newspaper, *Open Process*, that we first conceived of the book; after the paper was successfully suppressed by Dr. Hayakawa, we continued to do research into the underlying issues of the strike—once again, for propaganda purposes—and became convinced that the material we were uncovering had a significance well beyond our own campus. We do not think any of this reflects adversely upon either the accuracy of our observations or our ability to assess what we have observed. The best history is often written by those who have lived it. Categorically, they are neither more nor less capable of mastering their biases than professional historians; to their credit, their knowledge is first-hand, they feel about what they are writing, and their biases and vested interests are not concealed behind that pretense of objectivity and "neutrality" which is so much a part of the academic mystique. Ignorance is the only true basis for neutrality in certain matters; for those who know better, to remain neutral about the issues discussed herein is to abdicate to the powers that be with respect to one of the most important questions facing American society: whether its educational institutions will continue to serve a corporate elite, or whether they will serve the people; whether they will continue to oppress human beings or whether they will help to set them free.

January 1, 1970
W. B.
P. S.

CHAPTER I

Educating the War Babies:

THE POLITICAL ECONOMY

OF HIGHER EDUCATION IN CALIFORNIA,

1947-1960

In his Ph.D. thesis at the University of Chicago in 1958, Nathan Hare, the black sociologist who was to become chairman of the first Black Studies Department on an American campus, made some pointed observations about the changing character of American higher education. Citing Thorstein Veblen, Hare observed that higher education had traditionally been the near-exclusive province of a leisure class, for whom it served as a kind of social-cultural fetish. Veblen had defined the function of the university in terms of the eternal desire of gentlemen to distinguish themselves from the "lower classes" by means of time-wasting and nonproductive endeavor. Out of that function came the old notion of "liberal education," with its emphasis on "leadership training" and its careful preparation for the privileges and responsibilities of citizenship. With the advent of the postwar, technological, consumer-oriented "affluent society," Hare noted, the rising aspirations of the middle classes created in them a desire to emulate the old leisure class life-style. Higher education thus came to be seen as a social escalator, a way of acquiring that status of full citizenship which had previously been denied to all but a privileged few. That concept has come to be accepted by every segment of the population, and today, when a minority youth tries to make it out of the ghetto, he is told constantly, "To get a good job, get a good education."

What the educational system seems to promise is one thing, however; what it is actually able to provide is something else entirely. As early as 1947, a conflict was beginning to develop within California's system of public higher education which would severely plague the state's campuses some twenty years later. The conflict was one of priorities: on the one hand, college education was being posed as a passport across race and class lines in a society where race and class lines have remained intractable for all but a small percentage of the population; on the other hand, the state was in no position to sink millions of dollars into a system of mass public higher education unless it would produce tangible benefits for the dominant economic and political institutions in the state. The student strike at San Francisco State College, which lasted from November 1968 through March 1969, was not another manifestation of the "generation gap" or "irrational student protest"; rather, California was simply reaping the harvest of a conflict in educational priorities whose seeds had been planted twenty years before.

SOURCES OF THE CONFLICT

Public higher education in California goes back to 1865 and the passage of the Morrill Act, which made federal land available to the individual states for the purpose of starting public colleges and universities. Six years later the University of California at Berkeley was founded, a "land grant" college in a state which was still very much a part of the American frontier. Unlike the Eastern states, California had no private schools of comparable quality to its major public one, and there was never any question of whom the fledgling Berkeley campus was supposed to serve. A host of *de facto* social barriers prevented all but the children of the well-to-do from attending. The university quickly developed ties with California agribusiness which have lasted well into the present century: as recently as 1964, the U.C. Department of Agricultural Economics was grinding out propaganda tracts for the growers, urging extension of the notorious bracero program and debunking the problems of California's migrant farm laborers. In his book, *The Goose-step: A Study of American Higher Education,* Upton Sinclair devoted several chapters to the University of California which revealed, among other things, the following eerie precedent to the concept of "academic credit for community work," developed by student activists at San Francisco State in the mid-1960's (see Chapter III): "In 1913," wrote Sinclair, "there was a gas and electric strike; the president of the gas company, a member of the U.C. Board of Regents, called on his university for help, and the boys from the engineering department were given a full semester's credit for their service as 'scabs'."

During the 1920's the state capitol in Sacramento fell into the hands of the Progressives; as a part of their campaign to attract industry to the state, the scope of its public higher education system was significantly broadened. It was reasoned that California's industrial growth would require a large skilled work force as well as an atmosphere congenial to developing technology. Accordingly, a system of public junior colleges, whose stated purpose was to provide, tuition-free, two years of "terminal and vocational training" beyond the high school level to all who sought it, was established up and down the state. The Depression prevented the Progressives' aims from achieving immediate fruition, but World War II and the Pacific theater brought the defense industries to the state, and they continued to expand after Hiroshima and the establishment of a permanent wartime economy. Widespread government spending—for schools, colleges, welfare bureaucracies, but mainly for "national defense"—was supposed to insure continued prosperity and lend a measure of stability to an economy whose underlying tenuousness had been dramatized by the Depression. During the war thousands of Southern black, "Okies" and other poor whites, and Mexican-Americans from the Southwest states had migrated to California to work in the defense plants and naval shipyards; the threat of a renewed unemployment crisis in peacetime was staved off by the passage of the GI Bill of Rights, which institutionalized the notion that a good way to keep people off the job market is to keep them in school. Lavish federal contracts for defense research buttressed the income of the University of California and turned a relatively ob-

scure private school, Stanford University, into an academic power-
house, the self-styled "Harvard of the West."

By 1947 California's junior college system had grown to include fifty-five campuses with a combined enrollment of 61,000
students. But the general public, which supported them through
local property taxes administered by local school districts, was
becoming less and less satisfied with them. As the statewide association of junior colleges noted that same year, there was a growing public attitude "which hold[s] preparation for more advanced
college work to be the foremost principle of any school below the
college or university level. This attitude is based on social convention which identifies higher education with the professions and
white-collar jobs." Actually there was more to it than "social
convention"; parents knew as a matter of hard economic fact
that to subject their children to nothing more than two more
years of vocational training was to deprive them of a valuable
opportunity for higher salaries and successful careers. The University of California, which was educating 43,000 students at its
various campuses, had most of the prestige, status, "academic
excellence," and relative sovereignty of an elite Eastern school.
But it also had stiff entrance requirements which barred all but
the top fifteen per cent of the state's graduating high school seniors.

California's eight state colleges, loosely governed by the State
Board of Education and the State Superintendent of Public Instruction, represented a more likely alternative. These were far
easier to get into, and though they were primarily teacher training institutions they had, since 1923, been authorized to grant
bachelor's degrees. Most taxpayers saw no reason to support the
junior colleges with their local property taxes when the added
benefits of a four-year liberal arts curriculum could be made
available, at state expense, through the state college system. With
a combined enrollment of 19,000, the state colleges were so dispersed throughout the state as to make it impossible for large
numbers of students who could not afford to leave home to attend them. Accordingly, a number of local communities began
demanding that their local junior colleges be expanded to include
a four-year curriculum and that the state take on the burden of

financing them as it did the other state colleges; some communities were even demanding graduate instruction as well. The clamor became so great that the Liaison Committee of the University of California Board of Regents and the State Board of Education was obliged to issue a report denying the need for such expansion. *A Study of the Needs of Public Higher Education in California* (Strayer Report), released in 1947, advocated a policy of containment as far as the junior colleges were concerned. Though it was full of complex academic rationales to support that policy, the most cogent reason—mentioned almost parenthetically—was money: "The financial burden on the state would be overwhelming if it had to support fifty-five new institutions offering the third and fourth year of college . . . in addition to existing state-supported facilities."

The Strayer Report did not go into any details about the question of state finance, apparently being of the opinion that nothing could be done about it. Actually, it was not that the resources were not there; on the contrary, even then California had *potentially* one of the largest tax bases in the nation. But, as with most states, its tax structure is far too regressive to support real mass public higher education, except for the piecemeal two-year variety offered by the junior colleges. For all practical purposes, business and industry have never shouldered more than twenty per cent of the general tax burden; in the year 1968, banking and corporate taxes provided the state with only twelve per cent of its total income. Standard Oil of California pays no state taxes at all. The three biggest companies in the state's largest industry, agribusiness, pay no more than $50,000 a year. The retail sales, alcoholic beverages, motor vehicle, and gasoline taxes which make up fifty-five per cent of the state's general fund come largely from family income groups of under $10,000 a year; owing to the way business and industry shift their part of the burden onto the consumer, the sales taxes particularly tend to hit the poor hardest. The only truly progressive tax in the state is personal income, which accounts for twenty per cent of the general tax burden; even here, the "taxable income" of the very wealthy is never more than a tiny fraction of their total income. What it adds up to is a typically American dilemma: the group which controls the bulk of the state's wealth is the one group exempt from equitable taxation, forcing the state to tax those least able to pay.

For reasons that had nothing to do with philanthrophy, this very group—the corporate elite—had begun to take an intense interest of its own in the plight of higher education in the state in the early 1950's. The phenomenal industrial growth (largely centered around aerospace, electronics, and other defense-related industries) had created for private enterprise some exorbitant new expenses, among them a need to maintain a ready supply of skilled workers, elaborate facilities for research and development, and a small, highly-trained "technological elite" to operate those facilities. Naturally, the corporations were eager to see all three expenses borne by California's taxpayers, a goal which was in effect adopted as public policy in 1955, when the Liaison Committee released its sequel to the Strayer Report, the *Restudy of the Needs of Public Higher Education in California.* By introducing the concept of "differentiation of functions," which assigned specific roles to each of the three "segments" of public higher education, the *Restudy* proceeded to redefine completely the state's public colleges along lines dictated by the vocational needs of private industry. The junior colleges, said the report, were to engage in "technical training," the state colleges in "occupational training," the University of California in "professional training." The criteria were established for maintaining the proper relationship between the three, as follows:

> Industrial-technological economy requires more workers at a technical than a professional level. In the field of engineering, for example, estimates have ranged from six technicians for every professional engineer to as high as sixteen to one. In an expanding state economy, where the growth potential is much higher than for the average for the United States as a whole, technical personnel will be in increasing demand.

Accordingly, the principal concern of the *Restudy* was to maintain a large, smoothly-functioning junior college system which would assure that industry would never be at a loss for trained technicians.

Several obstacles stood in the way of this enterprising goal, the most notable of which was the existence of the state colleges. With both college enrollments and state population steadily on the increase, and the average middle-class parent totally enamored of the benefits of a liberal education, the state colleges were emerging from the relative obscurity of their traditional normal school status into a promising social escalator for at least half of the state's aspiring college students. Few could get by the prohibitive entrance requirements of the University of California, but nearly all high school graduates who were interested in going to college at all qualified for the state colleges. Given a choice between them and the junior colleges, most students were loath to choose the latter. With considerable alarm, the *Restudy* noted that where a given community had both a state college and a junior college in its midst, the junior college didn't stand a chance of attracting either students or community support. Clearly, this unequal competition had to be eliminated; hence, the *Restudy's* major recommendation: that no new state colleges be built before 1965, and that increasing enrollments be accommodated through expansion of existing institutions.

The logic of the recommendation seemed plain enough: There would be a large number of students who would not, for financial or other reasons, be able to leave home in order to attend college. A few carefully placed state college campuses would allow for the free development of junior colleges in the vast majority of communities where no other facilities existed, thereby insuring the proper balance between "technical training" and "professional and occupational training." But the scheme had one flaw: The *Restudy* had based its enrollment projections on figures which, computed in 1953, had already become outdated by the time the report was actually published. That same year, the growth rate of college enrollments took a sharp turn upward as a flood of servicemen, returning from Korea, entered school under the GI Bill. By 1957, when the wave of GI's had more or less subsided, the war babies were just reaching college age, and a new wave of entering freshmen pushed enrollment figures even higher. Where the *Restudy* had projected an enrollment increase of 38 per cent between 1953 and 1958, the actual increase was nearly twice that much; in the period between 1958 and 1975, the total college enrollments in California were expected to triple. There are limits to the number of students who can be accommodated simply through the expansion of existing plants, even under ideal conditions—and conditions were far from ideal. As early as 1956, there were requests for no fewer than nineteen new state college campuses before the state legislature, and individual legislators were beginning to feel the pressure from their local communities. They therefore rejected the recommendations for a freeze on the construction of new state colleges as unrealistic, and in 1958 the legislature allocated a record $82.1 million for the construction of new state college facilities. This figure accounted for one-third of the state's total expenditures for higher education in 1958, and two-thirds of the entire state college budget.

The *Restudy's* faulty enrollment projections were only part of the problem, however, for its cost estimates were even more inaccurate. The concluding section on cost analysis had declared, "in order to provide for higher education in 1965, at a cost level comparable to 1954, $226,974,000 will be required." Assuming that the 1954 level would not be totally adequate for 1965, the authors of the *Restudy* upped the figure to an estimated $293 million. By 1957, however, the actual costs of higher education in California had reached $276 million, and by 1960 they were to increase in excess of $300 million. The *Restudy's* ten-year cost projections had been surpassed in a period of five years!

Exploding enrollments were not solely responsible for this phenomenal increase in costs. Other factors stemmed from inflation and from the college's efforts to reorient themselves in order to meet the needs of industrial technology. The increased emphasis on research proved to be an exorbitant expense, even with generous federal and corporate funding; so did the emphasis on the more expensive curricula in such fields as science and engineering. As the fiscal situation grew bleaker, the growing competition between the state colleges and the junior colleges for students and community support was complemented by a new competition between the state colleges and the university for state and federal funding. Between 1948 and 1958 state college enrollments had more than doubled, but their operating expenses had increased by nearly 800 per cent. Capital outlay costs for new state college campuses made it even harder for the University of California to get the financial support it needed from the state. Moreover, the expanded state colleges were broadening their curricular offerings and beginning to infringe upon such traditional U.C prerogatives as research and development, graduate instruction, and "professional training." The University of California was an established "federal grant university"; it owed much of its enormous prestige to the fact that it had always enjoyed a virtual monopoly in California on federal grants for services rendered in research for the Atomic Energy Commission and the Defense Department. The state colleges had everything to gain, the University much to lose if a serious competition between the two was allowed to develop. In any case, the failure of the *Restudy* to resolve dilemmas such as this was apparent to all. For want of an efficient means of enforcement, its concept of "differentiation of function" was proving completely inoperable. For want of a way to finance its skyrocketing costs, the notion of publicly subsidizing private industry's job training and research expenses was threatening to pauperize the state.

THE MASTER PLAN

The full impact of the crisis was not lost on the state legislature, which felt it most directly through the continual clamor for new campuses and the nagging shortage of state funds. At the beginning of its 1959 session, the state assembly passed Concurrent Resolution 88, authorizing the Liaison Committee to draw up a "master plan for higher education in California, 1960–1975." The legislature's primary concerns were to eliminate the "unhealthy competition" between the various segments of public higher education and to impose a system of checks upon its "unwarranted expansion," while still maintaining at least the facade of a commitment to provide the opportunity for a state-supported education to all "qualified young people." Given the economic structure of the state and the direction mass higher education seemed to be taking, it appeared as though the Liaison Committee was being asked to reconcile two diametrically opposing trends. On the one hand, it had to overhaul the existing system in order for it to meet the corporate needs of the state in a more efficient manner; on the other hand, it had to display some semblance of concern for the public interest by providing for higher education on a mass, even universal basis.

The conflicting interests of the various segments seemed even more irreconcilable. At stake for the junior colleges was the matter of simple survival; competition from the state colleges was forcing them out of business, and their total enrollments were beginning to contain a smaller and smaller proportion of the state's lower division college students. The university was, to quote the Master Plan Survey Team, "concerned lest changes undermine its standards for graduate and professional education and jeopardize its premier role in advanced training and research." The state colleges were vying for official recognition as non-technical, liberal arts institutions, with a degree of increased prestige sufficient to put them on par with the university. They envisioned the latter end as attainable if the responsibility for their governance was taken out of the hands of the State Board of Education and placed under the centralized authority of a body appointed for terms of sixteen years. Complying with that request became one of the Survey Team's first official acts: a state college Board of Trustees was created with some of the prerogatives and most of the autonomy of the Regents.

The second recommendation to be listed in the Master Plan was of far more significance: "By 1975, 50,000 of the lower division students who will, according to our projections, be enrolled in the state colleges and the University of California should be accommodated in the junior colleges." Those 50,000 represented nearly half the students expected to enter the higher education system between 1960 and 1975. Diverting them was to be accomplished by jacking up the entrance requirements of the four-year schools so that the state colleges, previously open to between 50 per cent and 70 per cent of California's high school graduates, would now admit only the top 33 per cent of the graduating high school seniors, while U.C., previously ready to accommodate 15 per cent, was now closed to all but the top 12 per cent. All applicants to the four-year colleges would be required to take the Scholastic Aptitude Tests, which would determine their exact percentile rating according to a uniform national standard against which all students would be evaluated competitively.

Several reasons were given for diverting students into the junior colleges, which would, as always, remain open to all students who fulfilled the residence requirements. It would aid in controlling the "unmanageable size" of the state colleges and the university, while freeing them to concentrate more heavily on the upper division and graduate level work in which they were supposed to specialize. Junior colleges cost less generally, and they cost the state far less because they are financed chiefly by local taxes. Most significant, they could, while providing cheap, accessible education to all who sought it, simultaneously be utilized to reduce the number of students continuing within the higher education system as a whole. The Master Plan placed special emphasis on the "screening function" of the junior colleges: students were now forbidden to transfer out of them until they had completed their sophomore year, and an elaborate system of counseling and testing would in the meantime weed out "individuals who lack the capacity or the will to succeed in their studies."

The *Restudy* had failed to restrict the growth of the state colleges by freezing construction of new campus sites. The Master Plan found a new way, more efficient, less visible, and less risky politically. For most Americans, the gospel of academic standards, unbiased education, and objective truth is accepted unquestioningly; for many, it is a cherished ideal. If the State of California found it dangerous to state openly that it could not afford to educate *x* number of students, it could avoid doing so by invoking the gospel and claiming those students were not *qualified* to receive an education. The political and economic necessities of the state would thus be sanctioned with the blessings of academia.

Implicitly, the revision of state college and university entrance requirements and the redistribution of students throughout the three segments gave the *Restudy's* concept of "differentiation of function" a new lease on life; to enforce it, the Master Plan

Survey Team set up the Coordinating Council for Higher Education (CCHE). The original composition of the CCHE would have
included three representatives each from the respective administrations of the junior colleges, the state colleges, the university,
and the private institutions; later, when the Master Plan was
ratified by the state legislature, six gubernatorially appointed
representatives of the "general public" were added. The CCHE's
stated function was to advise the Governor, the legislature, the
Trustees, and the Regents with respect to three areas: review of
all budget and capital outlay requests of the various institutions,
interpretation of the "functional differentiation" between the
three segments, and planning generally for the "orderly growth
of higher education in California." An additional function, one not
spelled out in the Master Plan, was to serve as a buffer between
the individual institutions and the tax-paying public on the one
hand, and the state legislature on the other. Though the CCHE's
powers were theoretically advisory, in actual practice its "recommendations" would seldom if ever be overturned. A proposed
line-item budget for a particular institution could be presented by
the CCHE to the state legislators; the legislators, absolved of any
responsibility for having drawn it up, would simply vote it up or
down. A request for a new campus which the state could not
afford could be rejected on the grounds that it failed to comply
with the CCHE's overall scheme for the "orderly growth of
higher education" in the state. Most significant, private industry
could get pretty much what it wanted out of the colleges, since
plans for their development would be made by a sympathetic and
easily influenced body whose very *raison d'etre* gave it a blank
check to keep higher education carefully attuned to corporate
needs by regulating its operations and defining its orientation
and purpose.

The new, improved system of functional differentiation went a
long way toward eliminating the competition between the segments which had increased the cost and decreased the "vocational output" of the system of public colleges. The University of
California would specialize in graduate instruction and research,
giving it a virtual monopoly on federal and corporate grants. The
junior colleges, invested with primary responsibility for lower

division education, would engage in the screening and vocational tracking of students while reducing the operating costs of the system as a whole. The state colleges were now officially recognized to be the major institutions of undergraduate instruction, thus according them the bona fide liberal arts status they had sought so eagerly for so long. But in a larger sense the state colleges had been short-changed, for the prestige they sought to gain by placing themselves under the jurisdiction of an independent Board of Trustees was denied them when a sizeable portion of the Board's authority was preempted by the creation of the CCHE. It was no longer enough to have your own governing body; you now needed influence at the very top, and the academic hierarchy had just added another level of command.

Still, there were no indications as yet that any of the three segments had received a sufficient degree of preferential treatment to make it impossible for the other two to comply with the Master Plan's dictum that each segment "strive for excellence in its own sphere." And if the Master Plan did harbor any internal inconsistencies, they were easily overshadowed by the urgency of the situation it sought to address itself to, and by the immediate impact it promised to make in the area of state finances. Between 1948 and 1958, the cost of higher education in California had more than tripled, from 180 million to 554 million dollars, and by 1975 it would exceed $1 billion. The exorbitant capital outlay expenses for the new state college campuses had been a major factor in inflating costs to their 1958 level, and the state had paid for all of it. Shifting the enrollment burden over to the junior colleges eliminated this expense, at least as far as the State of California was concerned, and other operational expenses, cheaper at the junior college level, would be financed no more than 40 per cent by state funds. Moreover, U.C.'s clear field in the area of research meant uncontested access to as much as $200 million in federal grants by 1975, almost half its total instructional budget for that year. While it did not actually reduce the anticipated increase in the total cost of higher education over the next fifteen years, the Master Plan was willing to predict that the State of California would be paying for no more than $684 million by 1975, or less than two-thirds of the total cost. In so doing, it appeared to reverse the trend toward a higher education system financed almost entirely by the state.

Nevertheless, this did not prevent the Master Plan Survey Team from observing that the estimated cost of higher education to the state would begin to exceed projected state revenues available for it under "existing conditions" as early as 1961. If this bothered the members of the Survey Team, they gave no indication of the fact. It was suggested that higher taxes and bond issues for capital outlays could make up the difference—which was projected to be as much as $180 million by 1975. The Survey Team pointed out that California did not spend that much money on higher education when compared with other states; it ranked only twenty-fifth in the nation for average per cent of per capita state expenditures for public colleges. Given this, there seemed little doubt that the state was perfectly capable of increased generosity, and the concluding sentence of the Master Plan predicted loftily: "California can, and will . . . provide adequate support for an efficient program of public higher education to meet fully the rapidly changing needs of society."

Whatever its long-term consequences, the immediate benefits of the Master Plan were too good to pass up. It forestalled a crisis in college finance, resolved the difficulties engendered by the enrollment boom, restored the proper balance to the three segments, and rationalized the system as a whole with respect to the job market. It assured that the needs of the wealthiest and most powerful interest groups in the state would be attended to; at the same time, it gave taxpayers the impression that they were getting a good deal. More totally than ever, it made mass education a fixture in California by providing it with a degree of stability and a framework within which to operate. In 1960 the Master Plan was ratified, with minor changes, almost *in toto* by the state legislature; it was promptly hailed as a model system of public higher education and an example to the nation. Other states began formulating "master plans" of their own, and California prepared to enjoy the fruits of its own pioneering achievement.

CHAPTER II

An End to Silence:

THE ORIGINS OF THE
NEW LEFT IN CALIFORNIA,
1960-1964

THE HUAC DEMONSTRATIONS

The Master Plan was still before the state legislature in the spring of 1960 when the city of San Francisco learned, to its consternation, that it would again be expected to host the House Committee on Un-American Activities (HUAC). San Francisco had had unpleasant experiences with the congressional investigators in the past, but the hearings of May 12-14, 1960, were to prove unsettling beyond anyone's expectations. The three days climaxed on Friday the thirteenth with a harrowing and totally unprecedented scene: crowds of singing, chanting college students being drenched with high-pressure fire hoses and clubbed by police, dragged down the long flight of marble stairs of City Hall where the hearings were being held, and hauled away to jail.

Shocking as they may seem at first glance, the "City Hall riots" represent, in a larger sense, a particular kind of triumph: they have a historical significance which should far outlive the activities of the House Committee. Scholars have already begun to argue over precisely which event or which date can be affixed to the birth of the New Left in this country. Some cite the victory of the Cuban Revolution on January 1, 1959, which provided a new generation of radical youth with its inspiration; others point to the first sit-ins by Southern black students in February, 1960, which ushered in a new era of domestic resistance. A few would reach back to 1956 and the Montgomery bus boycott, which initiated the Civil Rights Movement.

As good a case might be made for May 13, 1960, at the San Francisco HUAC hearings. If we are to regard the white student movement as having an experience of its own—not merely as an adjunct of the black liberation struggle—then we must begin with the "City Hall riots," for it was there that white American, middle-class college students first made their presence felt.

While not as influential in 1960 as it had been at the height of the McCarthy era, the HUAC was still powerful enough to be destructive. In 1957, during one of its earlier visits to San Francisco, a Stanford University biologist named William Sherwood killed himself after being served with a subpoena, predicting in his suicide note that he would "within two days be assassinated by publicity" if forced to appear at a televised hearing. Many San Franciscans were profoundly disturbed by this incident, and when the Committee returned two years later with subpoenas for 108 Northern California school teachers, it aroused so much opposition that the hearings had to be cancelled. To be sure, the opposition was largely grounded in technicalities: since California had one of the most stringent systems of loyalty oaths in the nation, the proposed investigation was seen as a federal infringement on the prerogatives of the state government. Nevertheless, the Committee had suffered a significant defeat, and it vowed to return in 1960 to reestablish its influence.

The trouble began on Thursday, the first day of the proceedings, when a number of students also sought admission to the hearing room, partly to "see for themselves what was going on," and partly to break down that sense of isolation which made appearing before the Committee such an ordeal for its "unfriendly witnesses." Once inside, they applauded the witnesses' statements and snickered out loud when Committee Counsel Richard Arens asked informers questions like, "Within the framework of Communist operations, is there room for the concept of God and spiritual values as we were taught them at our mother's knee?" The Committee had issued 150 "white cards" to such groups as the Daughters of the American Revolution and other "friends of the Committee," which entitled the bearers to preferential admission to the hearing room. The cards were issued, according to HUAC investigator William Wheeler, "to keep the Commies from stacking the meeting. We wanted some decent people in there." Since the chambers could seat only 350 people and each white card could admit as many as six, the Committee was able to limit the number of students admitted to a handful. The others, appropriately enraged, began chanting, "Let us in!" and "Open the doors!" The cry was taken up inside the chambers, and at least one witness who joined in was roughly ejected by police in full view of the TV cameras.

No demonstration had been planned for Friday, but an even bigger crowd gathered in response to the previous day's events, and tension ran high as students were once again excluded from the chambers. At one point during the noon recess the students were promised that the "white card" policy would be abandoned and they would be admitted to the afternoon session on a first-come, first-served basis. The police disregarded this promise when the hearing resumed, however, and the outraged students again began to sing and chant, louder than before. The singing turned to startled shrieks when police, without warning, turned the high-pressure fire hoses on the crowd. Recovering from the shock, the students sat down on the floor and linked arms, facing directly into the stream of water. The hoses were then turned off and the police waded into the crowd swinging their nightsticks. Before the fracas had subsided, a number of students had been bloodied, some required hospitalization, and a total of sixty-four were arrested.

The "City Hall riots" had an immediate impact. J. Edgar Hoover said they were "the most successful Communist coup in twenty-five years." The news media spoke of an "explosive new generation" of college students "nobody knew was there." The damage done to the HUAC was probably irreparable, for it had always thrived on unquestioning public acceptance of its sensational exposés of domestic Communism. In the face of such a forceful show of opposition, the Committee ceased to monopolize public discussion of the subject, thereby losing much of its credibility. As for the students, they had inadvertently succeeded in dramatizing their very existence; the silence of the much-heralded "silent generation" was irretrievably broken.

EARLY STUDENT ACTIVISM IN THE BAY AREA

Though the student demonstrations at the San Francisco HUAC hearings were, to be sure, spontaneous and *ad hoc* in nature, they did not occur as an isolated phenomenon. For almost two years, students at the University of California's Berkeley campus had been in a state of quiet revolt against the tedium and banalities of conventional "college life," where a highly competitive, often irrelevant academic routine was augmented by such trivial extracurricular activities as fraternities, sororities and intercollegiate athletics. Increasingly, they sought involvement with the social and political issues of the "real world": SLATE, the student political party which led the opposition to HUAC on the Berkeley campus, was simultaneously engaged in campaigns against nuclear testing, segregation, capital punishment, and compulsory ROTC on the campus. The concern of its membership was not so much with particular issues or ideologies (outwardly, most of them were "motivated" by the old liberal values inherited from their parents) as with a desire to define for themselves the conditions of their lives and the social values to which they were to adhere. The HUAC was an obvious target for these students, since it had always been a primary factor inhibiting independent political activity; the legacy of its twenty-odd years of existence was an abounding fear of leaflets, petitions, and public identification with causes . . . in short, anything that might threaten one's personal security. The stated justification for opposing the HUAC usually involved complex legalistic arguments about constitutional liberties, but the main motivating force was a simple assertion of political maturity and a desire by student activists to assume the attendant responsibilities.

San Francisco State College had no group comparable to SLATE prior to the City Hall riots, but the traditional football and fraternity rituals had even less of a base there than they did at Berkeley. S.F. State was a "commuter campus"; few of its students took part in extracurricular on-campus activity. Many held part-time jobs, some were married; others, particularly in the School of Humanities, maintained close ties with San Francisco bohemia. Even in the late 1950's, the college's creative writing program attracted such denizens of the "San Francisco Renaissance" as Allen Ginsberg, Michael McClure, Robert Duncan, and Jack Spicer, who either taught or were students at the school. The first glimmerings of political activity at San Francisco State came on the heels of the Southern sit-ins: early in March of 1960, seven S.F. State students and a U.C. freshman named Douglas Wachter walked the twenty-five miles across the Golden Gate Bridge and through Marin County to San Quentin prison, where Caryl Chessman had been awaiting execution for the past eleven years.

Despite the pathetic turnout (the walkers were outnumbered by newsmen), the demonstration attracted considerable publicity, for the Chessman affair was already something of an international *cause célèbre*. The news media was fond of referring to Chessman as a "rapist-killer," though he had in fact neither raped nor killed; it was also charged that he was guilty of "crimes too horrible to mention," which, if uninformative, is a little closer to the truth. Chessman had allegedly committed fellatio; he was charged with kidnapping (at the time, a capital offense under California's "little Lindbergh law") on the grounds that he had, in the course of his unmentionable crimes, forcibly transported his victims from one parked car to another. Summarily convicted by a hostile court and sentenced to death, Chessman's execution was averted only when the court reporter at his trial died and left behind a shorthand record of the case which no one could completely decipher. While the appellate courts debated whether or not this was grounds for a new trial, the "little Lindbergh law" was repealed, complicating matters that much more. The execution was postponed again and again; balanced treacherously between life and death, Chessman found time to write three books, at least one of which was translated into several languages and widely read in Europe as well as the United States. As he emerged as an extraordinary example of personal rehabilitation, the various inequities of his case came to the forefront. Abolition of capital punishment had long been a stock issue of liberal and religious groups, but it had never gotten much support or even attention until it was dramatically illustrated by Chessman's ordeal. To a number of people with humane impulses, eleven years on death row was enough punishment for any man, especially when he had never taken another's life; to a generation of college students raised in the shadow of the atomic bomb, the Chessman case symbolized the insanity of the state's giving sanction to the taking of human life, not to mention the absurdities of the legal system.

The fight to save Chessman's life was a political baptism for a number of students, and, almost without exception, they found it a disillusioning experience. Hope had loomed when "Pat" Brown, a liberal and a Catholic, had expressed his opposition to capital punishment in the course of his gubernatorial campaign; hope faded when Brown, once elected and in office, began to vacillate. Eventually, he committed himself to commuting Chessman's sentence to life imprisonment—provided, however, that Chessman express the appropriate degree of repentance for what he had done. Chessman, who to the end of his life insisted that he was innocent of any wrongdoing, refused to change his story. This impertinence, finally, is what cost him his life.

As conventional channels proved more and more futile, the marches to San Quentin continued, increasing in size and intensity. The final march drew over five hundred people, who circled the prison walls and then maintained a vigil at the front gate until word came that the State Supreme Court had rejected a last appeal by a five-to-four margin. In despair, the protesters—no doubt with the Southern students in mind—sat down in the road, blocking the entrance to the prison. When police dragged them out of the way, they simply walked back to the road and sat down again. The process was repeated until the police grew impatient, manhandled several demonstrators and arrested at least one. Finally the execution was done, and the crowd dispersed quietly, some sobbing, and some silent.

Seven days later the HUAC hearings had begun in San Francisco. One of the first "unfriendly witnesses" to testify was Douglas Wachter, the University of California student who had participated in the first San Quentin march. Wachter had been served with his subpoena just before the final vigil, and few of his colleagues missed the connection.

POLITICAL AWAKENING AT SAN FRANCISCO STATE COLLEGE

"Operation Abolition" was supposed to refer to the code name of a Communist plot to undermine the nation's security program by attacking the HUAC; it became the title of the most talked-about documentary of 1960–61. Two days after the City Hall riots, the HUAC subpoenaed all films taken of the demonstrations and hearings by the local television stations, ostensibly for its own files. The two-and-one-half hours of footage was then shipped back to Washington, edited, given a soundtrack, and released at $100 a print as the authoritative account of what happened in San Francisco on "Black Friday." Within six months of the hearings, the film had more than paid for itself. Curiously, it did not bear any of the standard credits, either at the beginning or the end. Nevertheless, it imparted, to quote the San Francisco *News-Call Bulletin,* "the clear impression it [was] as much of a government document as the President's State of the Union message."

The film began with a trailer by HUAC Chairman Francis Walter, seated at an official-looking desk and flanked on either side by American flags. In grimly provocative tones, Walter advised the audience of what it was about to see: hard-core Communist agitators, after months of careful planning, engaging in the "long-time Communist tactic of inciting misguided students and other non-Communist sympathizers to perform their dirty work for them." More provocative than the spectacle Walter promised were the distortions of fact that actually followed. The film's time sequences were completely scrambled, its narration included outright lies as well as loaded terminology, and its careful editing supported the contention that the police had been deliberately and unreasonably provoked by the students instead of the reverse.

So pronounced was the self-parody of the film that students at S.F. State who had participated in the City Hall protest were anxious to show it on campus as a way of demonstrating their point that the HUAC was willing to resort to slander as well as intimidation in order to silence its critics. They quickly discovered that there was a civil liberties fight to be waged in their own back yard. Through innuendoes, complicated regulations governing public meetings, and a stringent commitment to "neutrality," the administrative bureaucracy of the college was able to enforce an almost total quarantine of on-campus political activity. Faculty members were not supposed to express opinions on subjects "outside their field of scholarly competence"; no meeting could be held to discuss "controversial issues" unless "both sides" were there to present their case; activities counselors were expected to find all sorts of practical excuses for discouraging students from doing anything which might cause trouble or embarrassment for the administration; outdoor rallies were permitted only under the most extraordinary of circumstances.

Through such techniques, the administration was able to delay the showing of "Operation Abolition" on campus for over a year, and the group which sponsored the showing, SCOPE (Student Council on Political Education, modeled after SLATE at Berkeley) was perpetually fighting for its right to exist. It was not until the Bay of Pigs invasion in 1961 that the group was able to make a dent in official policies. It did so by insisting on holding rallies to protest America's Cuban policy in front of the Commons, either without consulting with or without being restrained by the appropriate college authorities. Worse, SCOPE got a splash of newspaper publicity when it lent its active support to a similar demonstration downtown. Dean of Student Activities Alan Johnson was incensed enough over the former incident to personally storm out of his office and down to the Commons in an effort to break it up. The downtown rally, which threatened to have more serious repercussions, drew a blast from the President of the College himself, Glenn Dumke.

Dumke, who had been one of the principal authors of the Master Plan, had originally taught history at Occidental College, a small, private liberal arts school in Southern California, where he maintained close ties with influential Republicans in the Nixon camp. His narrow concept of academic responsibility and obsessive concern for "public image" had destined him to go far within the educational hierarchy of the state: shortly after the SCOPE controversy, he was promoted to Vice-Chancellor for Academic Affairs and, subsequently, Chancellor of the State college system. Dumke's attack on SCOPE was both characteristic and highly revealing. Student activists, he charged, had violated the tenets of academic freedom with their "actionist crusades based on passion rather than considered study and judgement." For Dumke, academic freedom was not a right but a privilege, "bestowed by a free society upon the academic profession in return for [its] providing the society with a selfless, objective search for truth . . . It is not, in my opinion, the right of faculty or students to use the state-supported facilities of an educational institution, and its convenient audience, to win converts to a political point of view. There is a difference between a lectern and a soapbox." Particularly disturbing was the prospect that "minority groups," by "using the college as a weapon to achieve their ends," were "misrepresenting the institution to its constituency, creating damaging public attitudes which influence it adversely in obtaining support for its work and, most important, in maintaining a public attitude which will continue to defend the concept of academic freedom."

Dumke's statement, and the almost universal disgust with which it was received on the campus, did a great deal to clear the air. Convinced that college policy was due for some major changes, a group of students, faculty, and activities counselors drew up a "Philosophy Statement on Student Activities" and took advantage of the confusion brought on by the impending turnover in the President's office to get it approved by the administration. Innocuous as it seemed, the Philosophy Statement was a kind of historical prelude, for its central premise—that "students are respected as adults and citizens in the community and, as such, have all the rights and responsibilities of adults and citizens to participate in college and community affairs"—was to become the crucial underlying issue of the Berkeley Free Speech Movement three years later. With its adoption began an eight month campaign, finally successful, for an outdoor free speech area on campus. Initiated by SCOPE members, the campaign was

soon taken up by the more respectable Forensics Union, and it
culminated in the construction of a twelve-by-eight foot wooden
speaker's platform in the northwest corner of the central campus
area, "dedicated to unrestricted freedom of expression." It was
the first such structure on any campus in the country. Presiding
over the dedication ceremony on October 15, 1962, with College
President Paul Dodd was the new student body President, Jay
Folberg of the Forensics Union.

With the dedication of the Speaker's Platform, SCOPE, the
group which had started it all, went into a state of eclipse. It was
not that the campus had suddenly become hostile or indifferent to
its brand of politics, but that its own most active members were
dissatisfied with the overly topical, *ad hoc* nature of their activities. The organization jumped frantically from issue to issue, here
organizing trips to Cuba, there recruiting volunteers to join that
handful of Northern whites who went South for the Freedom
Rides in the summer of 1962. But it never developed a concrete
program of its own; once its candidates were elected to the student legislature, there seemed to be nothing for them to do, for
student government was seen as inherently self-limiting and ultimately irrelevant—and SCOPE had found no way to broaden its
purview. A desire to "talk politics," not simply issues, led a
number of members, including most of the leadership, to form a
study group that sought to deal with the issues of the day in
terms of Marxian political analysis. A year later, the group gave
itself a name, the W.E.B. DuBois Club, after the great black
Marxist historian. Within two years it had spread far beyond the
San Francisco State campus to become a national youth organization supported by the Communist Party and, for a brief period,
one of the most active and influential of the campus political
groups.

THE SAN FRANCISCO CIVIL RIGHTS MOVEMENT

The Civil Rights Movement catapulted the DuBois Club into
prominence. At a time when large numbers of college students
were moved to action out of concern for the plight of the black
man, the DuBois Club was the only group, at least on the S.F.

State campus, which offered intelligent explanations for the rampant racism of which everyone was so suddenly conscious. Most Northern whites were full of sympathy and admiration for Southern blacks when they faced the fire hoses and police dogs in Birmingham, Alabama, in May, 1963. Their sympathy turned to dismay a few months later when the Civil Rights Movement came North; abruptly, the "Negro problem" ceased to be an abstract moral issue involving "racial discrimination" or "segregation," and became inextricably linked with the balance of economic and political power in a dozen different Northern cities. Humanitarian impulses needed to be supplemented with a critical understanding of the operation of American society. While fulfilling that function for Bay Area college students, the DuBois Club also gave new vitality to the tactics and theology of nonviolent civil disobedience, which generally disappeared as the Movement crossed the Mason-Dixon line.

The Birmingham demonstrations made an immediate impact on the San Francisco State campus. A black student appeared in the Commons one day, when the newspapers were full of Bull Connor's police dogs, with a sign that read simply, "My people are dying." Soon he was leading crowds of students in marches around the quad, then through the streets of the Fillmore district, one of San Francisco's two black ghettos. AS President Jay Folberg appointed Art Sheridan, the twenty-one-year-old black student, to head an AS-sponsored "Human Relations Commission"; when that failed to get off the ground, Sheridan started an organization of his own, the Direct Action Group (DAG), which was designed to turn student energies loose in the community. That summer proved crucial for San Francisco and the nation. For the nation, three months of turmoil in the Deep South, in which Northern whites were involved, climaxed with the March on Washington and the bombing of a Birmingham church. For San Francisco, it marked the beginnings of the United Freedom Movement, an uneasy coalition of such "established" civil rights groups as the NAACP, CORE, and the powerful Baptist Minister's Union. Actually, CORE was still relatively new to the area, but it soon attracted attention with its penchant for scattergun direct-action tactics. In August, twenty CORE members were

arrested in a protest over housing discrimination at the Select
Rental Agency, while scores more camped in the corridors of the
state capitol lobbying for passage of the Rumford Fair Housing
Bill.

In the fall, the Direct Action Group began investigating the
hiring practices of Mel's Drive-In, one of a chain of restaurants
owned by San Francisco Supervisor Harold Dobbs. On October
19, a group of pickets appeared in front of the drive-in, vowing
to be there "everyday after school until our demands are met."
The news media tried to ignore them at first, but this soon
proved impractical, for San Francisco was less than two weeks
away from a mayoralty election and the leading candidate was
none other than Harold Dobbs. Dobbs himself became panicky
enough to accuse his opponent, Democratic Congressman John F.
Shelley, of instigating the picketing; the Republican Supervisor
further claimed that if Shelley won, San Francisco would "become another Birmingham"—a statement which may have struck
too close to home; it was immediately denounced by the news
media as "irresponsible." By this time, the DAG had been joined
on the picket lines by other student organizations, including
Youth for Jobs and several chapters of the DuBois Club. Together, they formed an umbrella organization called the "Ad Hoc
Committee to End Discrimination"; within the structure of the
Ad Hoc Committee, Art Sheridan's leadership was effectively
supplanted by the better organized and more politically sophisticated DuBois Club people. On November 5, the Saturday before
election day, close to a hundred pickets, at least a third of them
S.F. State students, entered the drive-in, sat down at the lunch
counter and refused to leave. All were arrested, but by the time
their arraignments had concluded, it was clear that the sit-in had
had its effect. Shelley won an upset victory on Tuesday by such a
narrow margin that the black vote was probably pivotal; by Friday, Dobbs had capitulated on the other front by signing a comprehensive nondiscriminatory hiring practices agreement with the
Ad Hoc Committee.

Momentum gathered quickly. In February CORE launched its
"shop-ins" at Lucky Markets, protesting against hiring practices;
while a picket line circled outside, CORE members entered the

store, filled up shopping carts with groceries, and then left them
at the checkout counter when the bill was tabulated saying, "Sorry, that's too much." The tactics aroused a storm of criticism, but
they worked, for Lucky Markets capitulated early in March.

The ink was scarcely dry on the CORE–Lucky Markets agreement when the jails were being filled again. The Ad Hoc Committee had taken on San Francisco's largest tourist and convention center, the Sheraton Palace Hotel, after an investigation
revealed that only four per cent of the hotel's employees were
black. Negotiations between the committee and the hotel management, which had been dragging on since December 13, fell apart
late in February. On March 1, 128 demonstrators defied an injunction that enjoined them from picketing and were arrested for
contempt of court. What had started as a protest against job discrimination became a free speech fight as well, and by Friday
night, March 5, the hotel was ringed by well in excess of one
thousand pickets. A new injunction was served, but no attempt
was made to enforce it, and just before 10 o'clock the pickets
began filing into the hotel. They spent the night camped in the
huge, ornate lobby, spilling over into several adjacent corridors
as well, while feverish negotiations went on seven floors up. The
Ad Hoc Committee was trying to get the hotel management to
sign an agreement comparable to the one CORE had signed with
Lucky Markets a few days earlier. But the management was under pressure from the Hotel Owner's Association, which represented thirty-three of San Francisco's largest hotels and was obviously concerned that if one domino fell, others would follow.
Negotiations broke down at 4 A.M., at which point the Ad Hoc
Committee leaders decided that it was time to force police action.
One hundred and sixty-seven volunteers split off from the rest of
the group and sat down squarely in front of the main entrance to
the building, in violation of a city fire ordinance. The arrests
were completed by sunrise, but the sit-in continued through the
morning and into the afternoon.

Shortly after two o'clock a picket captain pushed his way
through the crowd of spectators and ran into the lobby waving a
piece of paper over his head. He was beyond speech, but none
was necessary. The exhausted crowd suddenly found the energy

to leap to its feet in a spontaneous demonstration, pausing only when Ad Hoc Committee leader Tracy Sims, an 18-year-old black S.F. State freshman, came into the room. Hoisted on the shoulders of several demonstrators, she shouted, "We came here trying to end the discriminatory hiring practices of the Sheraton Palace Hotel. We're coming away with an agreement covering *thirty-three* hotels!" The demonstration erupted all over again; it was a full ten minutes before the cheering, stomping, clapping, and waving of "V" signs subsided. An impromptu rally followed, at which the last to speak was comedian Dick Gregory. Then the pickets filed out of the hotel, leaving behind a small clean-up detail; after sitting-in for more than fourteen hours.

In his speech, Gregory said he saw "hope for America" in something that had bothered virtually everyone else—the fact that the demonstrators were seventy-five per cent white. Opponents of the Ad Hoc Committee used this as evidence that the Committee did not represent the black community and had no right to bargain for it, if indeed it even had the interests of the black community at heart. CORE Chairman Bill Bradley gave this argument a reverse twist. He maintained that blacks were relatively absent from the picket line because few of them could subscribe to nonviolence; and when the black community finally decided to act, San Francisco would really have something to worry about. Recognizing the consequences of racial separatism, Gregory saw it as a sign of hope when the composition of a picket line reflected the racial composition of the community, for it meant that in San Francisco at least, whites knew that civil rights was their problem, too.

" 'Ad Hoc Committee' had an imposing sound," read the editorial in the San Francisco *News-Call Bulletin* the morning after the sit-in, "but the group came from out of nowhere." A few days later the more enterprising *Examiner* had traced the Committee's origins back to the Kremlin, with the DuBois Clubs forming the principal link. White San Franciscans quickly found their pretext to condemn tactics they had applauded in Mississippi and Alabama: one of the most active and influential of the civil rights organizations was also a Communist front. But the spectacular success of the Committee had spread its influence far beyond the campus, and it was now a functioning part of the United Freedom Movement. Within seven days of the Palace demonstration, 107 more people were arrested for conducting a NAACP-led sit-in in the showroom of the Cadillac agency on San Francisco's Auto Row. The protest was again against what the activists considered to be discriminatory hiring practices. Resolution of this dispute was not nearly as dramatic as the previous one, but considerably more people were involved. Mass arrests occurred on two different occasions when negotiations, which continued through March and well into April, broke down; the day the NAACP finally signed with the Automobile Dealer's Association, thousands of people were massed along six blocks of Van Ness Avenue, ready to enter the showrooms again if talks should fail.

The agreement with the Automobile Dealer's Association proved to be the movement's final victory. Trials of the more than 500 cases of those arrested since February 29 had already begun when the Auto Row demonstrations concluded. The cases were tried in groups of fourteen or fifteen: the first won an acquittal; the second a hung jury; and another jury, hopelessly deadlocked, compromised by acquitting everyone except Tracy Sims. From then on it was all downhill. Judges were almost uniformly hostile and often flagrantly prejudicial in their conduct of the trials; black people were systematically excluded from the juries, and sentences were generally harsher than those meted out for similar offenses to civil rights workers in the South. The latter situation became painfully obvious when NAACP leader Dr. Thomas Burbridge, head of the United Freedom Movement, received nine months in prison for three misdemeanors. Almost worse than the sentences, however, was the demoralization that accompanied the trials themselves. Daily attendance was required of all defendants, many of whom lost their jobs or had to drop out of school as a result. Juries were frequently hung, meaning that a number of cases had to be tried over and over. As the trials dragged on, consuming time and energy and accomplishing vitually nothing, further demonstrations became very nearly impossible. CORE made a brave attempt to take on the Bank of America; its picket lines fizzled out when it became clear that no one could afford to get arrested again.

Since the movement had always relied solely on direct action to keep itself going, and since it had no more than the tacit support of the black community, the end of the demonstrations meant the end of everything. The hard core of DuBois Club members and other high school and college students who had formed the shock troops of the demonstrations vanished from the scene as inexplicably as they had first appeared, never having established any permanence or place in the daily pattern of events. A few were embittered enough to drop out of politics altogether; they became some of the original settlers in the hip colonies of the Haight-Ashbury district, which three years later was attracting far more attention than the sit-ins ever had. More simply found other areas of political activity in which to engage themselves. A number of DuBois Club people rang doorbells for the slate of liberal politicians, among them a young black attorney named Willie Brown who was running for the State Assembly, all of whom were swept into office on the wave of the sit-ins. But the organization itself, after such a promising start, soon deteriorated into one more small, sectarian campus political group.

Its undoing proved, in no small part, to be the undoing of the Civil Rights Movement; certainly it characterized one stage of the student movement. The DuBois Club had depended on direct action in lieu of a real base in the community, raising topical issues without projecting a comprehensive or functional approach to community problems. Moreover, it tended to rely upon liberal coalition politics rather than any *realpolitik* formula for dealing with power relationships, either to change them or to make them work to one's own advantage. And of course, there were the inevitable limitations of nonviolence and conventional civil disobedience, strategies that had more to do with public relations than with power politics. Theoretically, DuBois Club members understood the need for a "socialist revolution" in America; in actual practice, their rhetoric seldom went beyond the rhetoric of social reform; their critique of American society never indicted more than the most specific of social ills. Worse, their fear of red-baiting and their resultant need to continually conceal their politics prevented them from dealing with even these specific issues—jobs, housing, and so forth—in an ideologically coherent, consistent manner. This disease did not confine itself to the DuBois Club; up until the time of the Vietnam War, few mainstream student activist groups dared to make any serious criticisms of American society without first affirming their underlying patriotism or their desire to see the American dream come true. It was clear that a new style of politics had to be found if the student movement was to evolve beyond moral protest.

THE S. F. STATE TUTORIAL PROGRAM

While the DuBois Club was involving itself in local civil rights agitation, the successor to AS President Jay Folberg was moving in an opposite direction. As an avowed socialist and a dedicated activist, Tom Ramsey had entered into AS politics feeling that there was more to be gotten out of student government than the sandbox-to-soapbox transition that Folberg had helped bring about. Specifically, he had his eye on the $400,000 in compulsory student body fees collected each semester, over which the AS had nominal control, as a possible financial base for student work in the community. Like many student activists of the time, Ramsey was looking for a practical and effective vehicle for student energies and social concerns. And the time was ripe. Shortly after his election to the AS Presidency in April, 1963, Ramsey observed: "Civil rights has become the most emotionally charged, but intellectually frustrating issue on this campus." His idea was to direct those emotions and frustrations into meaningful community work under AS sponsorship, with at least some of the AS budget freed up to keep it going.

In July, Tom Ramsey attended the annual conference of the National Students Association (NSA) in Indiana. He quickly became disgusted with the "sophomoric level of discussion" and resolution-passing; worse, he suspected that the NSA was controlled by the federal government—five years before it was actually exposed as a CIA front. The trip might have been a waste of time had Ramsey not met and talked at some length with Bob

Moses, a SNCC field secretary, and Peter Countryman, founder
of the Northern Student Movement, both of whom had come to
the conference hoping to solicit support and recruit volunteers
for SNCC's work in the South. Countryman told Ramsey of additional projects that his organization was initiating in the large
Northern cities, among them a one-to-one tutorial program for
ghetto children rejected by the public school system. Ramsey was
so impressed by the description of the projects that he left the
conference two days early to hitchhike to New York. He spent
ten days in Harlem "talking to everyone"—from Black Muslims
to Domestic Peace Corps volunteers to a dozen different direct action and community groups—about what role white students could play in the Civil Rights Movement. In September he
returned to the S.F. State campus to predict, in an interview
with the campus newspaper *Daily Gater*, "by June we should
have three hundred to four hundred students working under
Negro leadership in the slum areas of the city."

Ramsey's plans quickly ran afoul of members of his own ticket
in the AS Legislature. The chief obstacles were Speaker of the
Legislature Bill Burnett and Assistant Speaker Marty Mellara.
On the surface, they were miffed by Ramsey's snub of the NSA;
the real bone of contention, however, was that Ramsey had no
intention of supporting Burnett as his successor to the AS presidency, since he considered Burnett to be overly ambitious. A
stalemate developed between the Executive and the Legislature,
and the student political party that Ramsey headed quickly broke
up under the strain. But by now the AS was, for the moment at
least, largely irrelevant; the campus was caught in the excitement
of the sit-ins, and few students paid much attention to the snip-
ing and backbiting of their elected representatives.

Ramsey soon realized that he would have to go it alone. Like
most of the politically active people on campus, he joined the
picket line at Mel's Drive-In. There he met Guy Sandler, a shy
and soft-spoken philosophy student, who had joined the DuBois
Club after talking to some DuBois people on the line and being
impressed by their political savvy. Ramsey approached Sandler at
school a few days later and asked him if he was interested in a
project that involved working with ghetto youngsters. The idea

was an "each one teach one" tutorial modeled after those developed by Peter Countryman. Since Sandler shared with many others a desire to "go beyond picketing" and liked the idea of working with kids, he agreed to help organize the project. Ramsey and he spent the next two months recruiting volunteer tutors among their friends and acquaintances, and seeking the help of Baptist ministers in the Fillmore District. Most of the ministers were suspicious, but one finally agreed to donate his church, a tiny storefront on Divisadero Street. Around the corner from the storefront was a large housing project, which, as Sandler wrote later, "looked like a zoo full of children. There were children crawling around everywhere . . . on the building's roof and down its sides. Some of these children were members of the church where we would tutor and the Reverend had told them of the extra school which was starting." Through the Reverend, the children were asked how they would want such an "extra school" to be run if they were the "Principal." Their response then became the basis for planning the program.

Finally, after the fifteen volunteer tutors had received some initial preparation, the first center was opened on February 29, 1964. Sandler was to write:

> Tutoring was scheduled for two times a week, from 7 to 9. A number of students from the second through eighth grades had been invited, but no one knew exactly how many would show. Ten children attended the first tutoring session. Then, a family of eight joined. The numbers grew and diminished, but at least some of the children came every time. And when more of them came to know that their tutors could be counted on to be there each time, and when they came to trust the sincerity of the tutor and could see it in the work prepared for them, they too would attend steadily and tell their friends. Soon new locations had to be found . . .

Few of the volunteer tutors were education majors; most of them came out of the social sciences and humanities, and had had little or no teaching experience. This bothered the tutors at first, so professors and graduate students from the School of Education were invited to lead orientations and workshops. They quickly proved unsatisfactory, however; as one tutor observed: "These 'experts' lacked a guts involvement in the subjects they talked about and were unable to communicate to the tutors on anything but a rarified, highly intellectual plane . . . [they] only talked about the theoretical aspects of reading and language skills without giving specific suggestions as to how to get a kid reading." Accordingly, the tutors were forced to develop their own theories, based upon what they could perceive for themselves. They knew, for a start, that theoretically everyone is capable of learning to read, yet high dropout rates and low reading comprehension levels alone provided enough evidence that few ghetto children were able to read without trouble. The fault, then, was not with the children, but with the schools and with the social conditions under which the children were forced to live, which together obliterated their self-image and prepared them for lives of poverty and degradation. The students' job as tutors was to try to restore that self-image and to give the children a chance to learn free of the social constraints and artificial molds into which ghetto children were supposed to fit. The children needed an education geared to their own needs, not those—as Sandler put it—"of some never-seen dream students" who were, in all probability, white, middle-class, and suburban.

Tutors were careful to eschew the authoritarianism of conventional adult-child relationships. They approached their pupils as equals, with whom they shared a mutual anxiety, a mutual hesitancy, a mutual inexperience, a mutual desire to learn and to be friends. Children learned at their own pace, with "lessons" drawn directly from their personal experience. The tutors knew little or nothing of phonics, monosyllables and polysyllables, or other "systematic" approaches to reading. Their standard approach was to suggest that the child draw a picture, explaining it with a story as he went along, and then write the crucial words of the story down on flash cards. Or perhaps the two would play or take an excursion; the tutor would write down the crucial words from the child's own vocabulary to describe what they had done. The language the pupil learned invariably reflected the language and life style of the ghetto, which his school teachers had no doubt tried to suppress. In watching the pupil learn to read, the tutor heightened his own social awareness. Gradually, the tutors came to realize that their inexperience was an asset rather than a liability—partly because it freed them from the authoritarianism that necessarily accompanies the "professional" approach, partly because it meant the program could be much more than simply a service that supplemented the work of the school system. It would, among other things,

> investigate and try in practice teaching techniques and theories of learning and motivation which no other agency had the time, courage, and flexibility to do on a similar scale. Not only are effective teaching techniques little employed in the poor community, they are also little known anywhere. So the tutorial program becomes a testing ground for innovations in teacher-student relationships, curriculum development, and student progress evaluation.

At the time of its inception, the Tutorial Program had one off-campus center, fifteen volunteer tutors, and a small sum of money Tom Ramsey had managed to siphon off from the AS Executive funds. Eighteen months later, when Roger Alvarado, a Latin-American student from the working-class suburb of Daly City, succeeded Guy Sandler as program coordinator, the program had twelve centers scattered throughout the city, 300 volunteer tutors, the official recognition and regular funding of the AS, and a $5,000 foundation grant. The phenomenal success of the program had begun to seriously worry its leadership. It had, from the beginning, operated under the assumption that poor education was a result, not a cause, of poverty, and that the program alone would not solve the problems which made it necessary in the first place. But as their understanding of the situation and their tutoring experience increased, program workers realized that cause and effect could not be separated. They attempted to close the gap by building relationships with the parents of the children as well. Often this was simply a matter of educational necessity: a visit to the home of one child whom his teachers had assumed to be dull and inattentive revealed that he was really hard-of-hearing. Then, too, ethically parents should know what is happening to their children. But, as Alvarado put it, "the most important element of the parent-tutor relationship is that it enables the tutor to gain some perspective of his or her child's background and environment." Tutors were implored not to "make the same mistake as the school system" by treating the child's problems in a vacuum and ignoring issues of culture, class, and race.

The process of "moving on the parents" had political repercussions of its own, for contact with the tutors quickly made the parents aware of how badly their children were being treated in school. There had never been any real, formal relationship between the S.F. State Tutorial Program and the San Francisco Unified School District, but the two parties had at least tolerated each other. Now, with tutors exposing the incompetence of the school district's teachers and talking about the prospect of "counter-PTA's," an open conflict seemed imminent. An even worse situation was developing at the Youth Guidance Center, where the program was attempting to work with children whose parents had been judged incompetent and who had been placed under the guardianship of the City. Tutors found that they were expected by the authorities to act as nothing more than whips of discipline, and that they had to justify any "fun" activities in which they and the pupils engaged. The probation officers were frequently hostile and rarely able to understand the subtleties of the tutor's work. The questions that arose suggested much larger dilemmas, with implications for the whole program: How much could be accomplished within an atmosphere of repression? Would it be better to openly attack the authorities and in so doing lose the opportunity to work with the children who so desperately needed help? At what point should the decision to do this be made?

Perhaps the best description of the overall situation came from Tony Patchell, one of the tutors in the program. With a mixture of eloquence and despair, he summarized the credo of the program, and, at the same time, its central dilemma:

It has been my belief that before the child dies and the man comes of age, before the freshness of vision is blunted or eradicated by poverty, fear, pain, each of us had within himself a certain indefinable spirit or capacity which should be, must be, nurtured and revealed. This I believe, but less strongly now than before. I do not think tutorial classes solve any basic problems; perhaps all they do is afford a few hours of relief and enjoyment each week for a few children. Perhaps we have only contributed more confusion to the lives of these children, since they now had had a taste of possibilities which they may not have had before. And perhaps those five or six students that we had to eliminate from the program because they were causing so much chaos were the really smart ones.

CHAPTER III

The Quiet Revolution:

THE DEVELOPMENT OF
THE S. F. STATE STUDENT PROGRAMS,

1964-1966

Early in December, 1964, the students at the University of California's Berkeley campus exploded the myth of excellence associated with California public higher education, sending shock waves through the academic community and the nation as they did so. Though its initial concern was to establish the right of students to engage in off-campus political activity, the Free Speech Movement quickly broadened in scope to encompass an indictment of the entire concept of the "multiversity" which Berkeley was supposed to exemplify. Involving some of the country's brightest and most promising students at a campus that was widely regarded as an academic Valhalla, the Berkeley uprising made an immediate and sensational impact; it remains a landmark in the history of the American student movement despite its failure to live up to its initial promise to revolutionize the institution at which it occurred.

While the Free Speech Movement was taking place at Berkeley, students across the bay at San Francisco State College were quietly engaging in an unpublicized struggle of their own. The ultimate stakes were the same, but the milieu could not have been more different. Instead of a nationally renowned ivory tower, it consisted of a drab, unimpressive-looking "streetcar college" which had been designated for mediocrity by the Master Plan for higher education. Owing to its location in a city which has traditionally been a center of radical politics and cultural ferment, it had attracted some outstanding professors and a generally intelligent, independent-minded student body. Its strongest departments were in the humanities and creative arts; its faculty liked to think of itself as being of university caliber. But the atmosphere on campus was deceptively low-keyed. College governance was entrusted to a remote, rigid, and notoriously unwieldy statewide administrative bureaucracy whose main concern was keeping operating costs at a bare minimum. For the moment, it was singularly indifferent to the activities of the students in its charge, and, rather than reacting against this anonymity as their Berkeley counterparts had done, student activists at S.F. State were able to use it to their advantage as they labored toward a new definition of their education, more in line with their own interests, priorities, and values.

The period from 1964 to 1966 saw an entire generation of college students become educated in radical politics. At S.F. State, this educational process took place at its greatest intensity and assumed a form that was completely unprecedented at the time and is not likely to be repeated in the future. The "form" was that of the so-called "student programs": initiated by student activists with the aid and encouragement of sympathetic faculty and lower level administrators, the programs evolved in an atmosphere of relative serenity and campus harmony, and within a few years they had become the pride of the college. Still, and despite their atypical nature, they bore an organic relationship to a particular phase of the student movement in the United States, and by living out that phase under optimum conditions, student activists at S.F. State were able to develop some of the best, most committed, most politically sophisticated radical leadership on any campus in the country. Beginning with the Fillmore Tutorial, the programs had by 1966 expanded to include the Community Involvement Program, the Work-Study Program, and the much-heralded Experimental College before their major impetus and

organizational model were taken up by the Black Students'
Union.

This particular phase of campus activism had begun in the
spring of 1963, when Tom Ramsey first hit upon the idea of using the Associated Students, and its $400,000 budget, as a base
for off-campus civil rights work. Ramsey's administration had
proved that radicals could get themselves elected, but it had
quickly bogged down due to personal rivalries and internal dis-
sension; beyond the establishment of the Fillmore Tutorial, it
had accomplished little of what it set out to do. Ramsey was
succeeded in office by a slate of candidates which included his
close friend Jim Nixon, a Canadian student named John Pearson, Guy Sandler and Ed Washington of the Tutorial Program,
and Joe Persico, the sophomore who headed the ticket. Once
in office, they wasted no time in trying to tap the resources of
the student body government for civil rights purposes. The Student Nonviolent Coordinating Committee (SNCC) had issued a
call for Northern white students to converge upon the state of
Mississippi over the summer, where they would teach in SNCC
"freedom schools" or participate in a massive voter registration
campaign. A thousand students answered the call, knowing full
well the danger involved in such a campaign. Ten students from
S.F. State had planned to go South, stopping en route at the
summer tutorial conference of the Northern Student Movement.
At its first official session, the new AS legislature voted to appropriate $3,000 to cover the ten students' expenses. Right
away there was trouble, although it was not entirely unexpected.
The Chancellor of the state college system learned of the appropriation and began applying pressure on the local administration
to quash it by claiming that it was a violation of Title 5 of the
State Education Code. The statute in question, which governed
all state college operations, stipulated that student governments
were "non-profit organizations" which could spend money only
for "educational purposes" and not for "political activity." The
definition of what constituted one as opposed to the other was
left very vague, and the final interpretation was the prerogative
of Chancellor Dumke. Having little or no sympathy for what
the students were doing, Dumke decided in this case that it was

illegal, thus touching off the first in a long series of skirmishes between S.F. State students and the Chancellor's office over the spending of Associated Students' monies.

Though the Chancellor had invoked the statute as a matter of political convenience, the furor over its interpretation went right to the heart of the students' intent. Campus opponents of the "SNCC Bill," as it was promptly labeled by the *Daily Gater*, argued that it was wrong to "spend Associated Students funds on activities that are of no benefit to students." To proponents of the bill, such reasoning was inexcusably picayune; the "educational process" was all but meaningless if its proper bounds were so tightly drawn as to exclude what was probably the most compelling moral issue of the day, and it was equally picayune to suggest that the issue had nothing to do with the welfare of students. Legally, the AS legislators could argue that the ten volunteers would not be registering voters—which was "political activity"—but merely teaching in the freedom schools. Beyond that, however, they were trying to establish a precedent which would enable education to break out of the classroom mold, become "relevant to the problems of the real world," and acknowledge its responsibilities with respect to pressing social issues.

Joe Persico and Jim Nixon, who had originally sponsored the bill, had anticipated a fight with the Chancellor's office if news of what they were up to got out. Their strategy was to involve both faculty and administrators in the project as "special advisors," thereby enticing them into accepting its major premise. Unfortunately, neither faculty nor administration rose to the bait, and hopes of a campus "united front" against the Chancellor's edict were further thwarted when the *Daily Gater* began to give the bill and its sponsors a sensationalized dose of negative coverage. Seven students were eventually able to go South without AS assistance, by means of collections taken up on campus over the summer to defray their expenses.

Even without the official blessings of the San Francisco State student government, the Mississippi Summer Project proved to be a climactic moment in the history of the Civil Rights Movement. The "invasion" of Northern white college students had its intended effect; beginning with the murder of three young SNCC workers in Neshoba County in early June, the Mississippi Summer Project focused the attention of the nation on the plight of Southern blacks. For the students involved, it was a true coming of age, but the triumph represented by the formation of the Mississippi Freedom Democratic Party was offset by bitter disillusionment when the MFDP failed to unseat the Mississippi "regulars" at the Democratic National Convention in September. Most of the seven S.F. State students who had gone down for the summer were present at the convention; a few, however, had returned to the campus to publicize their experiences and raise money for SNCC.

In the aftermath of the Mississippi Summer Project, the tenor of the 1964 national elections was strangely disheartening and somehow irrelevant. It seemed to a growing number of student activists that the more aware they became of social conditions that desperately needed changing, the more evidence there was that those in positions of authority would continue to equivocate, official institutions would remain unresponsive, conventional political channels would prove more and more futile. To civil rights workers who had risked their lives in Mississippi over the summer, there was no excuse for the shoddy conduct of the Democrats at their national convention, where even the party "liberals" were unwilling to take the most nominal political risks on behalf of Southern blacks. Northern cities were revealing themselves to be as infected with racism as the Deep South. In August, while Lyndon Johnson was denouncing his Republican opponent as a warmonger, his administration was ramming the Tonkin Gulf Resolution through an unquestioning Congress—an act whose chilling implications were not lost on everyone at the time. Driven by such incidents to abandon whatever faith they may have had in the powers that be to deal positively with social injustice, student radicals began to talk increasingly of building an independent power base outside the system. Rather than trying to sway those in positions of authority, they would challenge their authority by helping to organize a political alternative. The most logical place to establish it seemed to be among those who were themselves without power—the disenfranchised and dispossessed, those whom the system had victimized, those who were most isolated from the decision-making process. Once organized to fight for and defend their own interests, these people would form a powerful countervailing force against the interests which had manipulated and oppressed them in the past. Moreover, by demanding a measure of control over their own lives, they would give substance to the concept of democracy where conventional democratic forms such as the ballot box and representative government had failed.

This faith in the countervailing power of the poor and politically disenfranchised drew heavily upon the theories of Saul Alinsky, whose model of community organizing was coming to be accepted by more and more student activists.[1] For him, the process of effecting social change centered around the emergence of "radical constituencies," organized around their own self-interest and their own basic needs. Alinsky's approach was deliberately nonideological; it was for those who would be organized to determine the purposes and direction of their struggle, and the responsibility of the organizer, once he had lived among them long enough to get to know them, was to find out what they wanted and to show them how to get it. If he tried to channel their energies into any specific political direction, he would simply be manipulating people who had already been manipulated for far too long. Hence, the organizer acted not out of ideological commitment but out of moral imperative, and the faith that, given the chance, the people would find the proper path for themselves and that a viable political movement would emerge from their efforts. By 1965 community organizing had become the most important single concern of the New Left. Under the slogan, "Let the people decide," the Students for a Democratic Society sent teams of organizers into the black ghettoes of Cleveland and Newark and the poor white "hillbilly havens" of uptown Chicago. In Newark, at the behest of the ghetto residents, SDS members spent months fighting—unsuccessfully—for the city fathers to install a single traffic light at a dangerous intersection. Such was the depth of their commitment to the people they were working with.

[1] A Chicago-born sociologist with a number of scholarly publications to his credit, Alinsky had developed his theories while actually organizing poor people in the slums of Chicago.

THE COMMUNITY INVOLVEMENT PROGRAM

This particular phase of the student movement was already underway at San Francisco State College in the fall of 1964. The money that had been earmarked for the SNCC Bill eventually went into the rapidly expanding Tutorial Program, which had opened a number of off-campus centers and was even paying some of its coordinators a small monthly salary. At the same time, however, activists in and around student government were laying the groundwork for another vehicle to get students to work in the low-income neighborhoods of the city. The principal concern of the Tutorial Program had been educational rather than political; still, tutors in the program had quickly found that improving a child's reading skills meant dealing with every aspect of his life, and one of their constant frustrations was the awareness that the real cause of their pupils' problems—the wretched conditions under which they were forced to live—went virtually unchallenged by the mere act of tutoring. The Community Involvement Program (CIP), as the new undertaking was to be called, would encompass a broader range of activities than simply helping children learn to read. The founders did not at first clearly define these activities, except to say that the approach would be consciously political and as comprehensive as possible; in addition, it would provide the students involved with a major educational experience, deepening their social commitment while allowing them to develop their organizing skills and general political finesse.

The incubation period of the CIP lasted for nearly a year, during which time John Pearson, the Speaker of the AS legislature, and eleven other students embarked upon a lengthy research project to determine what projects would be best for the new program, what issues were most critical to people in the community, and what indigenous community groups the students could work with. At the same time, the CIP organizers attempted to define their relationship to their prospective off-campus constituency. They clearly wanted no part of the existing social services; their intention was to strive towards the ideal of "participatory democracy" and radical social change, not to bring about specific reforms or social improvement. Given the nonideological orientation of their thinking, as well as their own realistic assessment of the limits of their political efficacy as students, they did not attempt to become more specific on the direction their off-campus work would take. There was a great deal of discussion, however, of the CIP's role on campus. Initially, this discussion was simply a matter of necessity: if the fledgling program was ever to receive any money from the Associated Students, a way would have to be found to circumvent the restrictive nature of the Education Code vis-à-vis political activity and to escape the bureaucratic tentacles of the chancellor's office. Here, Pearson and his co-workers were able to come up with a scheme that was both ingenious and far-reaching in its implications. Tom Ramsey, who was at the time organizing for SNCC in Haight-Ashbury, was hired by the AS to teach a seminar in "community organizing." The seminar was to be sponsored by a sympathetic professor to give it an aura of academic respectability, and it was also to provide college credit for the students who would take it. All CIP staff and volunteers would officially participate in the course, which would substitute off-campus organizing for homework; as such, their community work would conform to the legal definition of "educational activity." The arrangement apparently satisfied the college administration, and soon it became the basic academic rationale for all of the community ventures that the CIP or the other student programs were involved in.

Students in the Ramsey seminar immediately recognized the significance of what they were doing. In arriving at an "acceptable" definition of education which was also in line with their own political and social concerns, they had succeeded where the SNCC Bill had failed. Simultaneously, the process of breaking down the college's traditional disengagement and its general lack of concern for the welfare of the community was filling a critical gap in their own education. Pointing out that "people learn best when they are working on real social problems," Donna Mikkleson, a veteran of the Mississippi Summer Project now active in the CIP, saw the granting of academic credit for community work as the first step toward "making it possible for people to be educated in solving social problems from a new perspective." That in itself was something of a breakthrough for the CIP workers, since the more committed of the student activists were always finding themselves on the verge of flunking out of school. By eliminating the need to take regular academic courses in order to maintain their student status, such credit arrangements freed them to devote more time to community work. More important, academic credits offered through the CIP were a compelling alternative for students bogged down in schoolwork they didn't particularly enjoy; their vague dissatisfaction with the remote and superficial quality of their education would find an outlet that was both fulfilling and of genuine social value. Here, a possible goal for the CIP might be having community organizing institutionalized as a regular training program within the college, the way engineering and business were in their respective departments; this was a notion that could cut both ways, however, and the students in the Ramsey seminar were wise enough to proceed with caution. They knew full well the distorting effects of an academic milieu, and they recognized the importance of preserving the integrity of their program and its basic political commitment. As Donna Mikkleson put it, "Even a seminar of this nature must not be allowed into the curriculum of the college unless it is organized by the students themselves and relates to the work mutually defined by students and community people. Otherwise, it could become another case of the college using communities as their laboratories or guinea pigs."

The CIP plunged into the first of its community action programs following an $8,000 appropriation from the AS for the 1965–66 school year. The initial emphasis was on youth work—a logical choice, considering the amount of attention given to the "juvenile delinquency" problem in the 1950's and early 1960's; but the CIP's approach was a far cry from the conventional social work techniques that were usually used to combat it. Del Sonsten, a CIP volunteer who had recently transferred to S.F. State from a Bay Area junior college, had made contact with a gang of teen-agers in San Francisco's Chinatown. Sonsten was a factory worker's son who had grown up in the "Iron Triangle" section of Richmond, an industrial city on the east shore of San Francisco Bay. He was not a very successful student; though he stayed at S.F. State for several years, he was never able to complete the academic work necessary to earn a degree. He was, however, extremely dedicated and hard-working, and he had a natural gift for organizing which drew heavily upon his own experiences on the streets of Richmond. The CIP was an ideal outlet for his talents; most of his academic life revolved around the program, and it was to provide him with the bulk of his college credits.

The gang members Sonsten was working with had all been arrested at least once, on charges of shoplifting, car theft, burglary, and the like; their parents were recent immigrants from Hong Kong who spoke no English and who worked at menial jobs in Chinatown's restaurants and garment sweatshops. Where the gang members had engaged in criminal activity, it was usually the outgrowth of conflicts with the police, the school system, or their parents, and the last thing that they needed was another authority figure. Instead, Sonsten put himself at their disposal, defining his task as one of facilitating whatever activities they might choose for themselves or of helping them find new ones. These activities came to include a series of Friday night discussion groups, excursions to the beach and elsewhere, sex education, and a regular newsletter. Increasingly, however, Sonsten found himself caught in the role of an intermediary, "trying to protect the kids from the institutions that were messing up their lives," as he later recalled. It didn't work, not because the gang members were unresponsive to his efforts but because, where conflicts developed, the institutions were more often than not at fault. Sonsten could not really remove the source of these conflicts; he could only try to see to it that the youths were not too badly incapacitated by them. In the Mission district, another CIP organizer, Ken Johnson, was having a remarkably similar experience with a group of Mexican-American youths. The difficulties of both these projects were similar to those of the Tutorial Program: they produced some rewarding personal experiences, but their encouraging aspects were more than offset by the knowledge that the framework within which the organizers were working rendered them all but incapable of dealing with the social conditions underlying the gang members' difficulties.

Sonsten was also involved in the CIP's next major venture, which was both more ambitious and broader in scope. Beginning in North Beach and the Mission District, student organizers started working with the tenants in a string of public housing projects that were scattered throughout the low-income neighborhoods of the city. The Federal Housing Authority (FHA), which had originally built the projects, was responsible for their maintenance, and it was as callous toward its renters as the most profiteering absentee landlord. Rats, roaches, and faulty plumbing were common to all of them, and the residents had established the initial unions in the hope of countering the deteriorating conditions in the housing projects. With the aid of the CIP, tenants' unions were set up in eleven different projects that averaged about 150 members each. The students canvassed the projects, recruited new members for the unions, used AS supplies to print leaflets, and set up self-help programs such as baby-sitting for project residents. At the same time, however, they realized the necessity of building a city-wide strategy through which to challenge the authority of the San Francisco Housing Commission, the local arm of the FHA. After months of patient effort within the individual tenants' unions, they were able to combine all eleven under a single umbrella organization called the San Francisco Tenants Issue Council (STIC).

Tenants' organizations similar to the one the CIP was trying to set up were, at the time, springing up all over the country. The 1964 Harlem riots had been preceded by a long and inconclusive rent strike by Harlem residents; two years later, Newark ghetto dwellers underwent an experience that followed the same pattern. In both of these cities, a major problem of the rent strikers had been the fact that it was often impossible to tell who their landlords were, even after the police had begun to evict them for non-payment of rent. The San Francisco tenants were more fortunate, since the FHA was a public agency which was supposed to be working to solve the low-income housing problem instead of aggravating it. Thus, the CIP could hope that rather than simply demanding repairs in the various housing projects, a city-wide tenants' union could attack the problem at its source. The major goal of STIC was to force the local Housing Commission to be more responsive to the project residents by giving them majority representation on its policy-making board.

STIC's plan was an ambitious one, but it never had a chance to get off the ground. In late summer of 1966, there was an outbreak of rioting in Hunter's Point, a nearly all-black slum in the southeast corner of the city, after the shooting of a black youth by a white policeman. As a direct response to the rioting, the tenants in the Hunter's Point union called a rent strike. From a city-wide perspective the strike call was premature, since many of the unions outside Hunter's Point were still not strong enough to risk such an action. Under the circumstances, however, the CIP could do little but try to spread the strike to the other ten unions, an effort which predictably failed. Tenants in the less-organized projects were fearful of isolating themselves, lest they be evicted from their apartments; the four unions which actually did go out on strike either settled separately or were forced to capitulate to the Housing Commission. To make matters worse, the local poverty agency (Economic Opportunity Council) moved in after the strike was broken and placed the leadership of the stronger unions on its payroll, thereby putting the unions out of business. STIC them completely collapsed, and most of the individual unions simply faded away. The student organizers were stunned; they had put over a year of painstaking work into the project and had come away with nothing to show for their efforts except some bitter lessons about such "enlightened" federal agencies as the Federal Housing Authority and the Economic Opportunity Council.

By the end of the 1966 spring semester, the CIP had expanded its staff to twelve organizers, who coordinated nearly one hundred student volunteers working in eleven community projects. Del Sonsten had replaced John Pearson as director of the program, and the AS had allocated $12,000 to the CIP for the coming school year. Though there was some concern that the program was expanding too rapidly and was not being selective enough in its project work, most of the staff felt that the hodge-podge of community projects supported by the program gave it both momentum and valuable organizing experiences in the community. That summer, the program's efforts were diverse enough to include a graphic arts workshop for ghetto children, an off-campus center in Oakland, a funded black repertory theater group (Black Arts West), an organizing drive against the San Francisco Redevelopment Agency's urban renewal plans in the Mission District, a community housing and job co-op in Haight-Ashbury, and support activities for the Delano strike and boycott.

The farm workers in the Delano grape fields had walked off their jobs in August of 1965, demanding a union contract from the DiGiorgio Corporation and a number of other large growers. From the beginning, the odds against them seemed insurmountable. Unionization of California's migrant farm laborers was long overdue; since the 1930's they had borne the brunt of the burden of maintaining the state's biggest industry, following the harvests up and down the Central Valley, living in ramshackle "company towns," doing hours of back-breaking labor for wages that were barely enough to live on. During the Korean War, the federal government had responded to a manpower shortage by authorizing the importation of immigrant labor from Mexico, under the bracero program; at the growers' behest, the program was extended again and again, long after it was needed, as a way of assuring a readily available supply of scab labor should the local farm workers ever try to organize. Now, under the leadership of Caesar Chavez, the National Farm Workers Association (NFWA) had called a strike, and it was honored by most of the grape pickers in the Delano area. The growers' response was to bring in busloads of scabs from as far away as Texas. Lacking any means of feeding themselves or their families, the strikers found themselves the object of a newspaper blackout and increasing harassment from the local police. Still, they managed to hold out through the first desperate weeks, and news of their struggle gradually began to get out. Grape shipments were turned back by union pickets on the San Francisco waterfront; a handful of clergymen and a growing number of college students started to respond to the NFWA's appeals for help.

To student activists, the grape strike had a special appeal. Many of them had read of the great labor struggles of the

1930's and wondered how they could have produced anything as complacent and politically conservative as the contemporary trade union movement. It was something of a revelation to them to learn that there was a whole stratum of workers whom the unions had not bothered to organize, whose desperate poverty clashed sharply with the popular image of the prosperous, satisfied American working man. Moreover, the NFWA had about it an air which was strongly reminiscent of the Civil Rights Movement: its rigid adherence to nonviolence, its idealistic, almost religious fervor, its promise of political regeneration for a long-dormant racial minority—California's Mexican-Americans. With the emergence of black power, many white activists had found that they were no longer needed or wanted in the black movement; in Delano, they discovered a close approximation into which they could rechannel their energies. Finally, student radicals who had become obsessed with their own sense of powerlessness took tremendous inspiration from the fact that a simple, determined people on the bottom of the economic pyramid could successfully defy the most powerful economic interests in the state.

The CIP became involved with the Delano strike in the spring of 1966, when it helped to send weekend car caravans of food and clothing to the beleaguered strikers. A "Huelga Week" was held on campus to educate students about the strike; fund-raising activities were organized around the city. CIP volunteers helped search out scab grapes on the docks and in the warehouses and prevent their shipment. Over the summer, after close to a year of bitter struggle with little outside support, the NFWA announced a national boycott of DiGiorgio products. The San Francisco boycott headquarters was set up in the home of Tony Patchell, a former tutor now active in the CIP, where an *ad hoc* boycott committee coordinated the picketing of several large stores which still carried DiGiorgio products on their shelves. The effectiveness of the boycott in San Francisco can be gauged by the fact that some eighty stores agreed to honor it, and the CIP was able to focus city-wide attention on the issue by picketing a DiGiorgio press conference. Another CIP worker, Gary Wagner, organized a fund-raising tour for the farm workers repertory group, El Teatro Campesino, which netted some $14,000 for the NFWA.

The *ad hoc* boycott committee planned to climax its publicity campaign on the farm workers' behalf by holding a mass march and rally during the first week of July. By this time, Chavez's movement had begun to acquire some powerful and respectable allies; after remaining dissociated from the grape strike for nearly a year, both the Catholic Church and the labor establishment threw their support to the boycott. Unfortunately, the price of their involvement in the support campaign was a good deal of "red-baiting" of the student activists who had supported the strike from its earliest days. The head of the *ad hoc* boycott committee was actually forced to resign just before the big march, and many of the student activists went with him. Publicly, Chavez willingly acknowledged that without student support the NFWA would never have survived its desperate first months; nevertheless, the influence of the Catholic Church, organized labor, and the Democratic Party were coming more and more to dominate the politics of the union. Naturally, it was disheartening for the students to have supported the NFWA during its most difficult times only to be spurned by the union just as it began to gain a measure of public support. Worse than that, however, was the fear of many student activists that the NFWA would end up by selling out the farm workers if it continued to make deals with the very people who had ignored the farm labor plight in the past. It was hard to find rational arguments to support such fears, but the students knew they were far from groundless. How much longer could the NFWA wholeheartedly represent the interests of the farm workers if it let itself be manipulated from above? Was it simply pride that caused the students to feel that the union was sacrificing its initial vitality simply because it had renounced their support? Whatever the answers to these questions, there seemed to be precious little the students could do about the situation, since they had, from the outset, committed themselves to working with the union on its own terms.

The sort of frustrations which the CIP encountered during its Delano support project were becoming more and more prevalent in the program. It was proving difficult for the student organizers to find a sustained role in any of the local community movements they were involved in; either their organizing efforts were hopeless from the start, as was the case with the Chinatown project, or, if they began to make some progress, the movements were promptly legitimized and the students' influence was replaced by a more "respectable" brand of politics. The students who were able to weather these kinds of disappointments were gaining some invaluable experience; for all its failure to make a perceptible impact in the community, the CIP was developing some highly competent and dedicated organizers while it involved a number of previously uncommitted students in off-campus work. That CIP organizers remained incapable of developing an off-campus base despite their skills only served to dramatize some of the major failings of the Alinsky method. Though the students had some very definite ideas about the kind of radical social changes that were needed, they had no clear blueprint telling them how to bring change about. The Alinsky method did not provide such a blueprint; the most it seemed capable of doing was strengthening the bargaining position of the poor within the existing power structure—a gesture that was ultimately self-defeating. So long as the authority of the institutions in control of the system went unchallenged, any effort to build an alternative would remain at their mercy. A redeeming aspect of Alinsky's approach (and most likely the one that wooed student activists) was that at least it went directly to the local level and recognized the people as human beings, capable of making their own decisions. But, lacking a critical overview of society and how it functioned, the Alinsky method ultimately left the organizers as helpless to challenge official institutions as the people they were trying to mobilize. Hence, their movements were prone to cooptation from above or disenchantment from below.

In spite of the short life span of its various organizing activities, the CIP managed to remain feverishly active. In the Mission district, a welfare rights organization was set up by Kathy Madden, a Peace Corps veteran who spoke fluent Spanish; she wrote a bilingual welfare rights handbook which served as a useful organizing tool for the core of welfare recipients she had gotten together. One of the group's more noteworthy ventures was its successful campaign to get Spanish-speaking welfare workers hired by the local welfare agency. At the CIP's rented community center in Oakland, which housed a number of indigenous social action groups, a community newspaper called *Flatlands* was started by the student director of the center, Gerry Leo, in an effort to counter the continual distortions of the problems of Oakland's minority poor by the reactionary Oakland *Tribune.* Leo was a former employee of the Oakland poverty program who had been eased out of his job after he tried to lead an insurgency within the EOC; he was soon thereafter hired by the CIP, and proved to be one of its most effective organizers. The community center also served as the headquarters for the Oakland school boycott in October of 1966, with the CIP bringing in a number of student volunteers to teach in the "freedom schools" while the boycott was in progress. In addition, the CIP got involved in three different "middle-class organizing" projects; these usually aimed to expose white racism and to work with high school students in the suburban districts around the Bay Area.

The swing toward middle-class organizing was a direct outgrowth of the black power upsurge within SNCC, which served notice to the white activists that they would have to get out of the black community and refocus their energies on their own turf. The transition was a natural one; as Stokely Carmichael explained, the best thing whites could do for the black movement was to "organize their own people," since white racism was what had necessitated the black movement in the first place. Yet many white radicals had a hard time facing up to the implications of Carmichael's demand; it meant they would have to develop a critical assessment of their own class background, coupled with an understanding of and empathy for a cultural style which most of them had already rejected. Moreover, their previous political experience offered them very little help or understanding of how best to reach their new constituency. In making the transition, many white organizers initially brought with them all of the rhetoric and all of the organizing techniques they had used in working with minority poor; they tended to treat the residents of the white neighborhoods and suburban housing tracts as if they were, in fact, blacks whose most immediate and perceptible hardship was the existence of white racism. Most of these student activists had no real grasp of the concept of economic classes; as such, the most compelling issues in the white community—taxes, inflation, accumulation of debts, social instability—were all but lost on them, and their early organizing efforts rarely got beyond appeals to altruism.

One of the first CIP workers involved in middle-class organizing was Chuck Crank, an energetic and outgoing student who had heard a Berkeley speech by Stokely Carmichael and was impressed enough by what he said to try immediately to put it into practice. He spent close to six months researching the conditions in San Francisco's Sunset district, a vast, fog-enshrouded expanse of middle-income housing facing the Pacific Ocean; not too surprisingly, he found it was rife with social discontent. Racism was everywhere apparent, and there was a tremendous amount of youth unrest in the area; among other things, it had the highest rate of car theft in the city, though police rarely shot at the youthful offenders as they were known to do in the black community. Even though he spent two years working tirelessly in the "white ghetto," as he called it, Crank was never able to channel that discontent into any kind of viable political organization; in fact, it was next to impossible for his organizing efforts to get any response at all from the residents of the area. As he tried in vain to break through their apathy, Crank became preoccupied with the "psychological oppression" he felt was at the root of the Sunset's problems. It was very real, but it was hardly an issue around which to organize people; only for high school students, whose alienation from their parents' life style and values was blatantly obvious, did it have any tangible meaning. Not surprisingly, the CIP activists in the Sunset district found themselves gravitating more and more toward the young people, whose rebellion tended to take self-destructive forms; a good deal of energy was put into trying to inject some political content into the drug-oriented "youth culture" that appeared to be undermining the parental function of the school system. Still, high school students were hardly a stable constituency, and, all efforts to reach the adults in the neighborhood having failed, the Sunset project was finally to burn itself out.

The disheartening lack of success of these early "middle-class organizing" projects was ample demonstration of the extent to which nearly everybody in the CIP owed their political consciousness to the Civil Rights Movement, and defined themselves accordingly. With the notable exception of Donna Mikkleson, who went on from S.F. State to do pioneering work with the GI coffee house movement, few CIP organizers were able to find a constituency with whom they could work well or be politically effective. They had a technique, but no context in which to use it; the sort of working relationships, based on a mutual reliance and trust, which they had hoped to establish with people in the community had not been forthcoming. At the root of the problem was their own social isolation as white student radicals, an isolation they knew would have to be somehow broken down if they were ever to bring about the kind of radical social change they felt was so desperately needed in America.

Its off-campus tribulations notwithstanding, the CIP was making a formidable impact on the college itself. In order to facilitate their work in the community, students in the program had made it their business to find out how decisions were made on campus, to develop contacts with faculty and administrators who could be of use to them, and generally to devise ways of milking the institution for all it was worth. The Associated Students had been effectively harnessed, but putting the structure of the college to work on their behalf was, for the students in the program, a far more demanding and necessary task. During his administration as AS President, Joe Persico had succeeded in getting nominal student representation on the faculty committees of the Academic Senate, the official educational policy-making body of the college. In terms of its stated purpose of giving students a real voice in the educational process, the concession was an exercise in pure tokenism, which was probably why the faculty readily agreed to it. But the AS activists were interested in the concession for other reasons: by giving them an ear to the activities of the faculty bureaucrats, it helped them develop a keen sensitivity to the intricate workings of institutional politics. Meanwhile, the process of acquiring academic credits for students who were engaged in off-campus organizing had already grown complex enough to warrant a separate program.

The Work-Study Program, as the new undertaking was called, grew out of the discussions in the Ramsey seminar. Lacking a cohesive or continuing role to play in community politics, the CIP was emerging more and more as a clearing house for a wide variety of off-campus projects, the main thrust of which was to get students working in those projects. As such, the organizational apparatus of the CIP began to defer towards the Work-Study Program, to the point where the new program would eventually outstrip the old. After some extended talks involving most of the CIP staff and a number of volunteers, Tutorial Program coordinator Roger Alvarado and Sharon Gold, a CIP organizer in the Mission district, drafted a detailed proposal for a degree program in community organizing. It included a meticulous four-year curriculum in community work, a pass–no credit grading system in lieu of the usual letter grades, and an autonomous administrative structure made up of students, faculty, and community people involved in the program.

THE EXPERIMENTAL COLLEGE

On another political front, the students were leveling their sights on an existing area of the college curriculum, the general education courses which were legally required of all freshmen and sophomores. Though it was supposedly designed to give students a "broad academic base" upon which to continue their education, the general education courses were in effect an academic obstacle course to weed out students who were unwilling or unable to put up with the requirements of the institution. Naturally, the courses were despised by students and faculty alike; so, to give incoming freshmen a more rewarding alternative, the AS set up a series of noncredit seminars. Taught by Joe Persico and an honors student, Cynthia Carlson, these seminars were oriented toward making the students aware of the conflict between institutional and personal values and encouraging them to think critically about the education they were getting from the college.

The students' burgeoning interest in educational reform was not entirely lost upon their professors. Two S.F. State faculty members, Jordan Churchill and Donald Garrity, attended a conference on the subject sponsored by the Danforth Institute during the summer of 1965 and returned to the campus bubbling over with good intentions. Both men were then on the rise in the academic hierarchy—Garrity was soon to be appointed Vice President for Academic Affairs, while Churchill was to become Dean of the School of Humanities—and they were appropriately eager to get in the good graces of students and faculty by showing sympathy for their latest and most pressing educational concerns. They pulled together a small number of faculty and administrators to discuss "making education at San Francisco State College more exciting and relevant." Among those who were invited to the early meetings of "The Group," as it was called, was an activities counselor, Claire Salop, whose job responsibility—making sure student conduct does not deviate from the administrative policy of the college—usually turns the most well-intentioned bureaucrat into a petty tyrant. Miss Salop had, however, initially defined her task as one of showing students how to get what they wanted from the system, and after five years on the job she was very astute at steering them through the bureaucratic maze in order to get a certain policy changed or a new one adopted. In 1962, she had been a prime mover of the Philosophy Statement on Student Activities; three years later she coined the term, "Quiet Revolution," to describe the work being done by the student programs. Now, she casually suggested to members of The Group that perhaps they might want to have some students included in their discussions. The Group agreed, so Miss Salop went out and rounded up Guy Sandler, Joe Persico, Cynthia Carlson, and Jim Nixon.

Sandler, who always spoke with unequivocal candor, thought The Group's attitude was paternalistic and its motives questionable, and he wasted no time in telling them so. The other students were more tactful; they continued to participate in the discussions after the former tutorial coordinator had stormed out, and at length their patience was rewarded. A common complaint of S.F. State faculty was that it often took a year or more to get a new course adopted into the curriculum, a situation that did very little to encourage such endeavors. The students expressed a similar desire to see more flexible curriculum procedures; so, to open up the college to new and "experimental" courses, The Group successfully politicked for the inclusion of a "special studies option" in the curriculum of most academic departments. Listed as "177's" in the college catalogue, these courses could be set up by any faculty member simply by writing up a course description and getting the approval of the appropriate department chairman. Though established primarily for faculty use, the "special studies loophole," as students called it, gave them exactly what they had been looking for. It allowed them to write up course descriptions for a particular community project, get a sympathetic faculty member to sponsor it, and offer it to anyone working on the project who was in need of academic credit. Yet not only did the special studies loophole provide the community activists with accessible credit arrangements; it also became the academic basis for the Experimental College.

The student usually credited with being most instrumental in the creation of the Experimental College was Jim Nixon, who by 1966 was a four-year veteran of student activism at S.F. State. Nixon had worked very closely with Tom Ramsey when the initial push to involve students in community work was being instituted, but he had never become as immersed in off-campus organizing as Ramsey had. Instead, he vacillated between becoming a serious philosophy student and involving himself in the political development of the Programs. Politics invariably won out, partly because Nixon saw himself as a revolutionary and partly because, even as a philosopher, he was always fascinated by the relationship between theory and practice. Though he continued to work closely with students in the community action programs, his role was not one of actual participation, but of devising organizational forms through which their on- and off-campus work could function effectively. Ever since Tom Ramsey had run for AS President, he had been deeply involved with the "student political parties" which were used, year after year, by Program activists to win student body elections, secure their financial base, and keep the machinery of student government at their disposal. Though most of the key people in the Programs had held AS office at one time or another, they considered it unpleasant but necessary "shit work," and Nixon was one of the few who make it a continuing occupation.

It was while he was serving as AS Vice President that Nixon first hit upon the idea of an Experimental College. Observing the CIP's difficulty in establishing an off-campus power base, he began giving more and more thought to the idea of mobilizing students as a political force in themselves, organized around their own grievances and their own self-interest. The bankruptcy of the education being offered by the college was taken for granted by virtually everyone in the Programs, whatever their field of activity; that the existing projects dealt with this bankruptcy only implicitly was, to Nixon and a growing number of others, an oversight student radicals could no longer afford to ignore. "The activists had a real stake in expanding their constituency," Nixon was to say later. "We wanted to create a situation in which students could become revolutionaries, and that meant dealing with every aspect of their lives." Teaching techniques developed by the Tutorial Program were a tacit rejection of the rigid classroom authoritarianism that characterized the college as well as the public schools. The CIP-Work-Study concept was a strong, if unarticulated, critique of the shallow, rarefied, and parochial social outlook of the regular curriculum. For Nixon, anti-authoritarianism and educational relevance were principles around which to organize the entire student body, not just those who drifted into community work; moreover, they deserved to find expression in a concrete educational philosophy which embraced them on a conscious, rather than intuitive, level. The college, mistrusted by a growing number of students, had somehow managed to escape their wrath; an opportunity was being missed to link up the activist tendencies of the Programs with the educational disenchantment of students at San Francisco State.

The idea of "parallel institutions of learning" in which radicals could put forth their own model of education was already gaining wide acceptance. European students had evolved a sophisticated concept of "critical universities" to attack the ideological assumptions underlying academia. In the United States, some of the more politically advanced of the student activists were beginning to look to a somewhat less rigidly structured "free university" as a way of tapping the widespread discontent with the educational system which had surfaced in the wake of the Berkeley Free Speech Movement. The "free U's" did not attempt to fit a particular ideological mold or political orientation that would tend to isolate them or limit their audience to those already convinced. They operated under the assumption that, within the framework of an educational environment that was truly open, the radical ideas which had been excluded from, or distorted by, the established academic curricula would emerge and win converts on the basis of their own innate vitality and pertinence to the contemporary situation. At the same time, by bringing together the best ideas of the student, radical, and dropout communities, it could create a focal point for all three, welding them together under a single attempt to find a workable ideology that addressed itself to all of their respective needs. The first and largest of the free U's was started in New York; others quickly sprang up around the country, usually near college campuses, and, at the time the Experimental College was in its planning stages at S.F. State, there were already two of them in the Bay Area, one in Menlo Park near Stanford University, and the other in Berkeley.

The founders of the Experimental College hoped to work a variation of the free university model which would give it an added dimension and a concrete political objective, something that the free U's lacked. The free U's were independent entities, often plagued by sloppy coordination and lack of resources. By functioning as a "college within a college," the Experimental College would be assured of adequate resources and a ready-made student constituency; AS money could be used to pay for staff, publicity, and other miscellaneous expenses, while credit arrangements could be worked out with sympathetic faculty through the "special studies" loophole. More important, however, was the political function the Experimental College would serve: in drawing students into its own program, it would simultaneously undermine the authority of the official college. The process of broadening the students' awareness of the sources of their own discontent would convert itself naturally into an attack upon the college, and the Experimental College would create the power base from which that attack would be launched. This scheme drew heavily upon the theory of "counter-institutions," which was popular on the student left at the time and was especially appealing to Jim Nixon. Central to the theory was a belief that the social institutions of the new society, to be built after the revolution, could be established within the existing one; if successful, they would hasten the revolutionary process. For Nixon, the value of the Experimental College would lie in its enabling students to test out their critique of the established educational system, to test their vision of the Utopia they hoped to replace it with, to persuade other students that that Utopia was a plausible and realizable goal, and to organize them to fight for that goal. In so doing, it would lend focus and direction to a student movement which was already very real, but still lacked a sense of itself and a concrete plan of action. A major slogan of the Experimental College organizers was "Blackmail them with quality," referring to the Experimental College's ability to reach students on a level the regular college couldn't; a second principle, aimed directly at the ingrained authoritarianism of the college, was expressed by the slogan, "Anyone can teach a course." The latter concept was enormously significant, since it underscored the basic rationale of the program: that of forcing students to take the responsibility for their own education, and, by extension, their own lives. This meant that they would have to begin thinking seriously about their own ideas, and the social and educational alternatives they wanted to project. As Jim Nixon put it, "If you have to teach something, you really have to know it." Once a real knowledge was forthcoming, the students would be in a position to incorporate their alternative concept of education into a set of demands and "move on the college."

The Experimental College got off to a promising start in the spring semester of 1966. A total of twenty-two seminars had been proposed, and at an impromptu registration 444 students appeared to sign up for them. As an added attraction, there was social critic Paul Goodman; he had been hired by the Associated Students under a new visiting professor program and had ended up teaching in the Experimental College, thereby lending his considerable prestige to the fledgling institution. There could not have been a more appropriate choice for this special task. Goodman had been one of the first to expose the failure of the American educational system and to attack the manipulation of the young by the established social institutions. During the FSM, he came to the defense of the Berkeley rebels by arguing that "students are the most exploited class in American society"; his books *Growing Up Absurd* and *Compulsory Mis-education* had made a tremendous impact on student activists. Moreover, the radical Utopianism which ran through all of his writings captured perfectly the essence of what the Experimental College was trying to do. Some of the other seminars that took place were "Perspectives on Revolution," taught by CIP organizer Sharon Gold; "Astronauts of Inner Space," set up by the poet Jeff Berner; "Nonviolence in a Violent World," taught by the famed pacifist Ira Sandperl; "Black Nationalism," "Competition and Violence," and an "Urban Action" seminar organized by a black student, Jimmy Garrett. Of the 444 students who signed up, 307 stayed with their seminars through the semester and 66 received academic credit for their work through the special studies loophole. During the semester, some 30 staff members and course organizers became involved in laying out an organizational structure for the program.

After the spring semester, the staff of the Experimental College embarked on a crucial summer evaluation project in order to determine what direction the program should take in the fall. In April of 1966, the popularity of the Experimental College had enticed Jim Nixon to run for the AS Presidency. He won by a landslide, as did the entire slate of candidates who ran with him. Nixon was later to regret having been elected, but the early effects were rather promising, especially when it led to a $24,000 AS allocation for the Experimental College.

The summer evaluation program consisted of a lot of busy-work and a conference on the Experimental College which attracted students and faculty from S.F. State and other colleges throughout the state. The most important event of the summer, however, was the dispute over the philosophical and programmatic perspective that the program would adopt. The opposing positions represented very clear social attitudes. On the one side were those who argued that the program should consciously build a coherent political strategy for redefining the educational priorities of the regular college. The other side argued that the Experimental College should provide space for various approaches to educational innovation by creating a "counter-environment of freedom." The first position favored a centralized program structure; its adherents often viewed things from a political vantage point, and they usually emphasized an institutional solution to social problems. The latter group opted for a decentralized program structure; they tended to emphasize the need for personal growth and development in a multi-purpose learning community. In the end, those favoring decentralization won out, and it was decided that the program would adhere to no specific perspective, nor have any determined direction. Instead, it would be made up of seven autonomous areas of study, and be open to anyone who wanted to make use of it.

To a certain extent, the genesis of the summer controversy can be traced to a related schism that developed around the use of "T-groups" and "sensitivity training" to facilitate the personal and work relationships of the people involved in the Experimental College. Jim Nixon was responsible for introducing these newly defined psychological processes into the program; as he was later to recall, "They seemed to be a handle on a whole variety of community questions that politics failed to deal with." And the benefits were quickly apparent: they broke down rigid power relations in a classroom; they provided valuable insights into the functioning of both political and social groups; and they could make people aware of their own repressed feelings. There was a danger of self-indulgence or even delusion, however, which seemed to have been the trap that some of the Experimental College staff members got caught in. By emphasizing a reliance on feelings, a "do your own thing" philosophy began to prevail at the expense of all other considerations. This "group faction," as they were called, then began to evolve differences with the "work faction," which had initially defined the Experimental College in institutional terms. The differences flowed over into the summer evaluation debate, where the "group faction" backed the plan for a nonstructured "counter-environment."

At first, business proved to be very good in the 1966 fall semester. During the two days designated for open registration, some 1200 people enrolled in 70 courses being offered through the Experimental College. The staff was, quite naturally, swamped with work; it was almost beyond their capacity to arrange for the necessary classrooms. A few of the seven autonomous areas managed to put together a good program, especially the Black Arts and Culture series coordinated by Marianna Waddy. Yet most of them, like the ill-fated Institute for Social Change and the Communications and Arts series, fell flat on their faces. By some yardsticks, the fact that the program had tripled in size meant that it was a phenomenal success deserving of its enhanced national reputation. In essence, however, the Experimental College had literally run away with itself, and most of the more perceptive staff members quickly realized that they had no influence on the overall direction and content of the program. The combination of the "anyone can teach a course" maxim and the mandate to "do your own thing," augmented by a flood of visionaries from the Haight-Ashbury, had resulted in a proliferation of such courses as "Zen Basketball," "Astro-Psychology," "Meta-Hamlet," and a number of "touchie-feelie" seminars. Such courses usually became hip social cliques; they included little if any serious thought or work. Moreover, they fostered an atmosphere in the Experimental College that was certainly apolitical if not downright anti-intellectual.

Enrollment had dropped off one-half for the 1967 spring semester, partly because the Experimental College fad was wearing thin and partly as a result of an effort to reorganize the program. By that time, though, the problems of reestablishing the Experimental College's original priorities were insurmountable: the activists in the Associated Students had lost their first student body election in five years, partly due to the opposition's success in exposing the mismanagement of the Experimental College; relations with the faculty and administration had begun to deteriorate; and the "do your own thing" philosophy had effectively supplanted the institutional objectives of the radicals. Where the

initial goals of the Experimental College had been to help build
the student movement and to reform the college, the new goals
were best seen in this statement by the former coordinator of the
Experimental College's newsletter: "The task before us consists
of developing processes which help the students get in touch with
his own Being, which help him to become aware of himself as a
Life-Force in the world, and explore and develop the potentialities of that Life-Force." This transition in goals led to the political emasculation of the program. Originally conceived of as a
vehicle to effect institutional change within the traditional college, the Experimental College had developed into an institutional safety valve for the very college it had hoped to revolutionize. To be sure, there were some excellent courses taught
through the program, and even some belated attempts to develop a nonauthoritarian theory of teaching, but these tended to
be the exception rather than the rule. For the most part, the
Experimental College became an educational playground for
bored or alienated students, and as such, it absorbed, ironically,
much of the discontent it had hoped to crystallize for political
purposes.

THE BLACK STUDENTS' UNION

Up until the spring of 1966, the Negro Students Association
(NSA) was the principal organization of black students on the
San Francisco State campus. The NSA was essentially a social
club; it showed little, if any, inclination toward organizational
involvement in the political issues that had captured the con-
sciences of the white student activists at the time. There was some
black nationalist sentiment among the membership, but it was
usually displayed in a penchant for black cultural awareness in
music or the arts. After Malcolm X was murdered on February
21, 1965, a rally to mourn his death set up by a few NSA members had attracted only a handful of black sympathizers. While
most of the black students on campus were in the NSA, their
foremost concern was to earn a college degree, and they didn't
seem to be involved in much else. Under these circumstances,
the NSA merely provided the black students with a convenient
and acceptable niche in a predominately white institution. But

there were social forces in motion that were affecting the lives of black people all over the country. The Civil Rights Movement had failed to meaningfully change even the most obvious manifestations of racism both in the South and the North. The polite civil disobedience of the sit-ins and marches was giving way to the angry civil insurrections of Harlem and Watts. Nonviolent attitudes implicit in a song like "We Shall Overcome" were being supplanted by a more militant outlook characterized in the slogan, "Burn Baby Burn!" And a movement that had started out by seeing integration as a morally just goal, was now rallying around "black power" as a political necessity.

Nowhere was this transition better epitomized than in the political development of SNCC. As early as 1962, SNCC was realizing that the effects of nonviolent demonstrations were limited; they could force the integration of a lunch counter, but they didn't even begin to deal with the fact that blacks were still politically disenfranchised in the South. This observation led SNCC to develop its voter registration campaigns. And when it became apparent that neither of the major political parties would satisfactorily represent black people's interests, independent political organizations like the Mississippi Freedom Democrats and the Lowndes County Black Panthers were experimented with. Equally important was the role of whites in organizations like SNCC. Even prior to the Mississippi Summer Project in 1964, a majority of SNCC's black staff members had opposed bringing white students into Mississippi. They felt that no matter how well-intentioned the whites were, they could not hope to be effective organizers in the black community. Whites had been trying to free black people for far too long, and nothing but misery had come of it. Nevertheless, the more moderate leadership in SNCC prevailed, convincing the others that the only way to expose Mississippi racism was to bring down the white kids, who would in turn lure the press. It was a calculated political act, and it worked fairly well up until the Democratic National Convention.

The Democratic Party's refusal to seat the MFDP at Atlantic City ended SNCC's attempts to work for political reform within the system. The bitter resentment that this event fostered was tacitly summed up by SNCC activist Bob Moses: "They told us to be responsible because the destiny of America was in our hands," he said after the convention. "We learned that it was not in our hands. We will pursue our own goals, and let the chips fall where they may." By 1965, Stokely Carmichael had injected the concept of black power into the political dialogue of a disintegrating civil rights movement, and defined it as the power to control the institutions in the black community, and, by implication, the destiny of black people in America. SNCC then became the first civil rights organization to adopt a black power position, and by so doing it ushered in a new phase of the black movement. No longer was integration a sanctioned goal; rather, the word went out that black people had to begin to define and organize themselves apart from white America. Only through such a process could they ever hope to become strong enough to effectively deal with the racism that seemed to saturate the whole society.

Jimmy Garrett had joined SNCC in 1962, and had worked in the South off and on for almost three years. In the summer of 1965, he was back home in Los Angeles, fund raising for SNCC, when the Watts rebellion broke out. He sweated out an entire night on the floor of his parents' house after the police had shot at him for standing on the front porch. During that same summer, Garrett had met Fred Thalheimer, a San Francisco State sociology professor who was involved in civil rights activity. They got to know each other while working on the same project, and Thalheimer suggested that he might enjoy attending S.F. State. Later in the year, Garrett came up to San Francisco, and while waiting to start school in the spring he got a job interviewing black people in Hunter's Point. Garrett had a natural talent for organizing, and he used his job mostly to become familiar with the Hunter's Point community. In particular, he got to know a number of young black men who were sympathetic to the new mood of black militancy, including a sociology student at S.F. State named Chuck Sizemore, who was also a member of the NSA.

Garrett had originally intended to concentrate on creative writing at S.F. State, but by the time the spring semester came

around, he was immersed in political activity. Along with Fred
Thalheimer, he was teaching a seminar in the Experimental College called "Urban Action," through which he got to know some
of the white radicals and how they had tapped the AS resources
to finance their social action programs. In addition, he was talking regularly with a group of black students about the implications of new concepts like black power and black consciousness.
Some of the students participating in these discussions were
Chuck Sizemore, Ed Washington, one of the few black students
in the Tutorial Program, Aubrey LaBrie, who was teaching a
course on black nationalism in the Experimental College, and
Marianna Waddy, a proud and energetic young black woman.
What they all quickly agreed on was that black students at S.F.
State had to begin to play a more active role in the struggles of
their race. With this in mind, the group began to take an interest
in the affairs of the NSA, which resulted in its total transforma-
tion in March, 1966. The name "Negro Students' Association"
was discarded in favor of "Black Students' Union" (BSU), and
Marianna Waddy was installed as the new president. Comment-
ing on the sudden emergence of the BSU, Miss Waddy said,
"This college had done little for black students except try to
white-wash them. We will now strive to incorporate the eminent
and profound concept of blackness into a new and positive image of black students on this campus."
    The impact of this new disposition of S.F. State black students
was first felt by the Tutorial Program. Since its inception, most
of the tutorial leadership had acknowledged the need to bring
black students into the program. But aside from Ed Washington,
who had himself tried unsuccessfully to recruit potential tutors
from the ranks of the NSA, very few black students got involved
in the Tutorial Program. Garrett, however, not only saw that
white students teaching black kids was almost a replay of the
Mississippi Summer Project, but also recognized that the program
was a ready-made vehicle for the black students to establish a
sound relationship with the black community. Even within the
tutorial staff meetings, there was a growing concern about ethnic
and cultural considerations, due mostly to the dependency and
paternalism that the "each one, teach one" philosophy seemed to

be producing. Questions about black-white relationships had been raised all along in these weekly meetings, but the lack of black tutors had stultified any meaningful discussion of the subject. Late in the 1966 spring semester, Garrett got together with Roger Alvarado, who was still the director of the program. The two agreed that as many black students as possible should become involved in the actual tutoring, and that the summer should be partly devoted to a comprehensive reevaluation of the entire Tutorial Program, with BSU participation.

The summer reevaluation project immediately turned into black-white encounter sessions. True to his word, Garrett brought a number of black students to every meeting, and the effect was a traumatic baring of racial fears and hostility. Invariably, the white students suffered most. It was hard enough to suddenly learn that the blacks did not take too kindly to them or to their efforts to help black children. It was even worse, however, when their own psychological motives began to surface. In spite of themselves, they deeply resented the black students for coming into the program, because their very presence altered it irrevocably. By telling white students that they could no longer tutor black children, the black students, in effect, were demanding an end to the emotionally fulfilling relationships that many of the whites had built with black youngsters. Such relationships were often extremely paternalistic, owing their origins to vague feelings of racial guilt; hence, the thought of tutoring white children simply wasn't appealing to the white activists. For their part, the black students felt that the role white students were playing was detrimental to the black child's own identity, as well as his image of black people in general. To be proud of his own race and heritage, the black child needed to be able to identify first and foremost with black people. In short, blacks had to start taking care of their own; they didn't want any more help from the whites because it could only perpetuate the vicious circle of dependency and oppression that had victimized black people since they were slaves.

By the end of the summer of 1966, the Tutorial Program started to reorganize itself in order to coincide with the wishes of the black students. As a result, eleven white tutors quit outright;

though they had begrudgingly acknowledged the legitimacy of the BSU's position, these students still felt they had been pushed out of a program that they had helped create. Most of the white students, however, stayed with their individual tutoring projects until the transition could be smoothly accomplished. The BSU began to actively recruit black students, and by November Roger Alvarado, who had supported the black students throughout the entire ordeal, stepped down as the program's director. He was soon succeeded by George Murray, a black English major who had twelve younger brothers and sisters of his own.

Another student program which initially attracted the interest of the black students was the Experimental College. Both Jimmy Garrett and Aubrey LaBrie had independently taught courses in the Experimental College during the 1966 spring semester, and it was mainly through them that the idea of developing a comprehensive black curriculum originated. There was literally nothing being offered at S.F. State that was oriented towards black people; there was hardly any black faculty to speak of—and the BSU was becoming very sensitive to these omissions. To fill the gap, Marianna Waddy took charge of organizing a Black Arts and Culture series, which was initiated through the Experimental College in the 1966 fall semester. The program attracted over 200 students to the eight seminars that it sponsored; some of the courses were "Black Psychology," "The Miseducation of the Negro," "Black Writers from Rebellion to Revolution," and "The History and Social Significance of Black Power." All of the offerings were taught either by the students themselves or by community people they invited in to assist with the program.

The BSU's utilization of the Experimental College led initially to more black-white encounter patterns. The black students had no intention of overrunning the Experimental College like some felt they had in the Tutorial Program; rather, they wanted the Experimental College to provide space and funds for the courses they planned to teach. Nevertheless, their very presence tended to threaten many of the white students in the Experimental College, something the blacks didn't hesitate to use to their advantage. A major flare-up came over the first budget that the BSU submitted for the Black Arts and Culture series. In comparison to the budgets drawn up by the other six areas of study in the Experimental College that semester, it was somewhat exorbitant, and many bitter words were exchanged before a compromise agreement was reached. Another revealing incident occurred at a meeting called to discuss Experimental College staff priorities, in which Jim Nixon and Jimmy Garrett got into a heated argument. In the middle of their verbal sparring, the telephone rang and was answered by Mike Vozik, an Experimental College staff member. With the entire room in dead silence, Vozik inadvertently said to the party on the other end of the line, "Call back later, Jim's busy handling Garrett and the BSU." Garrett countered with a few choice words of his own, whereupon he and his companions walked out of the meeting. These early experiences soon led to an uneasy entente, based strictly on each party's own self-interest; mutual trust between black and white radicals would be slow in coming. In the interim, the BSU proceeded to set up their own completely autonomous programs with startling speed. By the following semester, they had taken the Black Arts and Culture series out of the Experimental College, changed its name to Black Studies, and begun a long struggle to get the college to provide the resources for a Black Studies department.

The community aspect of the BSU's program, which included the tutorials, began to be put into operation in the fall of 1966. With the ubiquitous Marianna Waddy in the student legislature, the BSU's request for $9,550 was granted after only minor skirmishes (and a small coup that resulted in Miss Waddy being appointed head of the finance committee). Some of the earliest projects included a black draft counseling service in the Fillmore district and a community self-defense class in Karate. The major focus of the BSU's activities, however, was on the area's ghetto high schools. There, organizers aided the black high school students in developing their own programs to combat the oppressive conditions in the schools. High school BSU's eventually sprang up all over the Bay Area, and demands for black curriculum, more black teachers and "soul food" in the cafeteria became commonplace. In addition, the BSU started to work on a "special admissions" program, designed to get black high school students who couldn't normally qualify for the state colleges into San

Francisco State, with the financial and educational assistance necessary to help them stay in college once they gained entrance.

Marianna Waddy was replaced as BSU President by Jimmy Garrett in late summer of 1966. In a speech on "black power" right after he was elected chairman (the title of president had been done away with), Garrett hit on some of the new themes that were becoming increasingly important in the black movement. He characterized the condition of blacks in America as one of a "colonized people." "We are still slaves in this country," Garrett maintained. "We have yet to win our freedom from white America. Our struggle is no different from that of the Vietnamese, who heroically resist the white oppressor." This identification with the National Liberation Front in Vietnam was part of the belief that the black struggle in the U.S. had natural allies in the people of the "third world"—Asia, Africa, and Latin America. They also were colored people struggling to throw off the yoke of colonialism and its counterpart, imperialism. This colonial ideology, drawn mostly from the writings of the African revolutionary, Frantz Fanon, was quickly becoming the foundation for the "black liberation" struggle in America. Integration had been completely rejected; self-determination was the new objective. As Garrett put it, "What white people must begin to understand is that we are no longer striving for an integrated society; those days are gone. We are struggling for self-determination. Self-determination for our black lives; self-determination for our black communities; and self-determination for a black education."

CHAPTER IV

Broken Promises, Bleeding Hearts: THE COLLAPSE OF S. F. STATE'S LIBERAL CONSENSUS, 1966-1967

THE COMMONS BOYCOTT

The San Francisco State College Foundation is a $1.5 million "non-profit corporation" that is responsible for administering the Commons and the college bookstore. Despite relatively high prices and almost inedible food, the Commons loses money every year, while the bookstore invariably turns in an impressive profit. For years the Foundation's managers had steadfastly insisted that profits from one enterprise could not legally be transferred to the other. Accordingly, when the Organization of Student Employees (OSE), whose members received from $1.30 to $1.40 an hour for serving food and bussing dishes in the Commons, threatened to strike if their wages were not raised to $1.80 an hour, Foundation director Fred Avilez responded by raising food prices in the Commons by twelve to fifteen per cent.

Ever since Tom Ramsey had campaigned for student body president in 1963, the policies of the Foundation had been under constant dispute on the S.F. State campus. During his administration as AS President, Joe Persico had managed to achieve a kind of nominal student control over the Foundation Board of Governors, a nine-man body presided over by Presidential Assistant Glenn Smith. But while the four faculty-administration representatives on the Board were outnumbered by five students, only three of those students were AS-appointed; the other two were representatives of the college dormitories, whose food services were also provided by the Foundation, and, being administration appointees, they seldom voted with their fellow students. Leaders of the AS Programs had long viewed the Foundation's large profit surplus as a possible financial base to augment the limited resources of the Associated Students. Glenn Smith, on the other hand, saw it as a supplementary source of income for the college, to be spent in such areas as building improvements and capital outlay costs where the generosity of the state legislature was found wanting. The students did manage to get some money appropriated for an experimental nursery school in the college's married students' housing development, but it was usually Glenn Smith who got his way. Still, the AS representatives on the Board chose to continue working quietly with faculty and administration, gaining concessions where they could, maintaining the stance that they believed meaningful cooperation was possible, and striving behind the scenes to bring hegemony to their own ranks so as to put their one-vote majority to use.

This process had already begun to break down by the time the OSE made its strike threat. As early as April, 1966, the CIP had been instrumental in launching a campaign to halt the college's demolition of the $45-a-month married students' housing development known as Gatorville. The S.F. State administration had planned to do away with the dilapidated housing project in order to utilize the land it was on for institutional expansion; no provisions were made for the occupants, all of whom were students with families of three or more. In the dispute that followed, which in some ways foreshadowed the conflicts over the Morningside Heights gym at Columbia and "People's Park" at Berkeley, the students argued that the priorities of institutional expansion were secondary when measured against the needs of students—in this case, cheap and accessible housing. The "Save Gatorville" campaign was so successful in mobilizing support on campus that the college administration not only was forced to call off the demolition of the housing project, but also contributed $10,000 for the renovation of the apartment buildings. The CIP's role in organizing the opposition to the college's expansion plan did not go unnoticed by the local administrators. S.F. State officials were willing to tolerate and even encourage what the CIP did off-campus, so long as its activities remained unobtrusive; but when the administrators themselves became targets of CIP agitation, a number of them began to feel that the students were biting the hand that fed them. Shortly after, in the fall of 1966, when the CIP offered its services to the OSE in its fight for higher wages and a union contract, Glenn Smith, who regarded the Foundation as his personal domain, threatened a federal investigation. Like all of the Associated Students Programs, the CIP made liberal use of the job opportunities provided under the Educational Opportunity Act, which was designed to help students through school by hiring them to work for the institutions they attended. The federal government paid three-fourths of their salaries, the administration or student government the remaining one-fourth. A number of program workers, including those who organized in the community, were getting EOA money, and Smith's threat to "expose" to the federal government how its charity money was being put to use was not one which could be taken lightly.

The harmonious relationships of the "quiet revolution" were already beginning to show some ragged edges when the arrival of a new group on campus, under the aegis of another group, assured further deterioration of campus serenity. The first organization was the Students for a Democratic Society; the second, the lesser-known Progressive Labor Party (PL), whose genesis, like that of SDS, had its roots in the decline of the Communist Party of the United States. For years, the CPUSA had been the dominant force in American radicalism. It not only attracted the most members, but also made the greatest impact on American culture and American life. Communist organizers were instrumental in building up the CIO; some even became prominent architects of the liberal welfare state and other reforms of the New Deal. The doctrine of "social realism" dominated American literature during the 1930's and to this day continues to be an influence on most "serious" films coming out of Hollywood. Total failures as revolutionaries, the Communists had achieved considerable success as social reformers before the repression of the 1950's set in. During the McCarthy era, they adopted a strictly defensive posture, choosing to conceal their politics and, when attacked, hide behind a barrage of constitutional amendments and legalisms. This course proved disastrous; it was not hard for the Establishment to portray the Communists as insidious, super-secret agents of a foreign power when the Communists themselves responded by "going underground" and outwardly maintaining that they were respectable, patriotic Americans. Initially, the Progressive Labor Party grew out of a reaction within the Communist Party against this position, which PL saw as unprincipled, dishonest, and ultimately self-defeating. The dissident faction was further alienated by the eagerness with which the Communist Party fell behind the integrationist, nonviolent rhetoric of the Civil Rights Movement: PL preferred instead to identify with the exiled black leader Robert Williams, expelled from the NAACP and driven from the country when he asserted that black people should arm themselves in self-defense. The Sino-Soviet dispute provided PL with an ideological context; it officially split from the Communist Party, attacking the revisionist policies of the USSR and identifying strongly with the Chinese revolution.

Progressive Labor became deeply involved in the student movement around the time of the FSM, when it realized that something of great significance was happening on the campuses, even if a clear explanation for it did not yet exist. Through the May 2nd Movement, a campus front group, they sought to draw students into their organization on the basis of their opposition to the Vietnam war. May 2nd was the first student group to put forth, in a "New Left" context, a theory of American imperialism, a theory the student left was quick to adopt as the antiwar movement moved beyond moral outrage and sought to develop a systematic explanation for United States foreign policy. By the fall of 1966, PL had disbanded the May 2nd Movement in favor of working within the Students for a Democratic Society, the largest, most influential, and the most amorphous of the New Left organizations.

When the decision to move into SDS was made, Progressive

Labor organizers in San Francisco had been working for some time in the Mission district, trying to build a neighborhood tenants' union. There their path frequently crossed with that of the CIP, and a mutual suspicion quickly grew up between the two groups. CIP organizers saw PL as a tenacious cadre of rigid dogmatists, more interested in pushing their line than in serving the people of the community; the CIP workers, in turn, were regarded by PL as a muddled group of liberal reformers in the pay of the Establishment. The field of hostilities was transferred to the campus when a group of PL members began to set up the S.F. State SDS chapter in September, 1966.

Having arrived on campus, SDS needed a good popular issue with which to establish itself. Its interest in trade unions led it initially to make overtures within OSE; John Levin, a PL organizer, took a job in the Commons and began pushing for a more militant attitude within the union. When the OSE won its contract and the resultant fifteen per cent price increase touched off a storm of outrage on the campus, SDS launched a two-month investigation of the Foundation which revealed that, by continuing to run the Commons and the bookstore as separate enterprises, it was bleeding the students dry, while the AS representatives on the Board of Governors (at the time, they included President Jim Nixon and his Vice President and Treasurer, Tom Linney and Ira Schoenwald) were doing nothing to stop it. A boycott of the Commons was called for the first week of December.

Here SDS got some unexpected help. Jon McKinney, one of the principal boycott organizers, was an old high school friend of the City Editor of the *Daily Gater*, Phil Garlington. Cynical, contemptuous, whimsical, utterly without political commitments, Garlington was a Machiavellian character *par excellance.* He saw in the Foundation a potential issue which would scandalize the campus, a chance to do a favor for his old friend McKinney, and the prospect of embarrassing Jim Nixon, whom he disliked. The excesses of the "sensitivity" faction of the Experimental College were a staple of Garlington's columns, and he didn't hesitate to use them as an excuse to attack the entire complex of Associated Students programs. If the AS bureaucracy was a good target, however, Foundation director Fred Avilez was an even better

one. In a superb job of news management, the *Gater* began nee-
dling the Foundation and releasing information about it which
the SDS investigators had uncovered. Avilez panicked and ordered the management of the Commons and the bookstore not to
grant any more interviews; from that point on every article that
appeared in the *Gater* on the subject contained a meticulous
enumeration of the Foundation's various sins, then concluded
with the sentence, "Fred Avilez was not available for comment."
By the time the boycott was actually called, demanding a twenty
per cent reduction in food prices and meaningful student control
of the Board of Governors (with student representatives elected,
not appointed), the student body had become so mobilized that
the SDS picket line was ninety per cent effective, and business
in the Commons came to a halt.

The astonishing success of the boycott shocked the Program
leaders into realizing that they had isolated themselves from the
rest of the campus. Joe Persico and several other CIP workers
were the first to jump on the bandwagon and support the boycott. Jim Nixon was reluctant. He knew the boycott was liable to
destroy the "era of good feelings" between students and administration under which the Programs had grown and flourished; he
distrusted the style of mass confrontation and initially considered
SDS to be politically immature. He was, however, intelligent
enough to realize that it was too late to turn back the clock; if he
failed to be where the action was, then he knew he would become politically ineffective. In any case, the tactics the administration used to try and break the boycott indicated how wide the
rift had become. When the boycott committee brought in food
tables and sold home-made sandwiches to the students who honored the picket lines, Dean of Students Ferd Redell warned the
students that the Department of Public Health had declared their
tables to be a health menace and that the authorities would have
to be called in if the food was not taken away. The next day the
Gater called up the Department of Public Health and discovered
the "health scare" was bogus: City Health Director Ellis Sox did
not even know about the boycott. The administration's next
move was to try to split the OSE from the boycott by threatening
to lay off workers in the Commons if it continued. SDS had

made preparations for such an eventuality, however; the boycott had been called only after consulting with and gaining the support of the union, and the students threatened to shut down the bookstore as well as the Commons if the OSE was laid off. The final ploy, which also sought to be divisive, was partially to capitulate and lower food prices by ten per cent instead of twenty per cent, while keeping the composition of the Board of Governors intact. That was too much for Jim Nixon, who resigned from the Board in protest and threw his support to the boycott. However, Nixon's own underlings, Tom Linney and Ira Schoenwald, remained on the Board and continued to insist that the boycott "did not represent the majority of students."

When the boycott had completed its first week, a meeting was called at the apartment of one of the leaders, in the heart of the Haight-Ashbury, at which Program students and SDS got together to plan further strategy and attempt to coalesce their forces. The meeting was already well under way when the doorbell rang. One of the students got up to answer it and discovered a slight, sandy-haired man with an air of earnest deference about him. He was John Summerskill, the new President of the college. He stepped into the room where the astonished boycott leaders were talking and apologized for coming late.

Summerskill had begun his term as college President at the beginning of the fall semester; the boycott represented the first crisis of his administration. A 41-year-old clinical psychologist from Cornell, he had been brought out to S.F. State after his predecessor, Stanley Paulson, had suddenly resigned in an atmosphere of bitterness and mistrust. Paulson was offended when the faculty liberals in the Academic Senate had stalled at making him permanent President; for their part, the Senate's academic politicians were unhappy with Paulson because he had appointed Donald Garrity to be Academic Vice President over their objections. Once in office, Garrity promptly tried to undercut the Academic Senate's authority by setting up the Council of Academic Deans (CAD), a more conservative body designed to give the presidency advice more "prestigious" than the recommendations of the Senate. It was all too much for Paulson, who quit his job to return to teaching and research complaining of the "pressure cooker atmosphere" of the President's office, which no one had been able to hold for more than two years since the departure of Glenn Dumke. Summerskill was seen as a transcendent force, a man who could rise above politics and bring the warring factions together. His opening speech to the faculty in September, if somewhat out of touch with reality, must have sounded terribly reassuring: "You will not find me being a President in the power or authority of the word. Life is too full of problems to exercise prerogatives." Summerskill's approach to politics was basically that of a trained clinical psychologist: believing there to be no irreconcilable differences within the campus community, he felt that problems could be worked out if everybody simply "got together and talked things out."

Translating theory into action, Summerskill told the students at the boycott committee meeting that he felt their grievances were justified and he was sure an amicable solution could be reached. Promising to appear in the Commons Monday morning and speak in support of the boycott, he suggested that the students, for their part, talk things over with Glenn Smith. Smith undoubtedly had more personal hostility towards the boycott than anyone else on campus, so the students naturally assumed that Summerskill would pave the way for their visit. The President did show up in the Commons Monday morning, climbing upon a table to deliver a highly sympathetic speech which was nevertheless short on concrete promises. The boycott leaders, meanwhile, filed into Smith's office, only to discover that Summerskill had not even talked to him about the meeting. If anything, Smith was more put out than ever, convinced now that Summerskill was trying to put a knife in his back.

A detente of sorts had arrived by the end of the week, but it was far from amicable. After scandalizing the campus with stories of the Foundation's inequities and backing the boycott to the hilt, the *Gater* did an abrupt about-face. Pressure from the journalism department faculty, which felt that its charges were playing too partisan a role, provoked a front-page editorial declaring the boycott had "made its point" and it was "time to stop." Business in the Commons immediately began to pick up again. At this point the Associated Students politicos took charge; a

two-day moratorium on boycott activity was called so that elections might be held for a new, student-controled Board of Governors. Though suspicious of their motives, SDS was obliged to
accede to the AS leaders' plans, for it was admittedly not prepared to handle the mechanics of a student takeover of the Foundation. It had called the boycott simply to raise issues, establish
itself on campus, and to show that open confrontations, not be-
hind-the-scenes maneuvering and manipulation, got things done.
Having no program of their own for the Foundation, they had to
let the job of restructuring it fall into the hands of those who did:
a slate of six students, led by Peter Pursley of the Black Students' Union, won the election and took office after two months
of jockeying for power. Glenn Smith was forced out as the Foundation's kingpin, though he remained as the administration's
representative on the Board. College business manager Orrin
DeLand, however, quit the Board altogether, claiming in a huff
that students were going to drive the Foundation into bankruptcy. Actually, what Pursley was able to accomplish represented one of the last successful coups of the "quiet revolution."
Once the transfer of profits from the bookstore to the Commons
was arranged, the OSE received a $2.25 an hour union contract
and food prices were immediately lowered. Glenn Smith threatened to take all the vending machines out of the Commons if
these policies were not reversed; Peter Pursley countered by
threatening to raise food prices in the faculty-administration dining room if the machines were touched. Eventually, the new
Foundation was able to appropriate $12,000 to the Tutorial Pro-
gram, establish a $5,000 bail fund for S.F. State students who had
brushes with the law, and provide the infant Black Studies program with the earliest funding it was to receive from the college.

THE IMBROGLIO OF INSTITUTIONAL POLITICS

After the *Gater* had abandoned its crusade against the Foundation, it began redirecting its energies against the Associated Students. At the beginning of the fall semester, Marty Mellara had
wandered into the paper's office and volunteered his services as
"political editor," maintaining that he could come up with the

inside news on AS politics. After four years of repeated frustrations, Mellara was still trying to wrest control of the AS away from the Programs' leadership, and in Phil Garlington he found his most effective instrument to date. The years 1966–67 were particularly unsettling for the Associated Students. At the height of its national acclaim, with one prominent news magazine after another visiting the campus and singing the praises of the student programs, the AS was beset by fiscal mismanagement, bureaucratization, and increasing political irrelevance. The Experimental College, in particular, which was posed by the mass media as a panacea for student unrest, had fallen prey to some of the worst excesses of the burgeoning hip culture. When the Experimental College tried to stage a rock concert, an all-college "happening" in the manner of San Francisco impressario Bill Graham, it turned into an unqualified financial disaster. Another sizeable chunk of money was lost when poet Jeff Berner, who had been hired by the EC to teach an "Astronauts of Inner Space" seminar, took advantage of a badly worded contract and toured Europe while on the AS payroll. Readers of the *Gater* were quickly familiarized with these "scandals," as well as any backbiting or infighting that went on in the student government; where reality would not suffice, the editors would manufacture additional stories.

More important, the emergence of the Black Students' Union as the most powerful force within the AS Programs caused a good deal of anxiety on campus—something the *Gater* was not about to pass up. The BSU takeover of the Tutorial Program provided the opportunity for some scare headlines about "reverse racism," while AS money squabbles involving the BSU always managed to get a front page billing. Early in February, 1967, Phil Garlington facetiously announced in his column that he was running for Associated Students President. The joke caught on and Garlington began using the paper, and the various "scandals" it uncovered, to promote his own candidacy. Originally dismissed as a farce by the AS politicos, the City Editor of the *Gater* began to emerge more and more as a serious threat to their power. An "opposition" paper, *Open Process*, was started by CIP worker Gary Wagner with AS funds; the initial purpose of the new paper was to better familiarize the campus with the work being done by the Programs. It was, however, too little and too late. When the official campaigning began, Garlington steadfastly refused to recognize his presidential opponent, Peter Pursley of the BSU, whom he claimed to be a "puppet of Jim Nixon." In this clever manner the racial issues implicit in the election were neatly sidetracked. The fact that Pursley and the other black students on his slate were members of the BSU wasn't even alluded to; rather, they were derisively attacked as stooges of a white incumbent.

Garlington's own "Shape Up" slate was a curious amalgamation of political left-outs, most of them fraternity members, who ran the gamut from a *Gater* reporter named Dave Richmond to Steve Diaz, the son of a Cuban exile active in the Batista regime. The slate had been brought together by the AS Programs' old political nemesis, Bill Burnett, who had enticed Garlington to head it by offering to pay $1000 in campaign expenses out of his own pocket. The campaign itself was undoubtedly the dirtiest in S.F. State's history. It climaxed when the Shape Up forces released a leaflet written entirely in Arabic which accused Jim Nixon of being an agent in an "international Zionist conspiracy." Garlington eventually repudiated the leaflet, calling it a "tragic mistake," but not before it had been distributed among the college's Arab students.

At the same time, the AS politicos were under attack from the left. SDS had turned away from its initial success with the boycott to the less rewarding task of trying to build a constituency around its antiwar, antidraft activities. But although the campus community was virtually united in its opposition to American involvement in Vietnam—President Summerskill himself was prominent in the ranks of a large peace march in San Francisco on April 15, 1967—SDS had not found a way to capitalize on this opposition. A minor fracas occurred in April when SDS demonstrators escorted a Dow Chemical recruiter off the campus and were, in turn, verbally threatened by a group of athletes. Summerskill's response to the incident set the tone for the interminable debate on "college complicity" which was to follow: "I hate napalm and I think the war is wrong, but the principle of free speech is involved here . . . the college should be the last place to be touched by pressures, political or otherwise."

A more serious problem for SDS was the hostile competition for a student constituency that had developed between its adherents and those of the AS Programs. This competition led, in part, to SDS's decision to run four candidates of its own in the April elections, campaigning for, among other things, the abolition of compulsory student body fees—which would have effectively abolished the Associated Students as well. Though the SDS candidates polled only a small amount of votes, they undoubtedly drew support away from the Pursley slate. Garlington's sensational campaign tactics attracted the largest voter turnout the campus had ever seen, a sizeable portion of which was probably now resentful at having its ten dollars a semester in student fees spent by either hippies or black militants. The Shape Up slate swept the election by so narrow a margin that the results were contested for weeks afterward. Amid the tumult and shouting, two referenda passed overwhelmingly with little or no publicity: one called for the legalization of marijuana; the other, placed on the ballot by SDS, demanded that the college administration stop computing class rankings and sending them to draft boards.

Repercussions quickly set in at the first session of the Shape Up legislature. When visiting professor LeRoi Jones, who had been employed by the Associated Students for the spring semester, rose to ask for a $4,000 appropriation for a Black Communications Project (which would, under BSU sponsorship, put on plays in the city's black ghettoes), Finance Committee Chairman Steve Diaz gave a vitriolic speech accusing the BSU of everything from reverse racism to embezzlement. His charges touched off a near riot in which a table was overturned by BSU leader Jerry Varnado and a fist-fight was narrowly averted when the Speaker of the Legislature abruptly declared the meeting adjourned. The body reconvened the next day, and, under pressure from the college administration, narrowly voted to grant the BSU's request.

The Black Students' Union had, through tough lobbying tactics, managed to salvage an apparently hopeless situation, but the whole incident simply served to demonstrate to the other Programs that the new legislature threatened to wreak havoc with their respective budgets. At an emergency meeting of Program leaders, Roger Alvarado argued that it was time to move off the campus entirely and set up a "community college," independent of the regular institution. The chief barrier to such a course was, naturally, lack of funds, but here a bewildering turn of events gave the Programs unexpected help.

John Summerskill's official investiture as President of the College was scheduled for May 2, 1967. Some weeks before, he had told a group of SDS members that he could not act upon their demand for an end to class rankings without a mandate from the student body. When the passage of the SDS referendum in the AS elections provided him with one, he deferred to the faculty. And when the Academic Senate, which had its own reasons for opposing class rankings, voted to back up the SDS position, Summerskill still refused to act, claiming his hands were tied by Chancellor Dumke. This sort of vacillation led to a series of SDS-sponsored picket lines and sit-ins in President Summerskill's office, culminating in a demonstration-picket line at the inauguration ceremonies. The picketing failed to bring about its stated goal; indeed, the whole class rankings issue became irrelevant with the passage of the 1967 Draft Law later that summer, which granted 2-S deferments to all full-time college students. In his inaugural address, Summerskill had attempted to rhetorically outflank SDS, and to placate an enraged Chancellor Dumke, by calling for a "Center for Educational Innovation" to be set up as a separate division of the college. Characteristically, Summerskill sought to identify himself with the spirit of student activism on the basis of sentiment rather than concrete proposals; he had nothing to say about what such a "Center" would consist of, how it would operate, or even who would control it.

A few weeks later, with commencement ensuing, SDS threatened to demonstrate again, and Dumke warned Summerskill that he would lose his job if more demonstrations occurred. The harried President was then approached by Joe Persico, who suggested that students would regard the Center for Educational Innovation as meaningless liberal rhetoric if not an outright hoax unless Summerskill put some meat on his proposals. Summerskill was in no position to provide that meat, but Persico was; the

Program leaders had drawn up a detailed proposal of their own, encompassing work in progress and new projects on which they intended to embark. All they needed was proper funding; that was where the President came in. Persico had even written a speech for Summerskill, to be delivered at commencement in the event of an SDS picket line, the gist of which was an assertion that student radicalism was a healthy phenomenon and, rather than suppressing it, the college should find a place for it. The speech was never delivered, for SDS decided at the last minute to call off its plans. But Summerskill did agree to the omnibus proposal the Program leaders had drawn up, and promised to seek funding for it among his numerous contacts on the East Coast.

By this time, it was clear that Summerskill was as threatened by the changing political climate on the campus as were the Programs. Shortly after the disastrous first session of the Associated Students legislature, Bill Burnett and his political protégé Steve Diaz drew up a "white paper" that detailed the various crimes of the BSU and its activities, including as evidence quotations from plays and magazine interviews by LeRoi Jones. To these were added affidavits from two AS legislators who claimed they had been physically threatened by BSU members, and a statement that accused the college administration of countenancing intimidation and violence. The packet was signed by ten Shape Up legislators and sent to every member of the Board of Trustees, state Superintendent of Public Instruction Max Rafferty, and a number of state legislators.

The surprisingly cool reception which the Shape Up accusations received from the Trustees was probably due in no small part to a bit of clever sabotage work by Phil Garlington. Having no further use for either Burnett or the coalition he had put into office, and by no means sharing their blatant hostility toward the BSU, Garlington fired off two letters of his own to the Trustees. The first, bearing his own signature and the stamp of the AS President's office, was a blanket denial of the legislators' charges. The second, which was unsigned, corroborated the Shape Up charges and added a new one: that the college Administration Building was a hotbed of Communist activity. Somewhat uncertainly, the Trustees decided it was a "local matter" and, rather than taking any action, voted for the Chancellor's office to conduct an investigation of the accusations. A check of AS audits failed to uncover any illegalities, and the subsequent open hearing that was called was brilliantly handled by the BSU, whose membership packed the hearing room. The first to testify was Steve Diaz, who gave a rambling, emotional speech which reserved most of its fire for LeRoi Jones—"here to do away with large segments of the white population," as Diaz put it. Phil Garlington, who spoke next, flatly contradicted Diaz and then limited himself to defending the conduct of Summerskill's administration. Finally, Jimmy Garrett gave some lengthy testimony on the BSU's various activities, invited the investigators to visit the organization's offices, and answered the charges indirectly by pointing out that it was the Associated Students, not the BSU, which had hired Jones, and the administration, not the BSU, which was implicated in Diaz's attack. When he finished, the black students, who comprised most of the audience, left the hearing room. A few minutes later the meeting adjourned, the investigators having concluded that there was nothing going on at S.F. State to warrant action on their part.

If the BSU had acquitted itself, however, the pressure on President Summerskill was merely increased. The BSU handled outside attacks on its own, refusing to apologize for the activities it was engaging in. Summerskill, on the other hand, was openly sympathetic toward the black students while trying to make excuses for their militancy. Playing the apologist tended to undercut his own position, and, naturally, the BSU knew better than to back him up or depend on his support. In August, 1967, having failed to move the Trustees, Burnett, Diaz, and company took their case directly to the people of California. Burnett prevailed upon a Pinole businessman, H. E. Vandever, father of one of his fraternity brothers, to xerox 5000 copies of a short play by LeRoi Jones and various clippings from the student newspaper *Open Process*. The latter had been suspended by Summerskill at the end of the spring semester following the publication of its "Summer Love Edition." In its seven weeks of existence *Open Process* had transcended its function as "voice of the Programs" to become a flourishing "underground" newspaper. One of its regular contributors was Jefferson Poland, a seasoned campus activist, anarchist, and founder of the Sexual Freedom League whose column covered such diversified topics as masturbation, bisexuality, free love, and nudism. In addition to Poland's regular by-line, the Summer Love Edition included articles about a nudist camp and topless dancers, a long interview with poetess Lenore Kandel (whose *Love Book* was in the midst of an obscenity trial in the local courts), and a full-length picture of a reclining nude, complete with pubic hair. By and large, the campus community took such material in stride; but, unfortunately, the Summer Love Edition was never really distributed on campus. Shortly after it arrived from the printers, several thousand copies disappeared from the *Open Process* office, to reappear later in such unlikely places as the state legislature and the Chancellor's office.

The letter Vandever enclosed with his packet of quotations did not confine itself to attacks upon the *Open Process* staff or the BSU; rather, his condemnation was against the entire college. "This kind of activity makes one feel that the tax dollars being spent for higher education are being wasted," he wrote, "and I, for one, would like to see the situation investigated." Widely distributed throughout the state, the packet got a tremendous, though hardly surprising, response. One small-town newspaper after another editorialized against the "shameful goings-on" at San Francisco State College; dozens of chambers of commerce, joined in their protests by the statewide chapter of the Women's Christian Temperance Union, hastened to make their indignation known. Though the "Vandesmear campaign" was something of a campus joke, Summerskill found it hard to laugh. Vitriolic mail, much of it unsigned, came pouring into his office, and the jangling telephone became an ever-present reality. The San Leandro *Morning News* printed a particularly virulent four-part series which began with the assertion that "every student at San Francisco State College is being forced, indirectly, to support the violently militant Negro Black Panther Party!" It concluded with an exposé of the CIP's role in the Oakland school boycott which hinted that a Communist conspiracy was involved. The pressure became so intense that Summerskill

was forced to call a press conference to declare that the college was "under attack from a vicious, well-organized campaign
of a few right-wing individuals on and off campus."

The hysteria which the "right-wing campaign" succeeded in
arousing was symptomatic of a deteriorating political situation
that threatened the college from within as well as without. The
ultimate resolution of the *Open Process* issue was almost a satire
of institutional incompetence and bureaucracy. The original suspension of the paper was supposed to last only through the summer months. Still, with its every move scrutinized by the news
media, it took a "reconstituted" Board of Publications (the body
had, recognizing itself to be superfluous, voluntarily dissolved itself
toward the end of the 1967 spring semester) a full four weeks and
no less than five separate meetings before it could bring itself to
permit the paper to resume publication. Summerskill, who was
one of the major obstructionists in spite of his oft-expressed sentiment that *Open Process* was an asset to the college, declared at
one point that he was "sick of the whole business" and wanted
nothing more to do with it. Similar withdrawal symptoms were
evident in his opening speech to the faculty at the beginning of
the 1967 fall semester. Nostalgically hearkening back to the relative serenity of traditional classroom atmosphere, the beleaguered
President pleaded with students and faculty to abandon their political concerns, for politics was threatening to destroy the institution.

RACIAL STRIFE AND THE VIETNAM WAR

It was, to say the least, an unrealistic request. By October
1967, the Vietnam war had come to overshadow every other aspect of American life, and the movement against it was reaching
a critical turning point. The mass mobilizations of the previous
spring, while attracting a huge turnout, had failed singularly to
change official government policy. Especially among the youth in
the movement, there was a growing sense of futility with conventional channels of protest, which eschewed violence, remained
undefined politically so as not to "alienate potential support,"
and generally failed to challenge the legitimacy of the forces that

were perpetuating the war. An initial manifestation of the changing mood was The Resistance, a new group which advocated
openly confronting the Selective Service System by refusing to
cooperate with it in any way; the first of its "draft card turn-ins"
was scheduled for October 16. In the Bay Area a second group
was making plans through the summer for a "new kind of demonstration," one which would transcend the "moral witness"
school of protest by attempting to physically stop the operations
of the Oakland Induction Center.

"Stop the Draft Week" began on October 16, with hundreds
of young men massed in front of the San Francisco Federal
Building to hand in their draft cards to U.S. Attorney Cecil
Poole. Across the bay in Oakland, a group of pacifists who had
split with the Stop the Draft Week organizers over the issue of
nonviolence sat down in the doorways of the Induction Center
and submitted peaceably to arrest. The police were gentle and
scrupulously polite in hauling away the demonstrators, who included such personalities as Joan Baez and her sister Mimi Fari-
ña, poet Lawrence Ferlinghetti, and author and S.F. State professor Kay Boyle; it was like a ritual the details of which had all
been worked out in advance. The next day several thousand people moved off the sidewalks and into the street, hoping to prevent the busloads of inductees from getting through by blocking
traffic. The police, however, had a new tactic of their own: instead of arresting people, they inflicted as much physical punishment on the crowd as possible. No one who fell in the path of
the advancing police lines was spared; a number of reporters
were included among the scores of injured. By Friday, the demonstrators were ready to fight back. Numbering in excess of ten
thousand, they drew back as police lines approached, secured in-
tersections, and built barricades by hauling cars, park benches, and
debris into the street. They effectively closed off the Induction
Center and paralyzed most of downtown Oakland for several
hours before a large army of police, summoned from more than a
dozen different Bay Area communities, finally broke through
their lines.

When the demonstrators returned to the campuses, they did so
with a sense of exhilaration, and with the realization that they

could exert power far beyond their wildest expectations once they were willing to step outside the law and the self-imposed restrictions of nonviolence and proper decorum. By the time of the Democratic National Convention in Chicago a year later, police confrontations had become relatively commonplace in American life; but with the success of Stop the Draft Week, they had become a new and slightly terrifying frontier. A whole reservoir of previously untapped energies had been released, placing the antiwar movement in an entirely different context.

In the early 1960's, when Vietnam was simply an enigma to most Americans, opposition to American involvement was to a large extent confined to a handful of left-liberal academics who were well-informed enough to know about it. Marshall Windmiller, a serious, high-minded professor of international relations, spearheaded the "teach-in movement" at San Francisco State College by organizing the "Faculty Committee for Debate on Foreign Policy." The International Relations Briefing Center, which he had also set up, sought to perform a sort of watchdog role with respect to American imperialism, and to inform the students even if it could not actually influence the government. With an unshakable faith in the power of "the academy," as he called it, to bring about social change through its uncompromising search for truth, Windmiller was naturally concerned with the frequent incursions upon academic institutions by the military-industrial complex, and even more concerned that intemperate student radicals would, in their indignation at the fact, destroy the one institution which was their best hope for bringing the war to an end. With SDS vowing to renew its efforts to throw war recruiters off campus, and a group of athletes threatening physical retaliation if it did, the prospect of the Oakland violence coming home to the campus seemed ominously real. To bring the student antiwar movement back into the realm of reasoned discourse and persuasion (and to take the heat off Summerskill, whose administration was most immediately threatened by the furor over military recruiting), Windmiller proposed a college-wide "War Crisis Convocation" which would attempt to bring a reasoned consensus to the question of campus complicity.

The Academic Senate initially jumped at Windmiller's idea,

for it shared his anxieties about the sudden resurgence of student militancy and harbored within its own ranks a good deal of guilty concern about the college's relationship to the war machine. When the proposal returned from the committee, however, with the stipulation that decisions growing out of the Convocation would be made on a one-man, one-vote basis, with students on equal footing with faculty and staff, the Senate began to drag its feet. After reluctantly endorsing the proposal, it proceeded in the coming days to table or defeat every subsequent resolution concerning it—including one resolution that would have called for a moratorium on recruiting while the Convocation was in progress. President Summerskill, whose own endorsement finally had to be written by Marshall Windmiller, promised to secure the funding and provide the necessary rooms and then failed to do either for nearly a month; as a result, the Convocation had to be postponed twice. The faculty as a whole balked at interrupting the normal classroom routine to open what was frequently termed a "Pandora's box"; the conservative faculty were openly suspicious and hostile, sensing—not so unreasonably—an attempt by the liberals on the Academic Senate to isolate them politically. A marketing professor, Carl Larsen, actually went so far as to call the Convocation a "Communist plot." When Summerskill, displaying his usual insensitivity to political differences, offered up the gym for the plenary session, the head of the department of physical education—who heartily disapproved of the whole idea—objected that he had never been consulted. Out of Windmiller's attempt to create an atmosphere in which rational discourse would prevail, a climate of mistrust, hostility, and manipulation was already setting in.

On October 28, with the Convocation still struggling to get off the ground, the Black Students' Union held a program in the Gallery Lounge on campus. The two principal speakers were San Jose State College professor Harry Edwards, leader of the black boycott of the 1968 Olympics, and a slender, solf-spoken young man named Huey Newton, founder of the Black Panther Party. The Black Panthers had been quietly organizing in the Oakland ghetto for several months, attracting a brief splurge of publicity in August, 1967, when a group of them appeared, armed, in the state legislature to lobby against passage of a proposed gun control bill. Their armed patrols of West Oakland had succeeded in sharply curtailing incidents of police brutality and harrassment of ghetto residents, but the police had responded by stepping up their attacks upon the Panthers themselves. Twelve hours after his S.F. State speech, in which he talked of the necessity of black people arming themselves in self-defense, Huey Newton was driving through the deserted Oakland streets when he was stopped—perhaps for the hundredth time—by a police squad car. Full details of the incident which followed will probably never be completely known, but daybreak found one police officer dead, his partner wounded, and Huey Newton chained to a hospital bed with a bullet lodged in his stomach.

On November 6, a fight broke out in the offices of the *Daily Gater*. A group of black students had gone to protest the *Gater's* coverage of BSU activities, but their specific grievances reflected a situation which had been building for over two years. Long a thorn in the side of the Programs, the *Gater* had been particularly vicious, if oblique, in its attacks upon the BSU and its political philosophy. Jimmy Garrett's arrival on campus had coincided with the promotion to editor of a Peace Corps veteran and diehard integrationist named Dave Swanson who, having worked for the Civil Rights Movement in the South, was especially hostile to black nationalism. Subsequently, the *Gater* fell into the hands of Jim Vaszko, who as sports editor had made racist jokes about Muhammed Ali and attacks on Garrett and Marianna Waddy staples of his column. Program leaders had long puzzled over how to remove the *Gater* from the iron-fisted control of the journalism department and bring the paper under student control. But no one had found a way to bring this about, until Jim Vaszko, dismissing the BSU's complaints in a manner apparently offensive to the visiting black delegation, found himself in the midst of a full-scale brawl. While a *Gater* photographer sat quietly in a corner snapping pictures, the office was quickly demolished by the combatants. The tumult only subsided after Jim Vaszko had been beaten to the floor. Though no one was seriously hurt, the incident, loudly played up in the local press as well as in the *Gater*, flung the campus into a state of hysteria.

In their isolation on the campus, black students had always tried to protect themselves by maintaining an image of militant solidarity and cultural homogeneity. Even if it was not a monolithic organization, the BSU had tried and succeeded in giving that impression to the white world. An alien presence within the college community, it had managed to effect a kind of subtle psychological intimidation of whites on campus long before the *Gater* office brawl, which consequently touched off a flood of previously suppressed feelings of hostility and panic. Nine black students, who had been identified from the sensational *Gater* photographs, were immediately placed on interim suspension; the suspensions held for four of them after a hastily-called closed hearing provided a facade of due process. That the *Gater* staff members, who had participated in the fighting, may have had a hand in starting the melee was never even suggested; the black students were universally assumed to be guilty of a gratuitous act of violence. While more than a few white students privately felt that Vaszko was due for a good thrashing, they could not bring themselves to condone openly what the black students appeared to have done. The only exceptions were some SDS members who tried, somewhat quixotically, to portray the pummeling of Vaszko as a justified act of political violence. This posture, which irritated most of the campus, did nothing to bring the incident back into perspective. But the rampant atmosphere of guilt and paranoia in which the disciplinary hearings took place did not refute the SDS contention that the black students were being tried by a "kangaroo court."

Jim Vaszko, in any event, wasted no time in trying to get even with his accused assailants. Over the summer, President Summerskill's efforts on behalf of the Center for Educational Innovation had led him to approach several large foundations, and now there was a very real possibility of the Programs getting a Carnegie grant. On November 8, in his editorial column, Vaszko made some spirited remarks about the BSU and other "preachers of violence" and then announced that he had taken it upon himself to inform the Carnegie Foundation that the S.F. State Programs were unworthy of any financial assistance. The letter that he sent to the Carnegie Foundation condemned not just the BSU, but also the Tutorial Program, the Experimental College, and the CIP—in all of which Vaszko claimed the black students were "strategically involved." Students in the Programs got a quick glimmer of insight into why the black students had acted the way they did. Descending upon the Board of Publications with a twenty-page bill of particulars, they were met, as ever, with chronic stalling. The Board would not suspend Vaszko as editor without a "proper hearing" (which never took place); it would not even write a letter to the Carnegie Foundation correcting his allegations, claiming that it would merely "inflame the situation further."

By the time the Convocation finally got started on November 13, the campus was haunted by the spectre of political violence. Sandwiched between the arrival of the Navy and Marine recruiters, whose coming Summerskill had refused to postpone, proceeding with the understanding that none of the decisions growing out of it would be binding on the college administration, the "sober intellectual discussion" had an air of unreality about it. Playing heavily upon anxieties produced by the *Gater* incident, a group of students from Professor Carl Larson's marketing class circulated a "keep-the-campus-open" petition which urged the administration to preserve the right of students to consort with whatever recruiters they pleased and pleaded generally for protection from activist coercion. The "free speech" issue—indeed the whole Convocation—put student radicals in a difficult position. To appease them, Windmiller had agreed to stipulate that the legitimacy of the war was not under discussion; it was assumed that nearly everybody on campus opposed it. The problem with this assumption was that it reduced the discussion to a narrow and ultimately irrelevant question: given that the college had an existence independent from the rest of society, how was that "autonomy" best preserved? In the first plenary session, Professor Windmiller debated with a social science professor who, after assuring everybody that he was *"NOT* a hawk," said the college would jeopardize its neutral position in the society if it took a stand against military recruiting. Windmiller, after a long exposition on the conflict between military and academic values, said the college would jeopardize its neutral position if it did *not* take such a stand. Neither speaker suggested that the college might not have had any neutral position to lose. And neither made anything more than a passing reference to the war itself. A burning political issue was thus neatly posed as a simple matter of academic propriety.

SDS had, from the beginning, attempted to take a principled stand with respect to the Convocation, arguing that it was absurd to apply the concepts of free speech or college autonomy to the question of whether the college should aid and abet in the perpetuation of a genocidal war. Such a discussion, an SDS leaflet pointed out, "depends on a civil liberatarian notion that a kind of 'absolute' free speech is possible in a society that introduces a bias into every aspect of American life." But the radical group was, in a sense, in a bind of its own making. Having raised the issue of campus complicity (at a campus which had little or no important impact on the war effort), it was never clear whether its main intent was to mobilize students against the war, or simply to attack the myth of academic neutrality. Thus, while considering the Convocation as a liberal plot to coopt the antiwar movement, SDS members became its most active participants. They quickly discovered that within the context of the rhetorical hair-splitting and academic arguments, it was very futile to talk about Vietnam. SDS leader Alex Forman, who had agreed to speak on the panel, gave a witty, brilliant speech pointing out that students taking AFROTC enjoyed privileges far beyond those of normal students, and was received enthusiastically. When Forman became serious, however, and tried to read a statement by a Vietnamese survivor of a leprosarium bombed repeatedly by American B-52's, he was met with impatient heckling and uneasy laughter. With the "outside world" growing progressively more irrational and the campus thoroughly infected with that irrationality, the 3000-odd students who attended the Convocation no doubt sought to take comfort in the reassuring assumption that overwhelming social problems could be reduced to abstract formulations and academic platitudes. Under such circumstances, they were understandably repelled at the mention of bombed leprosariums and B-52's. Despite the motif of free discussion, there existed a certain gentleman's agreement as to what should or should not be talked about.

The Convocation ended on an appropriately absurd note when

the search for a consensus, taken to its logical extreme, ended in a ballot split twenty-seven ways. Of course, the results of the balloting were self-contradictory, but it hardly mattered. While students were still at the polls, the "keep-the-campus-open" petition, which had accumulated over 2,000 names from what was promptly dubbed the "silent center" of the student body, was presented to Summerskill on the Speaker's Platform. As if to demonstrate the futility of voting for any of the twenty-seven various resolutions that came out of the Convocation, the President again asserted that there would be no change in the college's policy on recruiting; then he accepted the petition and told his admirers, "This is one of the happiest days of my life!" Clearly the Convocation had resolved nothing; Summerskill, recognizing that tensions were basically unabated, called an emergency meeting of the faculty to discuss the whole issue of "campus violence." But, having no concrete proposals and no coherent direction to give the meeting, he only succeeded in aggravating the situation even further. The faculty emerged from what was later termed a "catastrophic mass therapy session" with a renewed sense of frustration and paranoia.

THE DECEMBER 6th DEMONSTRATION

The November 24th issue of *Open Process* contained a short piece of erotic poetry by Jefferson Poland, which the author whimsically dedicated to the head of the physical education department. The paper's editors had decided to include it quite casually, without expecting anything unusual to come of it. But the college was still living under the microscope. With publication of the poem, at least one state assemblyman and assorted other politicians and college Trustees began to howl for blood. With a Board of Trustees meeting ahead of him, Summerskill descended upon the Board of Publications and demanded immediate action. His demeanor suggested that more than a piece of erotic poetry was on his mind: complaining of a lack of student and faculty support for his administration, now in jeopardy again, he exclaimed, "I am an educator . . . If I can't do what I came here to do, then I am getting out!" The BOP passed a resolution saying that publishing the poem was poor editorial judgment. Summerskill was not satisfied; rumor had it he would settle for nothing less than suspension of the paper and its editors. The *Open Process* staff tried without success to get in to talk with him. A second BOP meeting was called, at which the requested suspensions were given serious consideration. But the Board decided against immediate action when it realized it would be violating the due process it had insisted on giving Jim Vaszko a scant two weeks ago. Summerskill promptly overruled the BOP. He suspended the paper, suspended its editor, Blair Paltridge, suspended Jefferson Poland, and departed for Los Angeles and the Trustees meeting.

The abrupt suspensions galvanized a sizeable segment of student opinion against the President, bringing together a strange and far from cohesive group of people under the banner of the Movement Against Political Suspensions (MAPS). To begin with, there was a host of politically unaffiliated students who felt that censorship was wrong, due process had been violated, and their rights had been arbitrarily abrogated by the administration. The BSU saw the *Open Process* issue as a way of winning white sympathy and support for its own four suspended members. SDS, isolated and confused by the intellectual gymnastics of the Convocation, saw a chance to rally a constituency at last. In addition, a coalition with the BSU would allow them to prove their revolutionary efficacy to the black students at a time when the attitude of the black power movement towards white radicals was decidedly cool.

On Friday, December 1, a rally was held on the steps of the Administration Building to call Summerskill on the carpet. Characteristically, the President emerged from his office and waded into the midst of the gathering, hoping to calm down the demonstration with a display of personal candor. "I'm the only college president you know who signs petitions and marches in peace parades," he began, and went on to remind the students of the pressures placed on him from above. He then apologized for his actions against *Open Process,* admitting, "I acted precipitously," and announced that, having been informed by the American Civil Liberties Union that he was on weak legal ground, he was lifting the suspensions of Paltridge and Poland. That made no

provision for the suspended black students, however, and Jimmy
Garrett was quick to point this out. Speaking immediately after
Summerskill, Garrett promptly accused the President of trying
to sabotage a promising alliance between black and white students by proceeding under the racist assumption that the white
students were concerned only about their own and would take no
action on behalf of the blacks.

The microphone was then taken by John Gerassi, a newly
hired professor of international relations. Gerassi was a former
editor of *Time* and, later, *Newsweek*, and the author of a popular
book on American imperialism in Latin America. As the *Time*
correspondent to the Punta del Este conference, he had met and
begun a friendship with Che Guevara. That, together with the
constant evidence of Yankee-inflicted poverty and exploitation he
found in his travels through Latin American countries, led him
eventually to quit his *Newsweek* job and begin writing more and
more for radical journals. By the time Marshall Windmiller approached him and asked him to teach at S.F. State, Gerassi was a
self-avowed revolutionary. As Professor Windmiller was to write
later, "While his views were not shared by all of us, we thought
they would enliven the dialogue between faculty and students
and precipitate controversy of educational value." Since his arrival in September, John Gerassi, the house radical, had been a
constant irritation to Windmiller, attacking the Convocation as a
fraud, refusing to give his students grades, and proving generally
that, to use Windmiller's own words, "he regarded the students,
rather than the faculty, as his peer group." Now Gerassi lam-
basted Summerskill, particularly his self-proclaimed dovish tendencies and his veiled references to pressure from above. "If you
really oppose the war," he thundered, "if you really oppose this
dehumanizing society that causes the war, you should stop worrying about losing your job and come down here and join us!"
Summerskill replied, probably quite honestly, "You can rest assured that I've given that a lot of thought, John."

Jimmy Garrett took the bullhorn again to announce the BSU's
plans for the coming week. If the students' five demands—they
included lifting the suspensions, student control of student publications, and an end to "political harrassment"—were not met by

December 6, a call would be issued for 5,000 blacks from the community to converge upon the campus to "take care of business." White students could do as they saw fit; Garrett added, with a note of irony, "We're not going to tell you what to do because we believe in participatory democracy."

That last remark emphasized the peculiar position of the white activists. Though they continually assured the campus that there would be no violence on December 6 unless the administration provoked it by calling the police, they really had no idea of what the black students were going to do, and the black students were not about to tell them. When December 6 arrived with the demands still unmet, the white students marched on the Administration Building only to discover that President Summerskill had ordered the doors locked and had sent the workers home. There was a moment of confusion; then an open window was spotted. One student hoisted himself up and climbed through it; Gerassi concluded that he had an obligation to follow and started to climb up himself. He met with resistance from a campus security guard and accidently broke the glass. While lodged halfway in and halfway out of the broken window, Gerassi was photographed by a number of media cameramen; his picture would appear in newspapers all over the country. With the window entrance temporarily blocked, the crowd sought another way to get inside the building. Here their own anxiousness helped them, for by surging against the glass door of the Administration Building, they inadvertently broke it and thus created an entrance. The halls began to fill up with people; altogether about three hundred went in, leaving a somewhat larger crowd outside. Many students were a little unnerved at how far things had gone; still, the atmosphere was relatively relaxed until some disturbing reports began filtering into the building from outside, causing the crowd outside to suddenly begin drifting towards the central campus area.

The Black Students' Union had not drawn its threatened 5,000 community people to the campus. What it had drawn was about three hundred black students from other Bay Area campuses, and a group of another hundred or so ghetto youths. The former either stayed on the steps of the Administration Building and harangued the crowd or went through the various other buildings dispersing classes. The latter simply roamed the campus: they swiped food and silverware from the Commons, broke into the bookstore and set fire to a Christmas tree, and engaged in shoving matches with reporters and petrified white students. The only serious physical violence occurred when some BSU members tried to bring the ghetto youths under control; this led to a few scattered fist fights. Finally, word came that Summerskill had closed the school for the day and the crowd drifted away. The President emerged from his office, where he had spent the entire afternoon shut up with a pair of police intelligence squad inspectors. "What we have seen here today," he told the battery of reporters in a shaking voice, "verges on civil insurrection."

Summerskill had refrained from calling in uniformed police on the advice of the police themselves, who correctly sensed the incident would burn itself out if left alone. Tactical restraint, however, is not liable to ingratiate a college administrator to either his Board of Trustees or the state political hierarchy. Within twenty-four hours of the "civil insurrection," virtually every California politican of any import was howling for Summerskill's job; an unprecedented emergency Trustees' meeting was immediately called for that weekend. The S.F. State faculty quickly rallied behind the harried President; the Academic Senate passed a resolution commending him for avoiding "what could have been a tragically violent situation." So did the student body; a huge crowd turned out for a rally called Friday by some individual faculty members. Four hundred dollars was raised to repair property damage that had occurred; six thousand people signed a petition calling for Summerskill's retention. The highlight of the rally was a five-minute period of silence, an apparent atonement for the windows which had been broken during the ruckus. Surprisingly, Benny Stewart of the BSU appeared and spoke briefly to the crowd: "In every revolution people are considered thugs at the time, but they are great patriots later. We're like mechanics and this place is due for a motor overhaul. We are trying to change it, but no one understands our language. What happened Wednesday was a failure of communication."

The Academic Senate had voted to send representatives down to Los Angeles to accompany the President at the Trustees meeting. Upon arriving they found the building under incredibly tight security, and all their academic credentials would not get them past the armed guards at the door. Summerskill testified for about an hour, repeating a favorite thesis that there would be "no peace on our campuses until there is peace in our cities and peace in Vietnam." San Francisco Police Chief Thomas Cahill spoke next, corroborating Summerskill's testimony that it would have been a mistake to call in uniformed police. Given that, Summerskill could not very well be fired; the Trustees voted instead to put him on sixty days' probation during which his continued "stewardship" of the campus would be considered. A second resolution, which also passed, made disruption of the normal functions of any state college punishable by mandatory suspension or expulsion. When the President of Fresno State College protested that this would give the local administrations no leeway in "extenuating circumstances," Governor Ronald Reagan shot back, "I can't see any extenuating circumstances with regard to force and violence on campus." Board members who tried to speak against the motion or in Summerskill's favor frequently found themselves cut off by points of order. The nightmarish atmosphere of the meeting was climaxed by a special report from Chancellor Dumke, who called for an appropriation of $100,000 to augment campus security forces—"our first line of defense," as he called them. Dumke also suggested that an additional $300,000 be appropriated in order to maintain "constant and effective liaison with outside police agencies to assure that these forces are ready to come onto campus at any time with their maximum amount of available force . . . We must face the possibility at some campuses of a riot growing into a general insurrection." To deal with the latter eventuality, the Chancellor called for an "insurrection alert mechanism" to assure the availability of even greater force where necessary. His plan was actually opposed by one Trustee who argued furiously that an appropriation of $400,000 was "woefully inadequate" and demanded nothing short of $1 million.

Much of the campus community watched the proceedings

broadcast live over San Francisco's educational television station. As Summerskill returned to the college, those students who had not abandoned the Movement Against Political Suspensions found themselves the most despised individuals on campus. The black students remained an enigma. BSU leader Jerry Varnado did show up at a MAPS meeting, and while his remarks seemed deliberately obscure, few of the white students in attendance failed to notice the gun placed ostentatiously on his hip. Partly to show the BSU it could hold out, partly because there didn't seem to be anything else to do, MAPS voted narrowly to have another sit-in Wednesday, December 13. The BSU's stance toward the rest of the campus astonished everyone by its contriteness. But the black students had already made their point—they could shut down the campus and they would do it again if they had to. Rather than let that happen, the faculty and the administration suddenly lent an extremely receptive ear to the BSU's grievances, and the black students proved to be as skilled at talking as they were at acting. The white radicals, reduced to a situation of complete political impotence, had no such options; the most they could do was act as a whipping boy, becoming the focus of all the accumulated resentments on campus. When they called their rally before the sit-in, a huge, incredibly hostile crowd gathered. Furious at the Trustees whom it was powerless to influence and even more furious at the black students whom the niceties of racial guilt would not allow it to condemn, the crowd vented its spleen upon MAPS speakers instead. As the heckling reached its crescendo, Summerskill descended grandly from the Administration Building and was greeted with an emotional ovation. "It's good to be back," he quipped boyishly.

Though he did announce that the journalism department had finally agreed to let go of the *Gater*, the President's subsequent speech reflected little or no change in his position on the five demands. That left the demonstration leaders with no alternative but to proceed as planned. A handful of students walked up to the Administration Building, while the crowd howled its disapproval. The seventy-five odd students who had agreed to sit-in felt certain that, under the new disciplinary regulations, their doing so would result in their immediate dismissal from the college. The crowd felt just as certain that it would result in Summerskill losing his job. As it happened, however, the only immediate casualty of the week's events was John Gerassi. Not surprisingly, the news media had made him into one of the major culprits of the December 6th demonstration, and he was placed on interim suspension shortly thereafter. Gerassi was then found guilty of "unprofessional conduct" by the Hiring, Retention, and Tenure Committee of the international relations department, which nonetheless concluded that his actions did not warrant his dismissal from the college. The committee was overruled by Summerskill at the urgings of Marshall Windmiller, who later explained his stance in a lengthy article in the *New York Review of Books*. Scrupulously avoiding any criticism of the Black Students' Union's role in the demonstration, Professor Windmiller flatly accused Gerassi of "trying to wreck the institution." Gerassi's suspension, like a rite of exorcism, accompanied the elevation of Summerskill to the stature of campus hero. In this way, an equilibrium of sorts was gradually restored to San Francisco State College.

CHAPTER V

Black Studies

THE STRUGGLE FOR

EDUCATIONAL SELF-DETERMINATION,

1966-1968

Between 1966 and 1968, the Black Students Union at San Francisco State College developed into an important model for black student organizations around the country. Two factors accounted for its vanguard role: its excellent caliber of leadership and its ability to exploit the singular situation in which black students on the campus found themselves. Through its system of leadership training and rotation, the BSU succeeded in developing a steady flow of organizers who were creative, flexible and politically adept. These activists did not hesitate to make the black students aware of their isolated situation on the campus or their privileged position with respect to the great majority of their race. By invoking a strong sense of duty and race loyalty, insisting on its autonomy within the college community, and proudly emphasizing black culture and consciousness, the BSU quickly emerged as the sole center of gravity for black students on the campus, involving them in a formidable array of programs and projects—from tutoring, to working in ghetto high schools, to setting up cultural affairs on campus, to serving in the AS legislature. Running through all these activities was a collective commitment to change, totally, the intolerable social conditions to which black people in America were subject.

Given this abundance of dedication and energy, it is not surprising that the BSU became the first college-based organization in America to give substance to the concept of Black Studies. Though the origin of a black curriculum at S.F. State goes back to the course on black nationalism taught in the Experimental College in the spring of 1966, it wasn't until a year later that the first Black Studies proposal was completed and forwarded to the appropriate college authorities. During the interim period, the Black Arts and Culture series had flourished in the Experimental College for a semester and had then moved over to the exclusive jurisdiction of the BSU. The transition was due in part to the strained relationships between the BSU and the Experimental College regulars, in part to the black students' desire to have complete control over all their various projects. What was most important, however, was that the black students had realized there were simply too many other programs that were seeking a slice of the AS budget. If Black Studies was ever to acquire the resources necessary to pay its projected costs, not to mention the prestige of recognition as a legitimate academic discipline, then it would have to be officially sanctioned and funded by the college. With this in mind, Jimmy Garrett began to work out a structure and rationale for the program, and by March 1, 1967, "A Proposal to Initiate an Institute of Black Studies at San Francisco State College" was officially presented to the Instructional Policy Committee (IPC) of the Academic Senate.

THE INITIAL BLACK STUDIES PROPOSAL AND THE CONFLICTS OVER IMPLEMENTATION

The first section of the proposal dealt with what Garrett saw as the central problem: the destructive effect of the "typical liberal education" offered by the college when imposed upon black students. Looking at the notion of integration as it is usually defined—since blacks were enrolled at S.F. State, it was "integrated"—Garrett argued, "There is no such thing as an integrated institution when the educational process is geared towards one group of students. It is a segregated institution with black pupils to give the college a liberal visibility." Where was the curriculum examining "racism from a black perspective"? "Where are the courses in Black psychology, Black history, African history . . . Black literature, drama, music, and arts?" The college having done nothing to rectify these "sins of omission," the black students who felt them most acutely had taken the initiative in establishing some black courses on the campus. To date, faculty and administration had done no more than pay lip service to the educational needs of black students; Garrett concluded, "This college has an obligation to allow room for alternatives to come about, and a separate college of black studies would be a beginning."

The second section outlined the structure and implementation schedule for Black Studies. It was suggested that a ten-man Board of Directors be established to govern the institute, seven of whose members would be selected, in essence, by the black students themselves. Nominees for the board would be chosen "on the basis of their work in the black community and their knowledge of the black community." The other three members of the board would include the President of the college, the AS President, and a faculty representative chosen by the Academic Senate. The board would be responsible for setting up the institute, overseeing the selection of its faculty and staff, and approving curricular offerings. As for implementation, Garrett suggested that the S.F. State Foundation immediately donate $7000 to the Board of Directors for the purpose of hiring an Executive Director; he, in turn, would be charged with recruiting faculty, developing a curriculum, and fashioning the overall program. The immediate objective was to organize the program around the model already established by the BSU; this was to be accomplished during the spring and summer so that by the fall of 1967 the Black Studies Institute could be functioning smoothly. The proposed budget for the 1967–68 fiscal year was $65,000, to be spent on salaries for a director of the program, five full-time faculty members, and six student assistants. Four college offices and classroom facilities were also requested.

The final section of the proposal addressed itself to the question of "special admissions." It was pointed out that one of the most urgent problems at the college was its rapidly declining percentage of black enrollment. Not only would the Black Studies Institute help to reverse this trend by attracting black students to its program, and hence to the college, but it could also develop a project in conjunction with the area's ghetto high schools which would work to "eliminate the exclusion of black students from entering San Francisco State College on the basis of white-oriented test scores." While still in its embryonic stages at the time, the special admissions project was destined to play a larger and larger role in the overall thrust of the black students' program.

Garrett concluded the proposal by dealing with the issue of racial separatism which many whites felt to be implicit in the notion of a black curriculum. Blacks, he insisted, had always experienced an enforced separation from white America, and it was precisely that separation which had given them different "standards, perspectives, and realities." This was why the Black Studies Institute had to be geared specifically to the educational needs of black students, who were "stunted in their academic growth in direct proportion to the development of their black consciousness." However, white students were not being barred from the institute; blacks were merely getting some long-overdue preferential treatment. As Garrett put it, "There is room for a minority of whites because everybody must learn. In any case, black students spend too much of their time justifying their blackness to white people. One of the purposes of this proposal is to eliminate that process . . ."

The Black Studies proposal spent the entire spring semester being tossed back and forth between the Instructional Policies Committee of the Academic Senate and the Council of Academic Deans (CAD). The IPC, where the black students had a good deal of support, immediately voted to begin a Black Studies program as quickly as possible. The CAD was more recalcitrant, requesting a number of discussions with the BSU before the implementation of the program could be considered. These contradictory responses had an ulterior source: Vice President Garrity had created the CAD specifically to counteract the power of the Academic Senate; both groups now claimed to have final authority to determine educational policy for the college, and the Black Studies issue had gotten caught in the middle. Black students grew increasingly frustrated as they realized their proposal was being used as a pawn in the dispute, and matters were not helped by some of the nit-picking questions they encountered from the

Academic Deans. At one point, the CAD claimed that the name Black Studies sounded too segregated, and suggested that it be changed to "Negro American Studies." Finally, Jimmy Garrett found a way to outflank, temporarily, both the CAD and the IPC. During the summer he managed to elicit a verbal commitment from President John Summerskill to hire any qualified person that the BSU selected to head the program. The two black professors that the BSU approached were both sociologists: Herman Blake, from the University of California at Santa Cruz, and Nathan Hare of Howard University.

In June of 1967, the Council of Academic Deans finally authorized the creation of a special "task force" to work out the details for the establishment of a Black Studies Department. Nothing was ever heard from the task force again; somewhere early in the game it "dropped the ball," as one high-level administrator put it later. By the beginning of the fall semester, the BSU's projected deadline for launching the program, Black Studies still had neither a director nor a department of its own. Though their patience was wearing thin, the black students had foreseen the delays and formulated their strategy accordingly. Over the summer Peter Pursley had inveigled the San Francisco State College Foundation into granting $20,000 to the unfunded Black Studies program. The money was used to finance the organization of a curriculum, insure its maintenance through the fall semester, and pay the staff members who were keeping the program going in spite of the college. In all, 368 students enrolled in eleven courses which were taught for the most part by the black students themselves. Tutorial coordinator George Murray taught a freshman English course in reading and composition for incoming black students who had trouble with these basic skills; Jimmy Garrett was the instructor of a "Miseducation of the Negro" course; Peter Pursley ran a seminar on "Group Processes" which was offered through the psychology department—to name but a few. There was one major drawback to this strategy: lacking the resources and the qualified professors of a bona fide academic department, not to mention official recognition, the Black Studies program had to spread its course offerings throughout the various existing departments of the college. Inevitably, conflicts began to arise over the courses that the BSU wanted certain departments to sponsor. In return for their approval, some departments insisted on reserving the right to decide who would teach the Black Studies courses and what material the courses would cover. Both conditions were, of course, intolerable to the black students.

The history department was a case in point. The black students had made contact with Roland Snelling, a self-educated expert in ancient African history. The history department had never bothered to offer a course in this subject, and the black students approached department chairman Ray Kelch with what seemed to them like a modest request: that Snelling be allowed to teach such a course through the department for credit. For the moment, they were not asking that Snelling be hired by the department, or even that he be paid for teaching the course—though, given the department's lack of an African historian, neither request would have been unreasonable. The chairman of the history department, however, was not even about to grant credit. Initially unsympathetic to Snelling because he lacked the conventional academic credentials, Kelch finally agreed to a series of interviews to determine his scholarly competence, only to conclude after a few sessions that further inquiries into the matter were useless. The department, he pointed out with unassailable logic, had no specialists of its own in ancient African history; how could it be expected to judge adequately whether this man was qualified to teach it?

About the same time as Kelch was working his academic Catch-22 in the case of Roland Snelling, a young American historian named Jerry Combs was unwittingly making himself the next focus of the controversy. Combs, who was relatively naive about the intricacies of campus and departmental politics, had read the Kerner Report and decided that it was important that he personally do something about the "white racism" which the report held was at the root of America's urban crisis. He then hit upon the idea of teaching a special course in the history of black people in America; unfortunately, he did not heed the advice of some of his students to talk to the BSU about the project before going ahead with it. As Combs admitted later, he knew the black students only by reputation, and he was more than a little apprehensive about approaching them. As a consequence, the black students did not find out about Combs's course until registration, by which time Snelling's African history course had already been successfully blocked by Ray Kelch. Naturally, they were furious: they literally cornered the unsuspecting Combs, accused him of being a racist who would only distort black history, and demanded that he give up his course and supply credit for Snelling's. Combs knew little of the Snelling affair, felt its connection to him was gratuitous, and refused to accede to the BSU's demand.

The situation came to a head on the first day of Combs's class. About a dozen black students showed up, as they had promised they would; they proceeded to air their grievances in harsh language, insisting that they would remain until credit was granted for the Snelling course. About half-way through a very tense session, the white students in the class recovered from their initial shock long enough to decide to leave the room *en masse* and confront Ray Kelch, whom they saw as the real cause of the trouble. Pouring into the corridor, they founded Kelch ensconced in a small coffee room a few doors down with Dean DeVere Pentony of the School of Behavioral and Social Sciences. A heated shouting match ensued, subsiding only after a ruffled Kelch had left the area.

Dean Pentony was present at the next session of Comb's class to face the onslaught of the black students, who had once again showed up in force. His apologetic defense of the department's posture did nothing to ease tensions. At one point Pentony tried to take the absent Kelch off the hook by claiming that no professor in the department was willing to sponsor the course, and Kelch had no choice but to respect the wishes of his colleagues. This failed to impress the black students, who suggested that if it were really the case then the entire history department was racist to the core. Pentony then offered to get Snelling's course approved through the friendlier anthropology department. The BSU refused, insisting that they were taking a principled stand against racism and nothing short of the complete capitulation of the history department would suffice.

The next day, however, some of the white students in the class found a way out of the impasse. They approached Richard Fitzgerald, a young history professor who had just finished graduate school and was teaching his first year at S.F. State; after listening to them, Fitzgerald agreed to sponsor the Snelling course himself. His grounds for doing so seemed firm enough: the anthropology department had recognized the legitimacy of the course, and Dean Pentony had maintained that the sponsorship of one professor was all that was needed for the history department to approve the course. The black students were satisfied with the arrangement: the Snellings course was taught for credit, and Combs's class was allowed to continue without further interruption. Only Kelch remained unhappy; when he learned of Fitzgerald's charity, he called the young professor into his office, accused him of "stabbing the history department in the back," and informed him by mail a short while later that he would not be rehired for the coming year.

NATHAN HARE AND THE SECOND BLACK STUDIES PROPOSAL

On the day of his arrival at S.F. State, having just been hired to head the Black Studies program, Nathan Hare was asked by President Summerskill to mediate the dispute that was raging in the history department. This was not the sort of role Hare had anticipated playing when he took the job, but he went ahead and talked to Professor Combs and the BSU leadership. As Hare was to recall later, "The black students readily convinced me that I would never acquire the Nobel Peace Prize, so I told President John Summerskill that I was not a peacemaker anyway." Summerskill had a stake of his own in Hare's appointment, since he had pushed it through, at the BSU's request, over the unfavorable recommendations of both Dean Pentony and the chairman of the sociology department. This time, the argument was not over academic credentials; Hare had plenty of those. Rather, it revolved around the fact that the BSU had been allowed to hand-pick the Black Studies director, a prerogative which normally belonged to the faculty.

Hare's personal history may have also served as a source of anxiety to some S.F. State faculty. The son of a sharecropper from the rural community of Slick, Oklahoma, he began picking cotton at the age of five to supplement his family's income, and, with his father's desertion, had become the sole support of his family at age ten. Despite this, and despite the fact that neither of his parents had finished grade school, he was able to complete high school with good marks and exceptionally high scores on the standardized aptitude tests. On the basis of his academic performance, he was encouraged by his high school teachers to go on to college, which he did at the age of sixteen.

Actually, Hare was not eager to remain in school; his main interest was in boxing, and he agreed to enroll at Langston College, an all-black teacher training institution in Oklahoma, only because he couldn't box professionally until he had turned nineteen. Working his way through Langston and boxing on the side, he continued to impress his teachers enough that they encouraged him to apply for a Danforth Fellowship—something unheard of at the college. Hare won the fellowship, and decided to go to the University of Chicago for his graduate work; while there, he continued to box as an amateur welterweight.

Living in Chicago brought home to Hare the pervasiveness of American racism. Even as a graduate student at the university, he was constantly exposed to discrimination in housing, jobs, and eating facilities, not to mention the bigoted attitudes of some of his white colleagues. Hare had always entertained a strong sense of racial identity and cultural pride; it was during these years that he began to look toward black nationalism as an alternative to the prevailing gospel of integration. He was particularly impressed by the community cohesiveness and rehabilitation programs practiced by the Black Muslims in the late 1950's, though he had little use for the religious aspects of the Muslim philosophy. By the time he had received his Ph.D. in sociology, nationalist sentiments and racial militancy had become the cornerstones of Hare's political perspective, so much so that they were to get him into trouble when he went on to teach at Howard University, a predominantly Negro institution in Washington, D.C.

Hare arrived at Howard in the fall of 1962, and quickly discovered that he had little in common with the vast majority of blacks on campus. His radical nationalism was not well-received by the privileged children of the Negro middle class—"Black Anglo-Saxons," Hare called them—, and it was even less well received by the Howard faculty. Only with the students from the West Indies, where black nationalism was more acceptable, was Hare able to find some common ground, and during his early years on the campus he became closely associated with these "outsiders." There was also friction between him and the officialdom of the college, particularly when he happened to make his views public. On one occasion, when the university administration announced plans to "integrate" Howard at some future date, Hare was quoted as saying that white people had more than enough colleges of their own to go to, and they surely didn't need access to Howard at the expense of needy blacks. For this breach of integrationist etiquette, he was informed that it would be unwise for him to make any further remarks on the subject if he valued his job. By late 1966, the black students at Howard had finally begun to catch up with him; he was asked to sponsor the campus's first black power organization, and he helped draw up a "Black University Manifesto" which was severely critical of Howard's "Negro" orientation. The latter proved to be one impropriety too many, and Hare was fired rather underhandedly during the summer. He immediately appealed his dismissal and was eventually to win the case; by that time, however, he had moved on to S.F. State, only to become involved in another embroilment.

Hare's initial intention, after losing his job at Howard, was to begin his career as a professional boxer. He had already won his first fight and scheduled a second when Jimmy Garrett engineered his appointment at S.F. State and persuaded him to accept, arguing that the black students at the college desperately needed his expertise. When he finally took the job in January, 1968, Hare was assigned to the staff of Academic Vice President Donald Garrity, who had been involved in much of the early politicking around the Black Studies Department and was seen by the black students as one of its major obstructionists. Garrity had arranged for Hare a large number of appointments with various deans, department heads, and other faculty members throughout the college. Hare began making the rounds, but he quickly discovered that there was a great deal of fear and resentment on the campus towards the BSU in general and Black Studies in particular. Since the program was still spread over a number of academic departments, temporary arrangements had to be worked out with each one of them so that Black Studies would continue to function on an interim basis until it could be consolidated into a single department. Hare felt that his first priority was to develop a proposal that could, with the approval of the proper authorities, get Black Studies started as an autonomous program. From the moment of his arrival on campus he had spent most of his time trying to mollify the anxiety of the white faculty and deans; by late April he had managed to complete a proposal which he hoped would answer all their questions and allow the Black Studies Department to become a reality by the fall of 1968.

"A Conceptual Proposal for Black Studies" initially dealt with two questions that were commonly asked about the program. Foremost among these was the question of why it was necessary in the first place. Dr. Hare pointed out that American higher education was in a state of crisis, owing to the students' alienation from, and resentment of, conventional educational assumptions. This tended to be "doubly so in the case of black students," who were "products of experiences which robbed them of a sense of collective destiny and involvement in the educational process." At S.F. State, the whole notion of Black Studies was an important response by the black students to these conditions. "It not only reflects their cries—echoed by others across the country—for a relevant education; it also represents the greatest and last hope for rectifying an old wrong and halting the decay now gnawing away at American society." Yet while black students at S.F State had pioneered the first Black Studies program in the nation, the failure of the college to respond positively to their innovation had only deepened their distrust and hostility for the institution, while causing the S.F. State program to fall behind those of other colleges and universities that had taken up the idea.

More generally, Hare maintained that the necessity for Black Studies, not to mention the basic elements for a viable program, was still misunderstood, and the concept was often diluted or distorted as a result. An example of this would be the tendency to see the aim of Black Studies "as the mere blackening of white courses in varying number and degree . . . while omitting from the program the key components of community involvement and collective stimulation." Dr. Hare was very explicit in his argument that the central purpose of a Black Studies program should be to "serve the educational needs of the black community as a whole." To accomplish this end, a collective or communal approach was essential if a real attempt was to be made to reach the entire community. The black students, for their part, would function within their communities rather than being lured away from them, and would be serving the people by extending to them the various offerings of the program. In contrast, a program that emphasized " 'rehabilitating' individual students and potential students by means of pride in culture, racial contributions generally, and regenerated dignity and self-esteem" would have little impact beyond the students who were fortunate enough to get into it. By being "individualistic in its orientation and only indirectly, therefore, or collective consequence," it would offer "super-tokenism at best, neglecting the important ingredient of motivation growing out of collective community involvement."

The second question concerned the fear of many white people (and some blacks) that Black Studies would perpetuate "racial separatism." More specifically, would white students be allowed to participate? Dr. Hare was admittedly ambivalent about the role of whites within the program. Since Black Studies was to be geared to the particular needs of black people, perhaps only those whites who intended "to work in the black community" would appreciably benefit from being exposed "to at least some portion of Black Studies." What Hare was leery about was the prospect of a situation developing that would permit white students to "flood Black Studies courses, leaving us with a Black Studies program peopled predominantly by white students." To circumvent this possibility, he suggested that established academic departments "increase their offerings in blackness," which would probably better serve the needs of the white students anyway. Whether such an arrangement lent itself to separatism was beside the point:

> The question of separatism is, like integrationism, in this regard essentially irrelevant. The goal is the elevation of a people by means of one important escalator—education. Separatism and integrationism are possible approaches to that end; they lose their effectiveness when, swayed by dogmatic absolutism, they become ends in themselves. It will be an irony of recorded history that "integration" was used in the second half of this century to hold the Black race down, just as segregation was so instituted in the first half. Integration, particularly in the token way in which it has been practiced up to now and the neo-tokenist manner now emerging, elevates individual members of a group but paradoxically, in plucking many of the most promising members from a group while failing to alter the lot of the group as a whole, weakens the collective thrust which the group might otherwise muster.

Once the fear of separatism had been dealt with, the question of academic standards inevitably came to the forefront. Hare met it head on, arguing that there was a pressing need to redefine totally the criteria for prevailing standards because they "evolved in large part from a need to restrict the overflow of recruits into existing professional niches." This "principle of exclusion" was particularly destructive to Black Studies, since it reinforced the historical exclusion of black people, particularly from institutions of higher education. Now the whole process had to be reversed: "We are facing the necessity for collective recruitment from a group that has been victimized in the past by racist policies of exclusion from the educational escalator." To overcome this, Dr. Hare proposed that an "admissions wing" be built into the Black Studies program. It would be responsible for developing criteria, other than the traditional standardized tests or high school grades, that could be used to determine the college potential of black students. In addition, it would develop special programs to facilitate the high school-to-college transition of the incoming students; these programs would minimize the dropout casualties by offering such services as tutoring, personal counseling, and even some remedial coursework. Through the admissions program, Hare projected that 300 additional black students could be admitted to the college in the academic year of 1969–70, with an appropriate yearly increase from then on.

The question of academic standards also came up in relation to Black Studies faculty. After citing a Ph.D. and a "string of 'scholarly' publications" as the two most conspicuous requirements for professorial status, Hare agreed that the program should take these specific qualifications into account when hiring faculty. However, he stressed, "it is essential (particularly in light of the current shortage of such credentials on the part of black candidates) to examine and emphasize the desirability of freedom to depart from those criteria without risking suspicion of 'lowering standards.' " A Ph.D. degree doesn't necessarily impart the ability to teach, nor does being published always indicate the presence of an exciting intellect; qualities like the ability to relate to students and a practical mastery over subject matter, as well as an enthusiasm for it, also need to be considered. As for the ethnic makeup of the Black Studies faculty, Hare contended that there would be an abundance of "qualified" black professors who would be willing to come to S.F. State because of the special nature of the program. White professors were not flatly ruled out; rather, they "would have to be Black in spirit" in order to be serious candidates—the same being true for "Negro" professors. Here again, Hare urged the white faculty to increase their course offerings in the study of minority groups through the established curriculum; this would hopefully accomplish what Black Studies was unequipped to attempt, namely, "the reeducation of white society."

The community involvement segment was the most novel and ambitious section of the proposal. As initially indicated, it was a pivotal element in Dr. Hare's concept of Black Studies, calculated to bridge the gap between the program and the black community:

> To develop the key component of community involvement, it is necessary to inspire and sustain a sense of collective destiny as a people and a consciousness of the value of education in a techno-

logical society. A cultural base acting as a leverage for other aspects of black ego development and academic unity must be spawned and secured.

Programmatically, the initial step toward establishing such a base would be to organize the students and interested community people into "Black Cultural Councils." The councils would sponsor a wide variety of cultural activities in the black community, using indigenous talent wherever possible. Dances, concerts, drama, street festivals honoring black heroes—all of these events would celebrate black culture at a level that would encourage widespread community participation. "Black Information Centers" would be set up to increase the flow of information within the community and to promote social awareness. Such centers might house a "Black Community Press Service" which could put out a free newspaper analyzing current events from a black perspective.

The other aspect of this community focus would be directly related to Black Studies as a program. Course lectures, especially those of general interest, would be held in the black community, perhaps in a church, thereby allowing non-students to better partake of them and the discussion periods that might follow. Ultimately, the goal would be to establish a Black Studies extension in the community, geared particularly towards adult education: "The Black race woefully needs concrete skills in a technological society, both for individual mobility and community development." To facilitate this approach, as well as to "increase the commitment of black students to the community," field work would be an important part of the program's curriculum. This would permit students to participate actively in the development of the black community while continuing their education; as "volunteer assistants" working wherever they were most needed (in schools, health clinics, job centers, community organizations, welfare agencies), they would be in a position to help "wed and cement community and curriculum practicums."

Dr. Hare rounded out his proposal by suggesting a "five-year plan" that would serve as a guideline for the development of the overall program. The first phase of the plan would be to set up a

Black Studies Department by September, 1968. This could be accomplished simply by combining all the existing black courses being sponsored by other departments throughout the college; in addition, the new department would have to get an official green light in order for it to proceed to recruit faculty and, more important, be assured of adequate funding. The second phase would involve "the inauguration of a major consisting of an integrated body of Black courses revolving around such core courses as Black history, Black psychology, Black arts, and the social sciences." This phase was scheduled for implementation by September, 1969. Hare also provided for an enrollment scale, projecting that the program should be in a position to serve at least 2,000 students by 1974–75. This was not a static projection; rather, it was intended to be flexible, aimed at satisfying "the developing needs for educational and socio-economic parity on the part of the black race." The concluding paragraph of Hare's basic argument read as follows:

> Black Studies represents a last-ditch, nonviolent effort to solve a grave crisis, a particular crisis in American higher education. To try and solve all the problems at once is to risk weakening the impact on the central crisis, although, like a stone tossed into a lake, the resulting waves might reverberate from shore to shore. Likewise, we recognize the need for a coalition, somewhere ultimately, of endeavors to improve and increase the educational participation of all ethnic groups. It is only that the assault must be both intraethnic and interethnic, for we cannot afford to lose the motivational ingredient of intraethnic *esprit de corps* and community involvement.

THE HARE-BUNZEL CONTROVERSY

While the Black Studies proposal was being circulated among the faculty and administrators at S.F. State, Vice President Garrity was assuring Nathan Hare that the Black Studies Department would be officially able to open its doors by the 1968 fall semester. Still, there were certain procedural hurdles to be cleared, the foremost of which were getting the approval of the Board of Trustees and securing the necessary funds from the State of California. For the present, then, the program would have to continue to function through the existing academic departments that were willing to sponsor its courses. In the spring of 1968, the Black Studies curriculum included fourteen different courses serving 413 students; though the program was gradually growing, it was still running into some stiff resistance.

The militant tactics of the BSU, particularly during the history department dispute, hadn't endeared the black students to the rest of the faculty. A professor's classroom was considered sacrosanct; to violate it through disruption was an unforgivable sin, no matter what the cause. The task of reconciling the growing chasm between the blacks on campus and a good portion of the faculty fell upon Dr. Hare; he continued to make the rounds, trying to assuage the fears of individual faculty members and wrangle a few courses out of the various departments where he could. At the same time, he had to keep the impatient black students, who warned him that he was getting the runaround, at arm's length. It was a task that would have taxed the most accomplished mediator, but to make matters worse, two very important departments still balked at allowing Black Studies courses into their respective curricula. Unless they had final say over who would teach the courses, as well as what their proper content would be, both the economics and the political science departments were adamant in their rejection of Dr. Hare's overtures.

The chairman of the political science department was an Ivy League-educated, influential faculty liberal named John Bunzel. An ardent admirer of the Kennedys, Bunzel had been chosen as a delegate to the 1968 Democratic National Convention on California's Kennedy-Unruh slate. When Nathan Hare arrived on campus early that year, the black students had already attempted to set up some Black Studies courses through the political science department. Neither party had offered a proposal acceptable to the other, however, and the black students suspected Dr. Bunzel of deliberately trying to obstruct their program.

In the summer an incident occurred which reopened old wounds. A fundamental argument the BSU and Dr. Hare had used when lobbying with recalcitrant departments was that they didn't offer any courses that related specifically to black people.

If anything, this was an understatement: there was next to nothing in the entire college catalogue that dealt with black people
in America, or Africa for that matter. Since few departments
were prepared to fill the void and Black Studies had been conceived for precisely that purpose, the departments were particularly vulnerable to this particular charge. The black students,
however, wanted not only the courses but the power to supervise
their own curriculum—something many departmental bureaucrats
were loath to grant, since it cut into traditional faculty prerogatives. Dr. Bunzel had found a way to circumvent this distasteful
possibility by authorizing a course through the political science
department in "African Government and Politics," in the summer of 1968, and hiring a professor to teach it in the fall. Needless to say, the professor's qualifications were impeccable, but she
had no relationship to the Black Studies program—which still
lacked the resources to hire its own teaching staff. As with the
history department, this development simply added insult to injury. It was humiliating enough for the black students to go, hat
in hand, to the various departments, only to have their proposals
rejected, but it was worse when one of those same departments
set up its own equivalent of a Black Studies course in lieu of
theirs. What both the black students and Dr. Hare saw as the
outright theft of their program carried with it the implication
that, as far as Bunzel was concerned, black people could not be
trusted with running their own affairs.

The festering antagonisms between Hare and Bunzel broke
into the open with the latter's publication of an article in *Public
Interest*, the trade journal for political scientists. Entitled, "Black
Studies at San Francisco State College," the article was primarily
an attack on the orientation of Nathan Hare's "Conceptual Proposal," but it also attempted to malign Hare's character in a
rather insidious manner. After noting that Hare "had recently
been fired from Howard University for what *Negro Digest* called
his militantly pro-black activities," Bunzel insinuated that Hare
had been hired at S.F. State solely to appease the Black Students' Union; moreover, his appointment had been made unilat-
erally by President Summerskill, against the wishes of the college's academic hierarchy. Reservations about Hare were,

according to Bunzel, completely justified, since his major claim
to distinction was his "angry and bitterly anti-white" public
statements. To prove his point, Bunzel supplied a number of
remarks supposedly made by Hare in the course of a speech at
Stanford University. (Bunzel had not heard the speech; he
gleaned his quotations from a highly inaccurate article in the
Palo Alto *Times.*) These statements he saw as "part and parcel of
the militant black rhetoric which derives its own satisfaction in
constantly putting down 'whitey' "—including, he added, those
who have what Hare called a "hunger for humiliation." The
statements were important to Bunzel because they provided "a
backdrop" against which Hare's "basic rationale and philosophy
[for Black Studies] . . . can be more clearly understood." Put
bluntly, Bunzel was accusing Dr. Hare of being a black racist,
and because of this any program that Hare was allowed to put
together would be racist as well.

Aside from the bitter personal animosity towards Hare, Bunzel's article questioned the efficacy of Hare's concept of Black
Studies in three major areas. The first dealt with special admissions, or "special quotas" as Bunzel insisted on calling them. "At
a number of universities militant students have demanded the
admission of specific numbers of Negroes," he wrote, "which
increasingly is being translated into quotas roughly equal to the
proportion of Negroes in the total population." Rather than view-
ing this as further evidence of the need to accommodate far
greater numbers of students in institutions of higher learning,
Bunzel asserted that "quota demands" would inevitably deny
other students a college education. Slyly injecting the spectre of
black anti-Semitism into his argument, he contended that "if
such quotas were to be applied, seven out of eight Jewish under-
graduates would have to leave." This was reinforced with a
quotation from a fellow liberal pluralist, Daniel P. Moynihan:
". . . if ethnic quotas are imposed upon American universities,
Jews will almost be driven out." Hare had, of course, at no
time suggested the use of ethnic quotas; special admissions was
simply an attempt to deal with the *de facto* exclusion of black
students from the college. While offering no alternative of his

own for the solution of this problem, Bunzel simply asserted that such a proposal would, if adopted, result in the denial of college access to *other* minority groups.

The second area of Hare's proposal of which Bunzel was critical—this time in a more direct manner—were the concepts of "collective stimulation" and "community involvement." Because Hare had emphasized that these two components were central to the notion of making Black Studies serve the educational needs of the black community, Bunzel concluded that the program was therefore designed to "get black students to stop thinking individualistically." As he put it, "the black curriculum is not explicitly designed to encourage black students to develop qualities of independence, skepticism, and critical inquiry—in a word, to think for themselves, but rather to intensify the motivation and commitment of all who enroll in the program to return to the black community and translate everything to which they have been exposed into black leadership and black power." That he should construct such a dichotomy seemed to imply that, deep down, Bunzel was convinced that Black Studies had no intrinsic academic merit, that qualities of scholarship which were taken for granted in other disciplines had to be stated "explicitly" here, lest they conflict with the program's emphasis on blackness and community service. With such an attitude, it was inevitable that the questions Bunzel asked about the program would be little more than thinly veiled accusations: what was to prevent the program from "substituting propaganda for omission, or, as some have said, new myths for old lies?" "Would this intellectual position be fully recognized and discussed in a Department of Black Studies?" "Would the Department at San Francisco St. mirror the views of the Black Students' Union, thereby reinforcing its political goals and purposes on campus?"

Bunzel balanced his assault on Hare's Black Studies proposal with a sympathetic account of an alternate model. Several of America's elite universities, among them Yale and Harvard, had already formulated programs in "Afro-American studies"; Bunzel applauded their efforts to overcome "the acutely difficult academic problems involved in developing a curriculum of Black

Studies." These "Ivy League universities . . . will be very much concerned with the academic substance and soundness of any proposed Black Studies curriculum." Yale, for example, had already approved a degree program in Afro-American Studies, and had even received a lucrative grant from the Ford Foundation to implement it. The problem here, ignored completely by Bunzel, was that even if Yale were to develop an extensive system of scholarships and special admissions for black students, it would be ludicrous to suggest that it would in any way be prepared to meet the educational needs of New Haven's black community. What it could do is cultivate what one Ford Foundation executive has called a "talented tenth." A select group of black students could, without significantly altering the educational priorities of the institution, be brought into Yale, given special attention, and bombarded with "Afro-American" courses with which they could identify. Such an approach impressed Bunzel, since its primary intent would be "to develop future academicians"; moreover, as Bunzel put it, "a Yale or a Harvard can insist upon and expect a considerable measure of intellectual discipline in all of its academic programs."

Beyond this kind of Ivy League snobbery, there are crucial issues at stake in the conflicting models of Black Studies posed in Bunzel's essay. It is not simply that in content one is radical and the other "moderate"; more important is the question of which would best serve the educational needs of black people. In a rejoinder to Bunzel published by the BSU, Hare maintained that the program at Yale is completely inadequate to the task, though it may indeed serve the interests of the Ford Foundation, Yale University, and the black bourgeoisie—in that order. In his eyes, there are three serious flaws in the Yale program: its courses are spread out over a number of different academic departments, leaving blacks with only nominal control over the curriculum as a whole; there is no community involvement emphasis in the program, which means that very few black people will actually benefit from it; finally, the "talented tenth" approach can only isolate a handful of bright black students from their communities, thereby lessening that sense of identification with and commitment to their race which is the educational and ideological basis for any serious "black curriculum."

Statistics tend to support Hare's fear that the Ford Foundation's "talented tenth" formula will impede rather than further the overall development of the black community. A study sponsored by the Deparment of Health, Education, and Welfare indicates that of the ten per cent of America's black population that succeeds in getting into college, only two per cent return to the black community upon graduation. The rest are "integrated" into white society, contributing whatever skills they may have learned in college to the economy of white America and lending a shred of legitimacy to the myth of "Negro progress." Meanwhile the black community, stripped of the trained manpower it desperately needs to overcome its traditional position of dependency, continues to languish.

Given this contradiction, and its obvious relationship to the privileged nature of higher education in America, it is not hard to understand Nathan Hare's unequivocal opposition to "talented tenth" recruitment schemes, Yale's Afro-American Studies program, and John Bunzel's academic rationales for both. "The 'academic problems' involved in developing a curriculum of Black Studies may be acutely difficult for Dr. Bunzel," Hare remarked drily, "but for us, the *political* problems loom much larger." This statement not only captured the basically irreconcilable nature of their argument; it went right to the heart of the entire controversy at S.F. State. After over three years of promises and procrastination, there was still no Black Studies program at the college. The black students had exhausted their patience; they had no more illusions about the flexibility of the system or college's ability to reorder its priorities. By July of 1968, after six months of bargaining and nothing to show for it, Dr. Hare realized that there would be no Black Studies Department in the fall, assurances to the contrary notwithstanding. As a newcomer to the college cast in the role of mediator, Hare had initially proceeded with caution and avoided becoming too close to the BSU. The BSU had, in turn, warned him that he was being duped by the college administration. Now, having found that out for himself, Hare allied himself totally with the black students, joining the BSU Central Committee late in August. Together they began laying the groundwork for the November strike.

CHAPTER VI

T.W.L.F.:

THIRD WORLD STUDENT ACTIVISM,

1967-1968

SAN FRANCISCO'S ETHNIC MINORITIES

San Francisco, like other major urban centers in the United States, is losing its white inhabitants. For the past twenty years the nonwhite population of the city has grown steadily, while the white population has increasingly joined the exodus to the surrounding suburbs. As of 1968, the total population of the city was approximately 750,000—240,000 of whom were members of various ethnic minorities. It has been estimated that if this trend continues, nonwhite people will comprise a majority of San Francisco's population by 1980. The present nonwhite population is, itself, a polyglot one, made up of peoples of African, Asian, and Latin-American descent. The black population numbers close to 100,000 or over thirteen per cent of the city's inhabitants. Orientals total 77,000 or nine-and-a-half per cent of the city's population; these include the Chinese (48,000), the Filipinos (17,000), and the Japanese (12,000). The classification "Spanish surname" is given to all of the people in the city who are of Mexican-American or Latin-American descent; they number about 66,000, or nine per cent of the city's total population. Taken together, these three groupings make up one-third of San

Francisco's inhabitants; as a cohesive entity, their most important
common bond is that they all bear equally the brunt of the
deteriorating social conditions that characterize America's
metropolitan areas.

Most of the city's black community occupies two ghetto
areas—Hunter's Point and the Western Addition (Fillmore district). The unemployment rate for black people in San Francisco
is an incredible thirty per cent, while another thirty-seven per
cent of those who manage to find work are paid so poorly that
they live below the poverty line, earning less than $4,000 a year.
About seventy per cent of the housing in black neighborhoods is
owned by absentee landlords, and some nine per cent of the
dwellings have been declared substandard. A redevelopment project in the Western Addition has been bitterly opposed by the
community; spearheaded by the Western Addition Community
Organization (WACO), black people have demanded a major
voice in the redevelopment planning, claiming that the relocation
process leaves them initially homeless, then unable to move back
into their old neighborhood due to the exorbitant rents being
asked for new housing. An explosive situation also exists in the
black community's strained relationship with the San Francisco
Police Department. Black policemen, comprising a mere five per
cent of the force, have broken with the Police Officers' Association, which claims to represent all of the city's policemen; accusing it of being a bastion of racism, they have set up their own
group, Black Officers for Justice, to counter it.

Conditions in the Mission district, where a large majority of
San Francisco's chicanos (Latin Americans and Mexican Americans) live, are in many respects even worse than those in the
black neighborhoods. The entire chicano community is essentially
bilingual, with Spanish rather than English being the primary
language. Fifty-four per cent of the residents in the Mission district can't read English at all. Housing poses another serious
problem: seventy-one per cent of the household units in the Mission are owned by absentee landlords, while seventeen per cent
of them have been rated substandard. A redevelopment project
and a section of a rapid transportation system, both being con-

structed in the area, threaten to drive rents up even higher than
the present level. Rapid transit, by increasing property values
across the board, creates increased rents even where actual housing conditions have not improved. The unemployment rate for
brown people in San Francisco is usually around twenty per
cent, as compared with four per cent for the city's white inhabitants. When the unemployed are added to those who work but
earn less than $4,000 a year, it turns out that *one-half* of San
Francisco's chicanos subsists on an income that is below the
statewide poverty line.

Of all the minority groups in San Francisco, the Chinese
community is relatively the worst off—a fact that is insidiously
concealed behind the Chinatown public facade. As a popular
tourist attraction, Chinatown has been promoted as a
"self-helping" community of successful businessmen, studious
and obedient children, hierarchies made legitimate by quaintness
and tradition, and a generally docile, contented, respectable pop-
ulace. In reality, conditions in the neighborhood are abominable; some of its unpublicized attainments include TB and suicide
rates that rank among the highest in the nation. Seventy-nine per
cent of the dwellings are owned by absentee landlords, and
forty-three per cent have been judged substandard by the federal
government. The overcrowding in Chinatown is astounding: next
to Harlem, it is the most congested area in the country— eight
times more crowded than the San Francisco city-wide average.
The average level of educational attainment in San Francisco is
twelfth grade; the average Chinatown resident has not even completed the second. The unemployment rate is fifteen per cent,
lowest of the city's nonwhite communities, but this by itself is
deceptive. Liberalized immigration laws, coupled with the inability of over half the Chinese population to speak English, have
created a large unskilled labor supply which the entrenched business hierarchy in the community is more than willing to exploit.
It is not uncommon for Chinese laborers to work up to fourteen
hours a day in restaurants, laundries, and garment sweatshops for
wages as low as a dollar an hour and less. In San Francisco,
close to sixty per cent of the Chinese community lives in poverty.

The poverty and oppression which engulf San Francisco's

nonwhite communities stem, in part, from the very social institutions which are looked to for a measure of relief. The Welfare Department is a prime example: supposedly created to help people overcome their condition of poverty, it actually functions to lock the poor into a vicious cycle of dependency and subservience. At the same time, it does not even provide them with adequate subsistence. The cost of hospitals and other medical facilities is so prohibitive, and the health care distribution system so ineffective, that nonwhite people in San Francisco have a much higher rate of infant mortality than the average for San Francisco, and their life expectancy is almost eight years lower. Similarly, the educational system, billed as a great equalizer, reinforces class stratification instead of alleviating it.

The public school system in San Francisco is a mammoth operation, serving over 100,000 young people in its elementary through junior college facilities. The impact of the white exodus to the suburbs is poignantly evident in the city's schools: six out of ten students are nonwhite, and where San Francisco's outlying suburbs are able to spend on an average of $1000 per student each year, San Francisco can manage a yearly average of only $603 per student. This shortage of financial resources, attributed to a shrinking tax base, results in overcrowding and undereducating which hits nonwhite students especially hard. There is no bilingual instruction for Chinese or Spanish-speaking students, even in the elementary schools where children from non-English speaking homes need help in making the transition. While the third graders at Alamo Elementary School, located in one of San Francisco's wealthier white neighborhoods, scored a year ahead of their grade level on a reading test, those at Golden Gate Elementary School, situated in the Fillmore district, were found to be more than a year behind.

These conditions have traditionally been reinforced by the *de facto* segregation in the San Francisco schools, something which recently prompted the Board of Education to propose that busing of students be instituted to bring about an integrated school system. It was literally too little and too late, however; for different reasons, neither the white nor the nonwhite communities actively supported the plan, and some elements in the white community vigorously opposed it. Consequently, the proposal was defeated after a good deal of sensational publicity, highlighted by a full-scale brawl at an open Board of Education meeting. With integration no longer acceptable as a solution to the failures and inequities of the school system, and no other alternatives even being considered, tensions and frustrations within the schools could only continue to mount. Already, a wave of rebellions had swept through the city's high schools during the 1968-69 school year.

The high school rebellions in San Francisco hit the schools where nonwhite enrollment has already been heaviest. Of the four schools (Balboa, Polytechnic, Wilson, and Mission) that experienced demonstrations or disruptions, nonwhite students comprised some seventy per cent of the total student population. All four schools specialized in vocational tracking: in 1966, they programmed eighty-two per cent of their students into either the armed forces, trade schools, or immediate employment or unemployment. A meager eight per cent managed to get into college. Lowell High School, predominantly white and specializing in academic tracking, sent fifty per cent of its graduating seniors to college that same year. The revolts in the vocational schools were never groundless; almost always, they revolved around a set of demands that the students had made on the school authorities. These demands were sometimes innocuous, like "soul food" in the cafeteria, and sometimes vindictive, like the removal of a "racist" teacher or principal; more often than not, however, they went right to the sources of the disaffection and discontent which permeated the schools. Demands for an end to police harassment of students in and around school buildings were a reaction to the prison-like atmosphere the students constantly encountered. Demands for a non-white curriculum, completely lacking in the high schools, and for more non-white instructors—only one teacher in ten employed by the school system was non-white—were among the most persistent at all of the schools. Finally, the students frequently expressed their resentment at being excluded from having a real shot at going to college.

JUAN MARTINEZ AND MINORITY ADMISSIONS

The lack of nonwhite students at San Francisco State College had been a source of some concern among faculty and administrators, particularly when the BSU began to point out that the total number of black students attending S.F. State had steadily dwindled since 1961, the year the Master Plan became operational. The BSU was working on a program to bring more black students into the school under the two per cent "special admissions" quota of students whom the Master Plan permitted to enter the state college system with academic entrance requirements waived. President John Summerskill hoped to venture even further in the recruitment of minority students to the college; in the early spring of 1967, he attended a local conference on the problems of minority students, the major outcome of which was the launching of the "College Commitment Program." Enlisting the support of such prominent universities as Stanford and the University of California at Berkeley, as well as S.F. State and San Jose State, the program was supposed to seek out minority students and place them in the various institutions participating in the project. The initial step was supposed to be for each of the participating institutions to hire someone to begin working on recruitment drives in the surrounding high schools. President Summerskill, for his part, followed through on this commitment: towards the end of the spring he handed the job of recruitment over to Juan Martinez, one of the two or three Mexican-Americans on the S.F. State faculty.

The son of a migrant farm laborer, Juan Martinez was born in Midvale, Utah, where his family worked in the sugar beet fields. He was the thirteenth child in a family of fourteen, and, due to his father's religious conversion in Utah, all fourteen were raised in the Mormon faith. Martinez spent his early years living in the Mexican barrios of Los Angeles; it was during the leanest years of the Depression, and his family was dependent on the weekly gunny sack full of food rations that they picked up from the welfare agency. When the crops were in season, the family would follow the harvest up and down the California Central Valley, with the children joining their parents in the fields. Because of the constant seasonal work, none of the Martinez children were able to complete a full year of school at any one time; instead, they either attended on a haphazard basis or gave up completely. Though Juan Martinez had managed to get as far as the tenth grade by 1942, his grades were poor, and his high school counselor finally convinced him that he was wasting his time and would be better off working.

After dropping out of high school, Martinez, who had just turned sixteen, moved with his family to Richmond, California. The United States had finally entered World War II, and the shipyards in Richmond were building warships around the clock. There was plenty of work, wages were high, and the Martinez family was able to live fairly comfortably for the first time. Juan Martinez continued to work in the shipyards until January, 1945, when he was drafted into the Navy; by the time of his discharge in the summer of 1946, the shipyards had virtually closed down, and his family was spread out all over California, many of them back working as migrant farm laborers. Jobs were scarcer than ever, but the GI Bill saved Martinez from having to return to the fields himself. In the Navy, he had been awarded a high school diploma on the basis of a test he had passed. Now, learning that the federal government was giving a subsistence allowance to veterans who enrolled in school, Martinez applied to Sacramento Junior College and was accepted in the summer of 1947. That fall, he enrolled as a twenty-one-year-old freshman.

Martinez nearly flunked out during his first year in college but managed to avoid doing so until he had begun to catch onto his academic work and even liked it. He completed two years of junior college and went on to get his B.A. at Brigham Young University, where his scholarly perseverance and his Mormon background had secured him a scholarship. By 1956, he had earned a Ph.D. in history at the University of California at Berkeley. He taught for a year at Brigham Young, then went on to teach for nine years at the State University in Flagstaff, Arizona.

It was while he was teaching at Arizona State that Martinez began to involve himself in the politics of the Mexican-American community. Having been born and raised in poverty and having escaped it through education, he was now eager to extend his good fortune to others in the brown community. The creation of the War on Poverty in the early 1960's had promised to give the poor a new lease on life, and it created a glimmering of political interest and consciousness among the Arizona chicanos. Martinez volunteered his services to the local poverty program at Flagstaff; much to his chagrin, he quickly discovered that the program was controlled by local Democratic politicians whose interests were often in sharp conflict with the pressing needs of the community. Brown people continued to suffer from unemployment, inadequate health care, miseducation and undernourishment, and the poverty program did little except to coopt indigenous community leaders by putting them on its payroll. Two years of working with the program was more than enough to convince Martinez of the futility of depending on government structures or programs to solve social problems. He quit the program in disgust, and in 1966 was approached by John Shover, who was acting as temporary chairman of the S.F. State history department, and offered a job. Martinez accepted, and began teaching at S.F. State in the fall of that year.

Martinez arrived at his new post only to become embroiled in a bitter feud with his department chairman, Ray Kelch. He had accepted the position at S.F. State with the understanding that he would be teaching a course in Mexican-American history, an idea which had been enthusiastically received by Professor Shover. Kelch, however, would hear nothing of it; he insisted that Martinez was needed to teach the established departmental courses to which he had already been assigned. The antagonism between the two men festered through the fall and spring semesters; during this same period, Martinez was developing into an outspoken critic of American capitalism and imperialism and an admirer of the Cuban revolution—a significant departure for him, since he had held much more conservative views throughout his academic career and had fulfilled his publish-or-perish requirements at Arizona State by writing a hostile book about the Castro regime. In part, his political transition can be attributed to his disillusioning experiences with the poverty program in Flagstaff; in addition, however, Professor Martinez was beginning to look for his political and intellectual inspiration to the revolutionary movements of Africa, Asia, and Latin America.

Toward the end of the 1967 spring semester, Martinez received a letter from the history department informing him that he would not be rehired for the coming school year due to lack of "positions and money." Having left a tenured position at Arizona State to come to San Francisco, he was understandably furious. He openly accused the history department of being "racist and reactionary," and took his grievances straight to President Summerskill. At the time, Summerskill was looking for someone to organize the College Commitment Program at S.F. State; as a minority professor, Martinez seemed perfect for the job. He was immediately appointed to head the program; over the summer the President was able to secure him a position in the social science department.

Martinez quickly learned that the development of an effective College Commitment Program was next to impossible. San Francisco's high schools did nothing to encourage or prepare non-white students to attend college, vocational tracking and counseling were so heavily emphasized that Martinez encountered attitudes of mistrust or disbelief when he offered students a chance to apply to S.F. State. Coordination with the other colleges supposedly participating in the program was virtually non-existent; many had, in fact, done nothing since attending the initial conference. After a few months on the job, Martinez decided to concentrate his efforts on getting minority students into S.F. State instead of relying on building the program; but even this proved to be an exasperating task. To begin with, there was no program except for what Martinez could do on his own: no staff or resources were available to him, nor were there any admissions criteria or mechanisms especially attuned to the needs of non-white students. There was the two per cent special admissions quota, but that was all: no implementation procedures, no financial aid for the needy students, no special orientation program, no advisors or tutors—and no funds with which to fill the gaps in any of these areas. Martinez complained continually about the insurmountable handicaps under which he was expected to work; the college administration would simply advise him to do what he could under the circumstances, since his working on the project was better than nothing. Concluding that nonwhite students would have to organize and resort to direct political pressure if they were ever to get anything from the college, he began sounding out various ethnic groups and nonwhite students on the campus. What he proposed was an alliance of nonwhite student organizations that would work together around a common educational and political program.

THE FORMATION OF THE THIRD WORLD
LIBERATION FRONT

The Black Students' Union, the most powerful and politically sophisticated of the minority group organizations on campus, was immediately receptive to Martinez's idea. The isolated nationalism which had characterized the BSU's early stage of growth was beginning to evolve into a more revolutionary form of nationalism, which took its direction from the writings of the Algerian psychiatrist Frantz Fanon. With the nonviolent orientation and assimilationist rhetoric of the Civil Rights Movement falling into disrepute, young black activists originally gravitated towards Fanon because of his emphasis on problems of black identity and the legitimacy, in clinical as well as tactical terms, of the impulse to revolutionary violence. Fanon's psychological speculations had a political basis, however, which was becoming more and more important to the black liberation movement in America. Originally the concept of "third world" was coined by Western journalists to describe the emerging nations in the UN committed to neither the U.S. nor the Soviet bloc. These nations were, in effect, pawns in an ideological battle being waged strictly between Europeans and their American descendents. (China was not included in the dispute.) For Fanon these "underdeveloped countries" of Asia, Africa, and Latin America were engaged in a common struggle against a common enemy—imperialism, whose defeat could be achieved only through the development of third world unity and revolutionary consciousness. By themselves, and without the benefit of a revolutionary ideology, the various nationalist revolutions were vulnerable to the superior technology, military might, and political subversion of the colonialists and imperialists; together, they represented the common interests of the vast majority of the world's people and could finally triumph over their oppressors.

The ideological orientation of Fanon's writings was first adapted to the American setting by the Oakland-based Black Panther Party, with whom the BSU had close ties. The Panthers viewed the black community as an oppressed "black colony" within the "white mother country," and applied to their own movement the same principles of "third world solidarity" that Fanon hoped to apply to the three continents of the underdeveloped world. This principle had special significance for American blacks, since, unlike the Algerians whose experience with the French colonialists provided Fanon with the empirical basis for his theories, they were an oppressed minority within a white society, not a colonized nation being ruled by a clique of white settlers. Isolated, they could be destroyed in the same way the German Jews had been destroyed; identifying their struggle with that of the Vietnamese, the Cubans, the Algerians, and dozens of other nonwhite peoples who were struggling against American military and economic power, they were part of a worldwide movement whose triumph could already be seen in Vietnam.

There was a similar element of practicality in the BSU's ready acceptance of the third world alliance at S.F. State. Its educational programs, like Black Studies and special admissions, were running into some stiff resistance from the college, and if the black students wished to continue to expand them they would need more muscle, for the stakes were growing larger. They had little in common with the white radicals, whom they regarded as unstable, but the other ethnic minorities on the campus seemed like perfect allies: they had common educational interests with the black students; they were also institutionally discriminated against; and their lack of political development would allow the BSU to assume a vanguard role in the new organization.

Two third world groups were actually organized in response to Juan Martinez's early efforts to arouse the interest of nonwhite students on campus. One was the Philippine-American College Endeavor (PACE); the other was El Renacemiento, which later changed its name to the Mexican-American Student Confederation (MASC). PACE was principally organized by two Filipino students, Pat Salavar and Ron Quidachay; its major emphasis was on tutoring and recruiting college applicants from the Philippine community, though later it developed a program of Philippine Studies. MASC was established at S.F. State in January of 1968, with primarily a cultural orientation. However, partly due to the urgings of Professor Martinez, who was their faculty advisor, the chicano students expanded their activities into the community, setting up a tutorial project and doing some work with the students at Mission High School. By the summer, MASC had linked up with eight other Mexican-American student groups on campuses throughout northern California in order to better coordinate the emerging chicano student movement.

Two other student groups, the Intercollegiate Chinese for Social Action (ICSA) and the Latin American Student Organization (LASO), participated in the discussions about bringing together a bloc of ethnic minority organizations, though they were hesitant to join the alliance at first. LASO had been founded at S.F. State in the spring of 1967 by native-born Latin-American students; its programmatic emphasis was social and educational, holding cultural considerations far above political ones. Within a year, however, LASO developed more social awareness; by the spring of 1968 it had merged with the Latin Tutorial Project, which had been started through the Work-Study Program and was operating in the Mission district under the direction of the former Tutorial Program coordinator Roger Alvarado.

Working closely with the students in LASO, Alvarado succeeded in involving them in tutoring and also in getting them interested in a Latin American Studies program which already existed at S.F. State, but was so inept that it had only graduated one student in eight years. When Professor Martinez approached LASO about his idea of a minority group alliance, it sent representatives to the meetings, but up until September of 1968, the Latin students participated only marginally in the third world student organization. Part of this was because they felt that associating with the alliance might jeopardize their chances of getting the curriculum and structure of Latin American Studies revamped; but LASO was also still somewhat uneasy with the militant revolutionary stance of the Black Students' Union.

The ICSA was organized on the S.F. State campus in the fall of 1967, with the help of Del Sonsten and the Community Involvement Program. Motivated by vague social concerns, the group worked as volunteers for some of Chinatown's social service agencies, among them the local War on Poverty office; they also set up their own project to teach immigrant Chinese teenagers to speak English. Most of the Chinese students attracted to the organization were from comparatively well-to-do families; they wanted to help improve the Chinese community, but not at the expense of their own social standing. The patient work of the CIP, however, succeeded in countering this missionary attitude in favor of at least a rudimentary political orientation; by the spring of 1968, the ICSA was soliciting Associated Student funds in order to set up a program of its own, independent of the social service agencies. The first two projects were an expansion of the English classes into a more inclusive tutorial, and a study of the Chinatown power structure which revealed it to be at one with the entrenched business hierarchy, the so-called "Six Companies" who enjoyed their prestige and power at the expense of the rest of the Chinese community. For much the same reasons as LASO, however, the ICSA still shied away from the idea of a third world alliance.

The vacillation over the third world question within the ICSA threatened to split the organization right down the middle. An insurgent group of Chinese students, led by a pair of City College transfers named Al and Mason Wong and supported by a militant Chinese street youth organization called the Leeways, demanded that the ICSA ally itself with the other ethnic minorities. After a seesaw battle within the organization, the insurgents were triumphant: Mason Wong was elected chairman in late spring of 1968, and the ICSA officially aligned itself with the third world coalition soon after. That summer it opened its own youth center in Chinatown and, in league with the Leeways, led a struggle to oust the director of the local poverty program, whom they had exposed as a pawn of the Chinatown Six Companies.

The talks leading to the formation of the Third World Liberation Front (TWLF), as the organization was to be called, gave rise to a loose coalition whose member organizations would still enjoy complete autonomy to do as they saw fit with respect to the policies established by the central committee. As for a program, the TWLF initially agreed to work toward three major objectives: additional special admissions quotas for all third world students; the creation of a program of third world studies, including the development of curricula and the hiring of third world faculty to staff it; and the rehiring of Juan Martinez, Richard Fitzgerald, and Nathan Hare. Actually, Fitzgerald was the only one of the three to have lost his job for certain, but Martinez suspected that his was again on the line and the BSU wanted assurances that Dr. Hare would be able to stay on at S.F. State permanently.

Toward the end of March, the establishment of TWLF was made public, and a third world cultural festival was held to celebrate the alliance. Dancers, singers, and musicians from the various third world communities joined in the festivities, which were modeled after the shows the BSU often put on to promote black culture. After the celebration, attended by a large number of curious third world students, the TWLF formed a partial slate of six candidates to run for office in the student body elections. The candidates included members of the BSU, PACE, LASO, and ICSA; they joined in a coalition with a group of white activists drawn largely from the programs, and called themselves the Community Action slate. After a lopsided campaign, the slate's candidates totally swept the elections by a margin of almost three to one, thus regaining control of the Associated Students and its $400,000 budget.

THE LAST DAYS OF THE SUMMERSKILL ADMINISTRATION

While the TWLF was in the process of developing itself organizationally and politically, John Summerskill was executing a strategic withdrawal from the office of the presidency. The increasing pressures of the job had not simply neutralized whatever effectiveness he may have had in dealing with the college's problems; they had also literally worn him down. On February 22, 1968, he called a press conference and announced his intention to resign, effective in September of that year. In his resignation statement, he placed the burden of responsibility for the deteriorating conditions at the college and the general plight of higher education in the state upon the administration of Governor Ronald Reagan. "Education is being seriously eroded by political interference and financial starvation," he warned. "The proposed budget for the coming year is inadequate to maintain operations at their present level and it contains practically no money to initiate new programs to meet public needs." Pointing out that the state colleges' line-item budgeting procedures made all but impossible the kind of fiscal flexibility that administrators needed to respond positively to a rapidly changing educational situation, Summerskill maintained that he had exhausted his ability to effect the necessary changes and grimly predicted that the situation would get worse. The resignation was somewhat surprising, especially since Summerskill had managed to survive the wrath of the Trustees after the December 6 disturbances; it shocked liberals throughout the state, who saw Summerskill as a renovating force in higher education. On the other side, conservative politicians like Reagan and State Superintendent of Schools Max Rafferty reacted with ill-concealed delight. Their good-riddance attitude was neatly capsulized by Governor Reagan, who quipped, "I hope he finds a campus where there are unlimited funds and no restrictions."

Actually, financial starvation was only one symptom of the institutional deterioration that plagued S.F. State. As students became more adamant in their demands upon the college, they were simultaneously learning that only so much could be accomplished within established structures and policies. The faculty, while cynically acknowledging their failure to provide cohesive direction in dealing with such pressing college problems as military recruiting and third world special admissions, self-righteously placed the blame for the mushrooming crises upon either the student rebels or on the despots on the Board of Trustees—depending on whom they disliked the most. S.F. State administrators, aside from constantly feuding among themselves, had compartmentalized specific decision-making prerogatives to the point where once a decision was made, it often conflicted directly with a previous policy established elsewhere in the academic hierarchy. In addition, many institutional decisions, once they had been made, were never carried out due to lack of cooperation or to lack of clearly defined responsibilities—a prime example of this being the ill-fated task force set up to implement Black Studies.

The chaotic history of the Carnegie Foundation proposal aptly captures the atmosphere of uncertainty and incompetence which characterized Summerskill's last months in office. After losing control of the AS for the first time in five years to Phil Garlington and the "Shape Up" slate, activists in the Programs had approached the college President, who had a high opinion of their work, and appealed to him to find some outside source of funds to make up for what was sure to be trimmed from their budgets by the new student government. Under the aegis of the "Center for Educational Innovation," Summerskill agreed; he approached the Carnegie Foundation and interested them enough in the idea to send a representative out to the college to look things over and to talk to the students who had drafted the proposal.

The representative's arrival on campus touched off a scramble for money and control of the program which all but obscured its initial intent. Having established the initial link with the Carnegie Foundation and gotten things rolling, Summerskill benignly turned the project over to his Academic Vice President, Donald Garrity. The students were openly suspicious of Garrity, and he quickly justified their suspicions by "opening up" the proposal to the entire college, advising a number of faculty associates to write up proposals they would like to see get a slice of the grant money. Since S.F. State's research budget had recently been slashed to the bone, faculty who had been left with no way to finance their pet academic projects responded to Garrity's benevolence with a good deal of enthusiasm. The Program students were enraged when they learned of Garrity's conniving; they contacted Summerskill and demanded that he come down to their offices for a conference. Dutifully, the President promptly appeared at the wooden construction huts on the south side of the Commons, where the Programs were housed; the students closed the door behind him, turned on a tape recorder, and be-

gan verbally raking him over the coals, finally eliciting an assur-
ance that the Carnegie Foundation was interested only in their
programs and no one else's. At a meeting held the next day,
(which was called at Summerskill's suggestion to iron out the
differences between Garrity and the students), Garrity and Summerskill ended up flatly contradicting each other: Garrity claimed
Summerskill had told him to open up the proposal; Summerskill
denied ever having done so. The students merely insisted that
Garrity have nothing to do with the proposal if they were to participate in it, and since the Programs were what had brought the
Carnegie Foundation out to S.F. State in the first place, Garrity
could do little but back down, leaving the students with full control over the writing of the final draft.

By the time the final draft was ready, Summerskill had resigned, taking with him his commitment to provide a letterhead
for the proposal and to present it personally before the Carnegie
Foundation. Throughout the spring 1968 semester, the proposal
was an on-again, off-again proposition, depending on whether the
Carnegie Foundation was listening to the students or to the college administration. Having lost control of the grant himself,
Garrity was doing everything he could to prevent it from going
through. For his part, Summerskill continued to insist that he
was doing all he could to secure the grant, but he was becoming
less and less convincing. Finally fed up with the President's eva-
siveness, the students left for New York themselves in early May,
without the letterhead Summerskill had never provided and without the faculty representative they had wanted to accompany
them. (The administration had refused to allow him to make the
trip.)

Upon arriving in New York, the students were astonished to
discover that Summerskill was there as well. He wasn't promoting the Center proposal, however; he was making speeches explaining why he had resigned and detailing the "political instability" at S.F. State which had driven him to it. Summerskill had
come in for some national attention following the December 6
disturbances; *Life* magazine had given him a lavish and highly
sympathetic spread portraying him as an anguished, high-minded
liberal being torn apart by pressures from the Left and Right.

Now, he was about to be appointed as an educational consultant to Senator Robert Kennedy; the image he was building for himself was predicated largely upon the assumption that S.F. State was a seething cauldron of insoluble social discontent. Needless to say, such talk did little to help the progress of the Carnegie grant, and the students were as furious at Summerskill as they had been with Garrity. They finally established a liaison with the Carnegie Foundation on their own, and succeeded in getting a provisional grant of $50,000 for the summer of 1968. The grant was scarcely worth the effort it had taken to secure it. The incessant politicking had forced the students to water down their programs and had a debilitating effect on their work. The programs had become so ambitious that some form of outside funding was unavoidable; at the same time, the students had become so dependent on that outside funding that when the money dried up, so did their programs. Happily, the BSU was able to devise an alternative strategy for continuing its work, but the white programs—the Experimental College, Work-Study, the CIP—were coming closer and closer to foundering.

While Summerskill and the Programs students were squaring off in New York, tensions were increasing back on the campus. In conjunction with its special admissions project, the TWLF had begun to help Juan Martinez recruit third world students from the local high schools though the College Commitment Program no longer existed, even on paper. During March and April, Martinez and the TWLF students did a good deal of work at Mission High School, meticulously explaining the significance of the two per cent quota to the students there. Most of the Mission students they talked to had already ruled out college; their counselors had always told them they weren't "college material," and this was the first they had heard of the special admissions program. Once they understood the opportunity that was still available to them, they were very enthusiastic. Aided by Martinez and the TWLF, some 200 Mission High School students, mostly chicanos, filled out applications for admission to S.F. State, as well as financial aid forms to enable them to stay in school once admitted. When the briefing and the filling out of forms were completed, the TWLF set up a campus tour for the students, during the course of which they were to formally present their applications to John Summerskill.

Summerskill was still in New York on the day of the tour, so the 200-odd students, accompanied by their TWLF guides, marched into Vice President Garrity's office. Garrity was taken aback by the invasion, but he managed to regain composure long enough to pass the buck to the Dean of Admissions, a newly hired ex-Army Colonel named Charles Stone. When the students crowded into his office, Stone informed them that existing quotas permitted him to accept no more than eighty of their applications. The students, who had been coached by Martinez, promptly informed him that the Trustees had raised the special admissions quota from two to four per cent at their April meeting; furthermore, urban campuses like S.F. State could utilize the unfilled quotas of other state colleges. They then suggested that he call the Chancellor's office, which had the authority to act on their applications. Stone made the call, with a few of the students listening in on the extension lines; the Chancellor's office corroborated what the students had said, but insisted that it only set guidelines and that it was up to the local administration to determine how those guidelines would be applied. After the call was completed, Stone's position was unchanged. He didn't have the authority, he said, either to accept all the applications or to guarantee that all the students who applied would be accepted. The students angrily demanded that he resign so that someone more responsive to the needs of third world people could take his place. Dean Stone, who was by this time completely flustered, took out a piece of paper and wrote out his resignation while the students watched approvingly.

Stone's letter of resignation was not taken seriously by the college administration, which would not even consider it. The local news media took it very seriously, however; somehow, they got wind of the story and made it into a front-page scandal. By the time it got into print, the story was that Stone had been forced to resign at knife point, and the Mission students had been put up to the job by Martinez, an unscrupulous agitator who was using the teen-agers for his own ends. Though Stone himself was to deny the story, it created a tremendous stir. A few days after the incident Martinez went to an emergency meeting in the Mission district and found himself faced with a hostile audience; after a good deal of explaining, a detailed resumé of the special admissions issue, and a recapitulation of his own efforts on behalf of the neighborhood's high school students, he earned an enthusiastic ovation. College officials were not nearly so appreciative. They knew the knife story was a total fabrication, but the affair had caused them a great deal of embarrassment and they were privately incensed over Martinez's pressure tactics on the special admissions issue. Consequently, Martinez was shortly thereafter informed that any chance he may have had of being rehired by the college was gone, and he would do well to look for a new job.

The firing of Martinez and the negligible progress of the special admissions campaign put TWLF in a difficult position. Some of the leadership of the organization realized that if the high school students they had recruited were to be admitted to the college, and Martinez were to get his job back, there would have to be some kind of an open confrontation. As a coalition of organizations, however, the TWLF alliance was still far too tenuous to allow such tactics. The BSU, most powerful of the third world groups, had a separate special admissions program which the college had already approved, and it was reluctant to jeopardize it by engaging in another confrontation. Under these circumstances, a faction within TWLF—including MASC, PACE, and some members of LASO—sought out SDS as a possible ally. Actually, SDS was not only in need of allies; it was in need of issues. After the setbacks of the fall semester, the white radical organization had continued to agitate around the issue of college complicity with the Vietnam war. Even in symbolic terms, the issue was rather weak: apart from the occasional visits by military recruiters, S.F. State's direct contact with the war machine went no farther than a tiny Air Force ROTC program with a total enrollment of twenty-nine students. The SDS campaign to get the ROTC contract terminated by the college attracted sympathy, but not much enthusiasm; though an SDS-sponsored referendum to that effect passed the student body elections in April by a margin of nearly two to one, there was little likelihood that many

students would back up the results of the referendum by taking
direct action against the college administration. Still, SDS members felt a moral obligation to rid the college of the Air Force;
and a coalition with TWLF seemed like the most likely way to
mobilize enough support for the mass demonstrations they knew
were necessary to get the administration to act.

President Summerskill, who had final authority over the
AFROTC contract, did not immediately respond to the SDS
demand that he honor the student referendum and terminate it.
Instead, he slipped out of the controversy for the moment by
dropping the issue in the lap of the faculty. "I have some serious
questions about the academic legitimacy of AFROTC on this
campus," he said, "but I think this is a matter for the faculty to
decide." The faculty, however, was still mainly concerned with
protecting the "neutrality of the institution." Their debate over
the AFROTC contract centered around the question of the "academic validity" of the program: faculty liberals maintained that
the AFROTC curriculum was established and operated independent of the college's regular academic standards, and since it was
directly responsible only to the Secretary of the Air Force in
Washington, D.C., the program did not warrant either the granting of academic credit nor the allocation of college facilities.
Such arguments induced the Academic Senate to vote, twenty-
four to four, in favor of canceling the AFROTC contract, and
to call for a ratification of their proposal by a full faculty meeting; however, they also served to disillusion the student radicals,
who viewed the faculty's approach to the issue as an absurd exercise in academic pretension.

The day after the Academic Senate vote, some 300 students,
most of them white activists, crowded into the AFROTC offices
in the psychology building for a "teach-in." They heard Professor
Martinez deliver a lecture on American imperialism in Latin
America, linking the ROTC issue with the TWLF demands by
asserting that both the Vietnam war and the denial of educational
opportunity to third world students were an outgrowth of the
imperialistic spirit. The students had drawn up a formal list of
four demands: the first three called for 400 third world special
admissions in the fall of 1968, the rehiring of Martinez, and the

allocation of eleven teaching positions to the TWLF special admissions program; the final demand called for termination of the AFROTC contract. The morning after the teach-in, Summerskill responded to the demands. The 400 special admissions, he said, had only to be cleared by the Chancellor's office; however, he was more equivocal about the other three. He was "doubtful" that Martinez would be rehired; he was "seeking" teaching positions for the special admissions program; and he would "abide by the faculty's decision" on AFROTC. At a mass meeting that afternoon, Summerskill's response was deemed unacceptable by the students, and 383 signed a pledge to stage a sit-in in the administration building if the demands were not met in full by 1:00 P.M., May 21. However, the TWLF was so badly split by this time that it would take no position on the sit-in, even though it was on record as supporting all four demands.

The split within TWLF was due primarily to a pair of factors. To begin with, the BSU had already elicited a series of concessions from the college administration for the fall semester—including 200 black special admissions, and a Black Studies Department with Nathan Hare as its official chairman. Beyond that, it was the only group within TWLF to have a stake in the Carnegie grant, which was still pending, and most of its leadership was still on probation as a result of the *Gater* office brawl. All these considerations militated against BSU participation in the sit-in. The second problem was that the stauncher supporters of Professor Martinez, in particular MASC and PACE, had set up the TWLF-SDS coalition without first getting the approval of the TWLF central committee. This so upset the leadership of LASO that they pulled their organization out of the TWLF a few days before the sit-in.

SDS was having some problems of its own regarding the impending demonstration. The deadline they had set coincided exactly with the beginning of the general faculty meeting to discuss the AFROTC issue; this led many faculty members and a good number of students to conclude that SDS wasn't really interested in getting AFROTC off the campus but sought confrontation for its own sake. Responding to these accusations, SDS pointed out that there were four demands, not one, and that the sit-in would

AN END TO SILENCE

be necessary even if the ROTC contract were terminated. Matters of principle were also involved: SDS had little use for the academic ground rules by which the faculty debate was being conducted; they viewed them as a calculated evasion of the war-related issues, and they frankly challenged the faculty's right to decide such questions independently. Nevertheless, the prevailing sentiment on campus was that SDS should wait until after the faculty meeting was over, especially since the anti-ROTC forces were expecting an overwhelming vote in their favor. At noon Tuesday, while the faculty was heading for its own meeting in the Main Auditorium, SDS held a rally at the Speaker's Platform, after which it led a crowd of students up to the administration building. The crowd numbered only 200, a little more than half the number of students who had signed pledges to sit-in.

Nor was there unanimity in the ranks of the 200 who honored their pledges. Once inside the administration building, a heated dispute broke out when members of the Progressive Labor Party (PL), who still tended to dominate SDS, attempted to barricade the building by putting chains on the doors. The rest of the students felt isolated enough without cutting themselves off from the outside completely; after a brief flare-up, PL backed down and the chains were removed. The sit-in was to be nonviolent, and access to the building would be guaranteed to anyone who wished to enter.

First to take advantage of the free access were the liberal faculty. Their own meeting had gone badly: Academic Senate Chairman Walcott Beatty had started it off by pleading with those in attendence to ignore the students in the Administration Building and address themselves to the issues, but his pleas were futile. The faculty conservatives, initially outflanked by the academic arguments against ROTC, now seized vindictively upon what they saw as the students' defiance of faculty authority. Speaker after speaker rose not to debate the merits of AFROTC, but to denounce in no uncertain terms the "student intimidation" and "student coercion" the sit-in was supposed to represent. They maintained that to cancel the AFROTC contract would be to capitulate to a "tiny minority of student dissidents." Frank Dollard of the English department informed his colleagues

that the campus SDS chapter was being financed by Mao
Tse-tung, and was met with a startling degree of credulity. The
anti-ROTC forces at the meeting were demoralized and inept;
still, they might have prevailed had they not consented to a conservative demand that the entire faculty, including those not in
attendance, be polled by mail. The mail ballot produced a 282 to
251 vote in favor of renewing the AFROTC contract, and the
enraged faculty liberals stormed up to the Administration Building to harangue the beleaguered students.

The faculty's decision on ROTC, and their shoddy conduct
during the general meeting, produced a measure of increased
support for the sit-in: by nightfall, the crowd in the Administration Building had grown to about three hundred. Closing time for
the campus was 10:00 P.M. and President Summerskill announced that police would be called to clear the building if the
students didn't leave on their own. Summerskill had very little
choice in the matter, since one of the conditions of his continued
"stewardship," as the Trustees defined it, was a mandatory use of
police when breaches of order occurred. At ten o'clock, with the
students still in the building, the San Francisco Police Department's notorious Tactical Squad arrived upon the scene. Authorized late in 1967 by Mayor Alioto as a "highly-trained mobile
unit to move into areas of high crime," the "Tac Squad" had
already earned a reputation for bullying and brutality. In January
it had attacked a student demonstration against Secretary of State
Dean Rusk at San Francisco's Fairmont Hotel; since then, it had
been used several times to quell disturbances involving youthful
"street people" in the Haight-Ashbury district. Now the Tac
Squad took up positions in a parking lot adjacent to the Administration Building as the order to disperse was read; all the students left except twenty-six volunteers who had agreed to submit
to arrest as a symbol of resistance. The tactic of token arrests
was agreed to by the students out of a recognition that it would
be foolish to have everyone hauled away to jail and expect the
sit-in to continue with any strength the following day. As it
turned out, the students who left the building got the worst of it.
While the twenty-six volunteers were led peacefully to the paddy
wagons, a crowd of about a thousand onlookers, at least half of

whom were curious night students, crowded around to see what was happening. Suddenly, without warning, the Tactical Squad charged into the crowd and began swinging riot sticks indiscriminately. As the terrified students were stampeded in every direction, a number of people, including AS attorney Terrance Hallinan, were clubbed to the ground. Hallinan, who was present at the demonstration to advise students of their legal rights, was singled out while trying to help a fallen girl to safety; his head was split open and blood streamed down his face. He was not arrested, however, until he had gotten to his feet and was making a statement to the press and the TV cameras; the police chose that moment to charge him with assaulting an officer and take him into custody. By this time the students' terror had turned to rage. Screaming, "Pigs off campus!", they threw anything they could get their hands on, including books, bundled newspapers, and even shoes, at the advancing police lines. Before there could be any further violence, the police quickly loaded up their vans and sped from the area. All told, eleven people were hospitalized that night, mostly for head lacerations that required stitches.

The Tac Squad's gratuitous display of muscle—the Chief of Police claimed it was necessary to "clear a path for the paddy wagons"—inadvertently gave the sit-in a new lease on life. Terrance Hallinan's bloodied face made the front page of both major dailies the next morning; as word of the previous night's events spread, there was a groundswell of support for the sit-in, and over 600 students joined in the occupation of the Administration Building when it reopened. Meanwhile a steering committee made up of six white students and six third world students had begun to negotiate with President Summerskill. The faculty, shocked by the police violence, called an emergency meeting at which the liberals regained the upper hand. Though they weren't able to reverse the AFROTC decision, they did push through a resolution stipulating that campus buildings should remain open on a twenty-four hour basis, thereby making it unnecessary for police to come and clear them. President Summerskill, who was as upset as everyone else by Tuesday night's violence, was more than happy to comply. About the only one to come to the defense of the Tactical Squad was Mayor Alioto, who blamed the violence on the students, referring to them as "street hoodlums."

The faculty's "open campus" policy did little to resolve the problems which the sit-in had created; in fact, Summerskill had been cast once again in the role of middleman, and nearly everything he did added to the conflict and general confusion. The Chancellor and the Trustees immediately demanded that he squelch the sit-in and close the building at the usual time. The Academic Deans and the President's own administrative staff urged him to agree to the two demands for special admissions, but not to give in on the rehiring of Martinez or the cancellation of the AFROTC contract. The sit-in, however, was finally gaining momentum: on Thursday about two dozen community leaders from the Mission district came to the campus to meet with Summerskill and voice their support for all four demands. Their pressure succeeded in getting Summerskill to agree to three of the demands, but the AFROTC issue remained deadlocked. During dinner Thursday evening, Summerskill assured his staff and the Academic Deans that he would abide by the faculty decision on AFROTC. Three hours later, after a negotiating session with the students and representatives of the Academic Senate, he had reversed himself: he now agreed to abide by the results of a student-faculty referendum which would settle the ROTC question once and for all.

The proposed referendum, which represented a compromise from all parties involved in the dispute, touched off a long and emotional debate between the students encamped in the Administration Building. In more ways than one, the sit-in had been a throwback to an earlier era: its adherence to nonviolent tactics, the incorporation of "participatory democracy" into the decision-making processes which governed the conduct of the demonstration, and the use of songs and chants to build the demonstrators' morale. Wherever enthusiasm began the ebb, an SDS member named Bruce Hartford, a veteran of the Mississippi Summer Project of 1964, would stand up and lead the crowd in singing "We Shall Not Be Moved," "We'll Never Turn Back," and other SNCC "freedom songs." The discussion over the proposed referendum was in a similar vein; it lasted for four hours, everyone got a chance to speak, and the arguments were delivered with an air of solemnity and moral earnestness. Those who favored the referendum argued that it would be easily won by the anti-ROTC forces, and for the demonstrators to reject it would be to isolate themselves once again from the rest of the campus and to show their lack of faith in their fellow students to come to the right decision. In addition, they argued, the referendum was setting an important precedent, since students would be voting on a matter of college policy on an equal footing with the faculty. Those who argued against the referendum saw it as an attempt to divert the energy of the sit-in into a cynical public relations ploy whose underlying hypocrisy could be measured by the fact that those who had the most to gain or lose from the outcome of the voting—the people of Vietnam—would have no say in the matter. Finally, PL's most formidable spokesman, John Levin, reversed the position that he and his followers had taken throughout the evening by arguing that, for tactical reasons, the students should agree to the referendum. A vote was called for immediately after Levin spoke; the referendum proposal passed almost unanimously.

As it turned out, the agonized soul-searching of the student sit-in did not make a bit of difference. Friday morning President Summerskill did not return to the campus; instead, he boarded a plane for Ethiopia, having been fired over a telephone at the airport by Chancellor Dumke. Some time before, Summerskill had been offered a comfortable Ford Foundation job at Haile Selassie University, but he had not intended to leave the country for at least another week, and his abrupt departure threw the campus into a state of literal anarchy; nobody knew who was in charge or what was going to happen. The student activists immediately reoccupied the Administration Building and waited for the new college authorities to declare themselves. The suspense continued through Friday afternoon; but finally that evening, Dean of Activities Jim Andrews informed the students that there would be no referendum on AFROTC, and that the open campus sanctions had been revoked. Behind these decisions was a hastily formed triumvirate consisting of Dean of Students Fred Reddell, Administrative Vice President Glenn Smith, and Academic Vice President Donald Garrity. After the 10:00 P.M. deadline passed, the police were called in and thirty-five demonstrators voluntarily submitted to arrest.

With the Friday night arrests, the four-day sit-in was virtually over; finals were scheduled for the next week, and further agitation around the AFROTC question seemed hopeless so late in the semester. However, there was a good deal of student discontent over the cancellation of the referendum; over the weekend, the remnants of the sit-in participants planned for a mill-in on Monday as an attempt to revive the AFROTC issues. The mill-in drew close to a thousand students into the Administration Building throughout the day. At one point, Reddell, Smith, and Garrity were all trapped in an office, which the angry students turned into a noise chamber by pounding on the walls and windows. The police were again summoned to aid the beleaguered administrators; somewhat, gingerly, they cleared the building of demonstrators and rescued the triumvirate in the process. By Tuesday, the activists could do little else but declare victory, having at least won three of the four original demands. The semester ended peacefully, and during the summer Robert Smith, a professor from the college's education department, was named as John Summerskill's successor.

CHAPTER VII

A Conflict in Priorities:

THE POLITICAL ECONOMY
OF HIGHER EDUCATION IN CALIFORNIA,
1960-1969

ROBERT SMITH AND THE "FACULTY REVOLT"

There is a certain irony in the state college Board of Trustees' choice of Robert Smith as President of San Francisco State College. In March of 1964, Smith had touched off a minor tempest on that campus when he resigned suddenly after seven years as Dean of the School of Education to return to teaching. The letter of resignation, which was made public, catalogued a growing list of frustrations which Smith had begun to encounter since the imposition of the Master Plan three years before. Though it was somewhat lacking in rhetorical clarity, his collegues received the document like a call to arms. Within a week of its receipt by College President Paul Dodd, over half of the S.F. State faculty, determined that Smith's resignation should not be an "isolated act of protest," signed a petition backing up his contention that the state college system was being mismanaged by its Chancellor and Trustees, and calling for an investigation by the Governor and the state legislature. The petition received sensational play in the news media and a measure of support from Dodd himself, who commented that its sponsors included "the recognized leaders of the campus . . . This is not a discordant segment but rather a solid group who, like Dean Robert Smith, are gravely concerned lest what appear to be tendencies toward centralization in the development of the new statewide system will dampen and diminish the 'creative spirit' which had made academic life at San Francisco so exciting in past years."

At its outset, the Master Plan had appeared as a godsend to the California state colleges. It offered them official recognition as bona fide liberal arts institutions, with all the increased prestige that accompanied it. Beyond that, it eliminated the yearly scramble for funds and competition with the University of California by creating a delicate balance of power between segments and centralizing control of the eighteen campuses under a single Board of Trustees which would represent their interests and give them a stable framework within which to function. Now, after three years of the Trustees' authority, many of the state college faculty were coming to the conclusion that they had actually been better off under the state Board of Education. While allowing faculty salaries, sabbaticals, research opportunities, travel expenses, and fringe benefits to lag farther and farther behind national norms, the fledgling Board of Trustees had taken a zealous interest in the internal operations and management of the campuses in its charge. The most crucial aspect of this new emphasis was the introduction of line-item budgeting into the state college system. As an economy measure, this accounting system strictly detailed the precise amount of money that each operation (departments, campus maintenance, administration, etc.) at a particular state college would be allocated annually. This made it virtually impossible for the individual campus to have fiscal, and hence institutional, flexibility—especially where new educational needs arose than hadn't been anticipated in the previous year's budget request. As a result, either directly or indirectly, traditional faculty prerogatives in such areas as curriculum, personnel, and admissions standards began to erode; the administrative structure at the local campus level was systematically weakened; and strong presidents at least two campuses were, as Smith put it, "picked off quietly behind the scenes." Frustrating as the breakdown of local authority must have been for an administrator like Smith, it spelled disaster for the faculty, which traditionally relied upon the President's office to mediate between their interests and those of the lay officials who are finally responsible for

the institution. As such, the virtual emasculation of the state college presidents by the Trustees left the faculty with no say at all
over how the colleges were to be run and, consequently, no way
of checking the sudden deterioration of their own position. A
quarter system was imposed upon some of the state colleges over
the protests of the Statewide Academic Senate; a "Master Curricular Plan" was drawn up in the Chancellor's office and instituted without faculty approval or even prior consultation; a set of
"administrative guidelines" were laid down that required the various campuses to overhaul their bureaucratic structure. Locally
developed plans or suggestions were summarily rejected or ignored; the drive for a stronger state college graduate program
was diverted into the establishment of a complicated, seldom-used
"joint doctoral program" with the University of California, which
no one in the state college faculty wanted.

The root causes of these conditions within the state college
system were not attacked in the S.F. State petition, and there
was more than a grain of truth to the Trustees' defensive contention that the protesting professors were mainly concerned with
feathering their own nest. But Robert Smith, who was more than
a little surprised when the news media dubbed him the "leader of
the faculty revolt," brought a broader perspective to the issue
than did most of his colleagues. For Smith, recognition of the
state colleges' liberal arts status had been achieved at the expense
of everything else; the Master Plan had "snared them in
mid-flight" during their "rapid and turbulent transition from the
functionalist, normal school tradition towards something akin to
the multiple-function land grant universities," of which the University of California was a prime example. To check this trend,
"stubborn efforts [had] been made to press them into a mold of
'essentialist' liberal arts presuppositions," and the result was "a
superficial concept of elite education inappropriate to a state college system." By the time the Master Curricular Plan had been
imposed, most state college faculty had begun to realize that their
academic base was actually being narrowed under the pretext of
broadening it. Smith was also concerned with the stiffening of
entrance requirements, as much for its resulting rigidity as for its
exclusiveness. In an implicit critique of the admission-by-

percentile-rating syndrome embodied in the Scholastic Aptitude Tests, he observed, "Colleges should not reject the student of promise because of identifiable specific deficiencies . . . A good college must be willing to bolster weaknesses as well as extend strengths." Similarly, the diversion of students to the junior colleges would "seriously restrict the educational opportunities of students of limited financial means and those of high native competence but limited cultural opportunity." What piqued Smith the most, however, was a dictum of the Trustees restricting the size of two metropolitan campuses, San Francisco and San Jose, to a full-time equivalent enrollment of 12,000 students. Departing momentarily from the jargon of the professional educator, he anguished, "The premise that land is too costly to permit expansion is a travesty to the community and its youth . . . How is it that we can build freeways but not colleges in metropolitan areas?"

Even in 1964 Smith was intelligent enough to see the connection between the Trustees' aggressive interest in the internal management of the state colleges and their singular lack of concern with seeking support for them, financial or otherwise, from the general public or the state. Most of the signers of the S.F. State petition saw the Trustees' incursions upon their privileges and prerogatives as a simple abuse of power by men who, not being academics themselves, failed to understand the complex processes of running an academic institution. For Smith, the Master Curricular Plan, the quarter system, and the streamlining of local administrative machinery all fell into a common pattern—all were economy measures, designed to reduce the cost of the state college system. Accordingly, he was less concerned with restoring the balance of power between faculty and Trustees than he was with "extending the services of the institution, whether or not there is an active demand," to those who would be most hurt by the cutbacks. With an uncanny prescience, he speculated as to the ultimate consequences of the "restrictive ideology being institutionalized within the state colleges":

Undue centralization at the top forces increasing pressure on those further down the hierarchy. This reduces the scope of their discretion and thereby releases conservative or reactionary forces which are intolerant of even the most trivial deviations from rigidly prescribed patterns of behavior. Those forces eventually impinge upon the students, rendering them anxious and fearful, prone to either conformity or revolt.

Though it served as a minor source of embarrassment to the Trustees and to the administration of Governor Pat Brown, the "faculty revolt" was largely ineffectual. The legislative investigation it had managed to provoke petered out as soon as it became clear that the Trustees had more political collateral with the Sacramento politicians than any of their employees. Six months later, the Berkeley students through the Free Speech Movement posed a far more serious challenge to the direction and implications of mass public higher education in California; within another two years the state college system would come under attack from its own students as well. By that time, however, the political climate in California had decisively shifted to the right, accelerating the process which Smith had bemoaned in his letter of resignation. In the 1966 gubernatorial election, the liberal Democratic incumbent, Pat Brown, was swamped by his reactionary Republican opponent, whose campaign included a stern promise to "get tough" with rebellious students being educated at the taxpayer's expense.

THE FAILURES OF THE MASTER PLAN

Ronald Reagan, who was overwhelmingly elected Governor of California in 1966, has been widely portrayed as a political curiosity, a kind of strange mutation of the electoral process; actually, he represents the natural outgrowth of that most logical of political phenomena—the taxpayer's revolt. "Government is the people's business," he said in his inaugural address on January 5, 1967, "and every man, woman, and child becomes a shareholder with the first penny of tax paid." Arguing that the state, operating at a deficit, was in the throes of a fiscal crisis, Reagan took office vowing to "cut and trim and squeeze until we have reduced the cost of government, and it will involve every department of government." The new policy went into effect with the slashing of the state mental health budget, and within a few months the deteriorating conditions in California's understaffed, overcrowded mental hospitals had already become something of a national scandal. The state colleges and the University of California were next to feel the bite; Reagan proposed a ten percent reduction in both of their budgets, at the same time threatening to impose tuition upon the two institutions for the first time in the history of the state. The tuition fees—$400 a year at the University and $200 a year at the state colleges—were justified not so much on the grounds that the state needed the extra revenue as on the grounds that students were getting a free ride and that having to pay for their education might be "a good thing for them." As Reagan put it, those who went to school to "agitate and not study" might thereby be induced to "think twice."

The enormous appeal of such a seemingly contemptuous attitude toward the general welfare may be shocking, but it is not hard to trace. In California as elsewhere, the mid-1960's heralded the impending collapse of the public service bureaucracies, whose increasing costliness was accompanied by an increasing insensitivity to the needs of those whom they were supposed to serve. For all the tax dollars expended on them, they had failed to contain urban unrest and social disintegration, failed to rationalize the contradictions in the economy of the state, proved woefully inadequate to the task of providing for the taxpayers in such areas as jobs, housing, transportation, health care, and education. California's vaunted system of public higher education proved no real exception to this trend. The Master Plan's pretensions to democracy and "equality of opportunity" notwithstanding, the public colleges—despite their rising costs—had grown progressively more inaccessible to the income groups under $10,000 a year, which bear the brunt of the tax burden in the state. The way students from those income groups are dispersed throughout the three segments of public higher education under the Master Plan is in itself ample demonstration of the fact. They comprise less than a third of the enrollment of the University of California, one-half the total enrollments of the state colleges, two thirds of the total enrollments of the junior colleges, and—needless to say—an even higher proportion of those who do not get to college at all. Yet the State of California spends twice as much on the education of a University student as on that of a state college student, and three times as much on the education of a state college student as on that of a junior college student.[1] If few taxpayers from the lower income brackets consciously realized that they were subsidizing the education of the children of the rich, most of them were aware that few of the benefits of the state's mushrooming higher education budget had filtered down to their own children.

The income distribution patterns throughout the three segments—and the unequal levels of state support for each segment—are far from accidental. The concept of "differentiation of functions," so crucial to the Master Plan, had originated with the *Restudy of the Needs of California Public Higher Education* in 1957.[2] According to the *Restudy,* the functions of each segment were to be defined in terms of the job market: the junior colleges would engage in "technical training," the state colleges in "occupational training," and the University in "professional training." The Master Plan, while in essence preserving this definition, tended to soft-pedal it by shifting the emphasis from economic considerations to supposedly academic ones. Thus, the state colleges were to be the major institutions to undergraduate education; the University's major field would be graduate instruction and research; the junior colleges would specialize in teaching the lower divisions; and all three would "strive for excellence in their own sphere." Differentiation was not in quality, but in different grade levels and areas of concentration; the diversion of students to the junior colleges, accomplished by raising the entrance requirements of the four-year schools, was justified by the contention that the junior colleges could expend more resources and devote more attention to their freshmen and sophomores than could either the state colleges or the University.

The Master Plan had scarcely been enacted into law when it became apparent that the concept of functional differentiation and "excellence in your own sphere" was an impossibility if not

---

[1]This needs to be qualified, since junior colleges are financed chiefly by local rather than state taxes. The general pattern is unchanged, however; local tax structures, which rely primarily on property taxes, are if anything more regressive than the state's.
[2]See Chapter I.

an outright fraud. Budgeting policies stated implicitly in the Master Plan itself saw to it that more would be spent on undergraduate education at the University than at the state colleges, and more would be spent on the lower divisions of the state colleges than on the junior colleges. This graduated pattern of preferential treatment is carried over into virtually every area of institutional operations. The University receives far more in capital outlays, though the state college system has added more new campuses since 1960. Faculty salaries at the university level are five to ten per cent higher; the average university professor earns $1,000 a year more than his state college counterpart, while for full professors the gap is nearly $3,000. Administrative salaries at the state colleges lag even farther behind, and most of the state college administrations are forced to "bootleg" positions from the faculty budget simply to assure themselves of adequate staffing. The state college faculty has one of the heaviest workloads in the nation; they have less time for sabbatical leaves, fewer paid assistants, almost no opportunities to do even instruction-related research. Nor do they enjoy the most elementary kind of contract rights: in 1964, an accounting error in the Chancellor's office led to an across-the-board 1.8 per cent pay cut for all senior state college faculty, which violated the terms under which most of them had been hired. When certain faculty members protested and took the matter to court, however, they lost their case—none of those terms had been in writing, so they could not be held as binding upon the state. Given such conditions, the faculty exodus from the state college system since the imposition of the Master Plan is hardly surprising. The faculty turnover rate and the percentage of unfilled vacancies has climbed steadily, to a formidable 21.8 per cent in 1966-67, while the percentage of state college faculty holding doctoral degrees has plunged downward.

Strangely enough, the differences in the prospective programs of the state colleges and the University are not as great as one might expect. The University does enjoy certain prerogatives in the area of predoctoral instruction and research, but these were designed by the Master Plan primarily to give the University uncontested access to federal grants, not to make it specialize in graduate education generally. The real differentiation between the

two segments shows up not in their programs, but in the budgeting and execution of those programs. A state college student has
less spent on his education, less sumptuous facilities in which to
learn, larger classes, and professors with less impressive academic
credentials. He receives, in essence, a cut-rate, low-cost, and decidedly inferior version of a University education; the state college system offers nothing that is not better provided by the
University.

Lest there be any illusions about the junior colleges specializing in the lower division education of students whose college careers will continue past the fourteenth grade, it might be helpful
to recall in greater detail the original language of the Master
Plan. A section devoted to "standards for selection and retention
of students" maintains that entrance requirements of the
four-year schools have been raised so that junior colleges can
"relieve them of the burden of remedial work." Since they are
open to anyone with a high school diploma, the junior colleges
are, we are told, able to salvage a number of "late bloomers"
whose high school records do not permit them to attend anywhere else and give their academic careers a new lease on life—if
they do well, they can transfer to a four-year school. Even on the
face of it, it is somewhat specious to suggest that these "late
bloomers" are getting a second chance, since prior to the Master
Plan, many of them would not have been disqualified from attending the senior colleges in the first place. But observe how
they are "salvaged": procedures for transfer to other institutions
are tightened; "vigorous use of probation and threat of dismissal"
are employed, ostensibly to "help some 'late bloomers' flower
sooner"; retention standards are kept "rigid enough that taxpayers' money will not be wasted on individuals who lack the capacity or the will to succeed in their studies." The junior colleges
are, in short, more exclusive than they pretend to be; they admit
students indiscriminately only to weed them out systematically.
Since many of those students are there precisely because their
high school educations have been so inadequate, they frequently
cannot cope with the rigid retention standards; or if they do, they
find that the kind of education they get is virtually indistin-
guishable from high school. The latter become disillusioned and

drop out, or are channeled by their counselors into vocational courses designed to discourage them from continuing beyond the sophomore year. Thus, only a relatively small number of entering junior college freshmen actually finish out their two years; the proportion of those who go on to a four-year school is often as low as 5 per cent and is seldom higher than 15 per cent at any junior college.[3]

This process can be more easily understood in the context of the tracking system, which was instituted in the California public schools as a way of aiding in the shift in enrollments away from the four-year schools. Designed to determine which of the three segments, if any, a particular student will attend once he reaches college age, the tracking system evaluates all students competitively on the basis of their scores on the so-called "objective tests"—the IQ and College Board examinations. Students are tracked as early as the second grade, the purpose being to separate the college material from the "less academically inclined." Invariably, the prophecy is self-fulfilling; while money and attention is lavished upon the former, the latter's education is an exercise in social control at its crudest, with only half-hearted attempts at remedial course work and, later, vocational training. If preferential funding of college-track programs is most responsible, certain psychological elements are also important. An experiment was conducted in New York City with a group of teachers who were told that certain of their pupils, in fact selected at random, were "late bloomers" whose work would soon show dramatic improvement. Surprisingly, the children really improved; thinking them to be somehow different, the teachers treated them with greater patience and respect, and they responded accordingly.

In effect the "objective tests" are no less arbitrary than the experimenters in designating "exceptional" children. Edward

[3]The high level of attrition at the junior colleges is completely deliberate, though the policy tends to be a tacit one. At the College of San Mateo, the transfer rate is normally around 5 percent. A "College Readiness Program" for third world students was instituted to persuade them to continue their education, and succeeded in getting 90 percent of them to do so. Whereupon the director of the program was promptly transferred to another job. One of the reasons given by the college administration was that he wasn't putting enough students into vocational training. Shortly thereafter the program was effectively disbanded by the Board of Trustees of the college.

Thorndike, the "father of intelligence testing," believed that non-white people were genetically inferior; statistics have shown that a child's IQ, especially as he grows older, is a remarkably accurate index of his family income. But this says nothing about how these tests actually operate, so some examples are in order. A group of questions on the Stanford-Binet IQ tests for young children involves the use of wooden building blocks which nearly all middle-class parents buy for their children. Unfortunately, most children from poor families have never seen such blocks before the day of the test, so they cannot hope to compete with children who have spent hours playing with them in their own homes. Similarly, standardized tests generally place an emphasis on verbal skills which sets the student who comes from a "bilingual" home, or who is accustomed to speaking something other than conventional English, at a serious disadvantage. In these and other areas, the tests reflect an orientation and range of experience which is more often than not completely alien to most students from minority or working-class backgrounds.

It cannot be stressed enough that this kind of bias, far from being incidental, is inherent in the whole concept of objective testing. Implicit in the notion that all students can be evaluated according to a uniform national standard is a complete disregard for social, ethnic, or cultural differences; where such differences are not acknowledged, standards of "conventionality"—and, by extension, standards of academic achievement—are subject to the most flagrant kind of manipulation. High-paying jobs are available for only so many students once they get out of school, and only so many can be educated at state expense in a public four-year college. Instead of helping students who are academically "disadvantaged" to overcome their difficulties, the tracking system slowly but deliberately screens them out of the educational system, keeping them in school only so long as it is expedient to keep them "off the streets." To be sure, such conditions reflect a nationwide educational malaise, but it is particularly revealing to observe how they have affected California's public colleges under the Master Plan. If the incorporation of the College Board Scholastic Aptitude Tests into the state college and University of California requirements explains the relative exclusion of lower income youth from either institution, it also explains why at San Francisco State College alone, imposition of the Master Plan was followed by a gradual drop in black enrollment from 12 per cent of the student body in 1962 to 3 per cent in 1967—this, in a city whose public schools were rapidly approaching 70 per cent non-white.

Basically, the "remedial education" offered by the junior colleges is simply an extension of the same process; it carries the tracking system to the collegiate level. An elite of "successful" students is cultivated at the expense of their fellows, whose options are reduced to a narrow range of "careers" as mechanics, hairdressers, technicians, or secretaries. Their eventual fate only further substantiates the contention that functional differentiation under the Master Plan is really nothing more than a rigid enforcement of the *Restudy's* "job market" concept of education: the rich get richer and the poor get vocational training.

In essence, Governor Reagan's tuition proposal was intended to reinforce class stratification and institutionalized racism. In 1968, Occidental College President Emeritus Arthur Coons published a memoir of his experiences as head of the Master Plan Survey Team and as Chairman of the Coordinating Council for Higher Education (CCHE), the watchdog body the Master Plan created. According to Coons, who favored tuition, its primary function would be to aid in the planned diversion of students into the junior colleges. Effective as they were at keeping certain segments of the population out of the four-year schools, devices such as the raised admissions standards and the tracking system had failed to "disqualify" enough students to sufficiently reduce the enrollement squeeze upon these institutions. Both the state colleges and the University were, under the Master Plan, supposed to maintain a 60 to 40 ratio of upperclassmen to underclassmen. The underfinanced state colleges had no choice but to adhere strictly to this ratio, but it meant that as early as 1964 San Francisco State alone would be turning away up to 7,000 qualified students every year, and by 1968 the state college system as a whole would be turning away a growing army of students equal to one-fifth of its total enrollment. The more prosperous University of California was reluctant to turn away any qualified students; so, despite repeated ineffectual protests from the CCHE, it consistently failed to bring its proportion of lower division students into line. As an economic measure, tuition was not simply an extra source of revenue for the state; more important, it could, by erecting one more barrier to attendance at the senior segments, reduce the cost of those segments where the manipulation of academic standards had failed to do so.

The "tuition-free principle" of public higher education is something of a tradition in California, dating back to the Progressive Era. Accordingly, Reagan's plans met initially with a good deal of resistance, but the Governor was more than willing to bide his time. Since taking office, his public stance toward the state-financed four-year schools—particularly the University of California at Berkeley—has been one of barely concealed, unremitting hostility. Reagan's arrogant, often needlessly provocative methods in dealing with campus disturbances have baffled and enraged the liberals, but they have been remarkably successful in building a public climate more favorable to the idea of tuition, even as a simply vindictive gesture.

THE UNRUH PROPOSAL: A NEW LIBERAL ALTERNATIVE TO THE MASTER PLAN

There is, of course, another side to the same coin. Early in 1969, at the height of the S.F. State strike, the state legislature's Joint Committee on Higher Education released a report that called for the overhaul of the California higher education system. The committee was dominated by liberal Democrats such as former Assembly Speaker Jesse Unruh, for whom the entrenched and increasingly obvious racism of the Master Plan was as dangerous as it was embarrassing. The product of a liberal Democratic administration of ten years before, the Master Plan was now condemned by the committee as an "expensive failure." The concept of segmental differentiation and the graduated system of funding for each of the segments had, they said, given birth to a "class-caste system" whose political consequences were becoming too serious to ignore. Their report called for consolidation of the three segments under a single twenty-four-man Board of Regents, gubernatorially appointed and free from "political influence." The Board would be advised by seven different "regional governing bodies," which would gauge the educational needs of their respective areas and formulate an academic and institutional program accordingly.

With rhetoric often reminiscent of the Ford Foundation's Bundy Report, which first put forth the ill-fated decentralization proposal for the New York public schools, the Unruh committee dwelt at length upon the state's failure in the area of minority education, and reserved special fire for the "elitism" of the University of California which was, it contended, chiefly responsible for the situation. Its critique of the Master Plan in this regard was intelligent and to the point:

> The better the student, according to conventional standards of achievement and ability, the more spent (on the average) for his instruction . . . This must, in our judgment, be regarded as a major, if implicit, pedagogical and philosophical premise of the Master Plan . . . This notion is nowhere more evident as it is in the [recommendation] . . . that a greater proportion of less able freshmen and sophomores be diverted to the junior colleges where expenditures per student are lowest.

> In no small part this policy results from the effort to build and maintain the reputation of the University of California in competition with four or five elite private eastern universities. The growth of the University's prestige and stature . . . has been achieved at a great cost, the denial of resources to other institutions. It is all too clear that not all public institutions can seek to obtain such stature . . . Accordingly, the "best" students and a disproportionate share of available resources have been concentrated in the University.

Like the tuition proposal, this is an explicit recognition that higher education in California remains a matter of privilege. But, as with tuition, recognition alone does not bring about an end to the educational double standard. Here consideration must be given to the role played by the private colleges and universities; though they are relatively few in number in California, their interests figure more prominently in both the Master Plan and the general orientation of the CCHE since 1961 than do all of the University of California's ivy league pretensions.

According to Arthur Coons, representation of the private institutions upon both the CCHE and the Master Plan Survey Team was a matter of political expediency: "They happened to have as Trustees, presidents or among their alumni persons importantly placed in influence or in the total power structure of the state, so that considerable heed to their voices . . . had to be given." As the Master Plan neared the end of its first decade, the vested interests of the private schools in the planning of public higher education were growing more and more pronounced. This was not a phenomenon confined to California: in 1968 the U.S. Department of Health, Education, and Welfare observed, "Unless the costs of production of services by private colleges and universities change drastically, their resources will fall short of projected requirements by $500 million in the next two years and a full $1 billion by 1972–73." A study of America's twenty wealthiest private institutions, released by *Fortune* Magazine in 1968, also revealed that all twenty were in desperate financial straits; with the end of the spring of 1968 their aggregate deficits were already in excess of $3 million, and by 1978 they would have risen to "close to $110 million, 17 per cent of their operating budgets. The twenty have no idea where the money needed to cover deficits this size will come from." For less prosperous schools, needless to say, the situation is far worse. Federal grants already play a large role in financing private schools (53 per cent of their combined budgets in California), and for some it has not been enough; a number of urban campuses, most notably Columbia, have been driven by their fiscal difficulties to such entrepreneurial activities as real estate speculation in the black ghetto.

Given such conditions, there is clearly a contradiction inherent in exclusive, expensive private schools coexisting with tuition-free public ones of comparable quality. Either the public schools must be systematically downgraded somehow, or the private ones will literally be driven out of business. The two are forced to compete not only for students and federal grants, but in such mundane areas as faculty salaries, which can account for as much as half the instructional budget of a given institution. Obviously a professor with more job openings to choose from can demand more for his labors, unless his prospective employers are able to work out collectively some kind of system of wage freezes. So it goes in California: a major preoccupation of the CCHE since its inception had been with holding down the level of faculty salaries at the state colleges. That those responsible for governing the state colleges have actually aided in this process is not surprising when one considers that even the public segments draw heavily—almost exclusively—upon the business community for their trustees or regents. In 1968 no less than six state college Trustees had vested interests in one or more private institutions, several to the point of sitting on their Boards of Trustees like an interlocking directorate.

Here is the central problem with the Unruh committee report: while it attacks the elitist aspirations of the University of California, it defends the traditional role of the private schools, whom it claims have "set standards of quality instruction" for the public institutions. Such a posture raises serious questions as to whether the report's frequent references to the need to "equalize" the University of California with the other two segments means to bring the latter up to the University level or simply to downgrade the University, with the private institutions, rather than the state colleges or the taxpaying public, standing to gain most. And the report's contention that segmental differentiation and "lack of parity" between segments is responsible for the inequalities of the system emerges as, at best, a half-truth.

The real question is one of state finance. By systematically taxing those least able to pay, California in effect assures that quality higher education at public expense will never be available to more than a privileged few. With considerable eloquence, the Unruh committee argued that the extent to which its proposed reconstitution of the state higher education system approaches the old University of California levels of quality depends on the taxpayers' willingness to support it—where there's a will, there's a way. Yet all the rhetoric in the world about the value of higher education in a democratic society—and the Unruh report is full of it—does not alter the fact that household units in California are already being taxed to the saturation point, and there is little likelihood that Jesse Unruh or anyone else in state government will ever seriously suggest that Standard Oil of California begin sharing a portion of its $400 million in annually reported profits with the people of the state.

Since there is obviously more to them than a simple desire to provide an alternative to the segmental governing bodies, the "regional boards" deserve a closer look. To justify them, the Unruh committee alludes to a report prepared for the CCHE in March, 1968, by Frederick E. Terman, Provost Emeritus and Dean of the School of Engineering at Stanford University. The purpose of the report was to study the engineering programs being offered by the various academic institutions around the state with a view to increasing their efficiency. As the CCHE observed in authorizing the report, engineering was "a relatively costly program, and the unnecessary duplication of engineering curricula is highly undesirable." The kind of material Terman confined himself to presenting says a good deal about how he sees his responsibilities as an educator; in full, it consisted of a computation of the "instructional costs index" of every engineering program in the state, a figure arrived at by dividing the total teaching payroll of a given program by the product of its enrollment and the total number of units for which its students are enrolled. The interpretive sections of the report conclude with the recommendation that three state college engineering programs whose "instructional costs index" was too high or whose yearly output of baccalaureates and graduate degrees was too low be phased out by 1969.

Terman has been associated with Stanford University since his own days as a student there; his personal history, and the recent history of his *alma mater*, might be termed a paean to Cold War America. When he became Dean of the School of Engineering in 1946, Stanford was an "underprivileged," even second-rate institution in a state whose academic landscape was dominated by the University of California. By the late 1960's it had blossomed into one of the most powerful and prestigious academic institutions in the country, its rise to prominence coinciding with the emergence of a huge defense-electronics industrial juggernaut in the Palo Alto area. The Palo Alto-Stanford complex had, in fact, become the second largest research and development center in America; and, according to Undersecretary of Defense David Packard, Terman is, "more than any other single individual, responsible for this amazing development. It was his vision that the academic community and the business community of the adjacent area could and should work together for the benefit of both."

In Palo Alto the two have grown so intertwined that separation would be next to impossible. Packard himself is a member of the Stanford Board of Trustees; Terman sits on the Board of Directors of Packard's Palo Alto corporation, a multimillion dollar enterprise whose biggest customer is the U.S. Department of Defense. Terman is also Vice President of the Stanford Research Institute, one of America's leading chemical-biological warfare and counter-insurgency research centers, and a trustee of the Institute for Defense Analysis (IDA, of Columbia fame). But his real claim to distinction lies in his pioneering efforts on behalf of the Stanford Industrial Park, a unique arrangement whereby the University leases its land and lends its research facilities and personnel to literally scores of local industries in a major cooperative effort. The Industrial Park has, according to Terman, "sparked a second California gold rush, serving as the focal point for over 206 scientific and technological companies doing $1 billion business annually." So successful has it become that by 1969 Terman was already making plans for a similar complex in the Dallas-Fort Worth area, centered around Southern Methodist University, and for a totally new private graduate university in New Jersey, wholly sponsored and supported by a group of corporations.

Such direct collusion with corporate interests demands a good deal from an academic institution, and Terman sets some stringent standards of efficiency for California's engineering schools in his report to the CCHE. Chief among these are a high degree of specialization in curricula, large class sizes for maximum output, and de-emphasis on teaching generally. According to Terman, the volume of a teacher's work should be evaluated not in terms of his unit load but in terms of *productivity*, to wit: "A faculty member who lectures six hours a week to forty students has twice the productivity of an associate who lectures twelve hours a week to ten students . . . if the institution fills the first position with a superior teacher at a salary 50 per cent higher than that received by the man who carries the heavy teaching load, the teaching of the superior instructor is still less expensive to the institution than the man who meets many small classes." A teacher's productivity can be further increased, Terman points out later, if students receive their lectures over closed-circuit TV. Mutual agreements between academic and local industry, such as those pioneered by Stanford, can increase output and decrease costs still further, as often industrial representatives are willing to come and lecture to students for free.

The kind of educational experience engendered by this approach makes no pretense of attending to the needs of the individual student. It is extremely difficult for him to engage in meaningful discussions with a closed-circuit TV. He cannot develop his faculties of critical thought when his course work is too specialized to be placed in any kind of social perspective. He cannot participate in or take any responsibility for his own education, which is therefore reduced to a purely passive act of consumption. But all this is not to say that Terman is unconcerned with quality. Quite the contrary; in one section of the report, after an elegaic description of California's phenomenal postwar industrial growth, most of which is centered around defense-related industries, he observes:

> The new industrial character . . . is strongly oriented towards science and advanced techology. It involves sophisticated and highly intellectual aspects of aeronautics and space, scientific instruments, computers, solid-state electronics, microwave tubes, systems analysis . . . These are the so-called "growth industries" whose growth is achieved through innovation . . . [their] success depends upon intellectual input rather than natural resources, cheap labor, or proximity to markets. Those companies which have the best brain-power will excel in creation of new products and will therefore grow faster and be more profitable than their competitors.
>
> Graduate work, particularly in engineering, makes an impor-tant contribution to such a situation. It is no coincidence that in

the last twenty years California: (1) has experienced a phenomenal growth in these technological industries; (2) has three of the five top engineering schools in the country; (3) has become the largest producer of a master's and doctor's degree in engineering . . . In the kind of competition that exists, it is academic excellence, rather than quantity of bodies, that counts, and California will get nowhere if it scatters its resources over so many new graduate programs that each is too small to be effective and too weak to be attractive. The leading position California has achieved during the past 20 years, which is the envy of the nation, has been achieved primarily through the efforts of only three institutions . . .[4]

Terman defines "academic excellence" the same way he defines everything else—in terms of corporate needs. Yet the flagrant elitism of his educational philosophy is perfectly consistent with his antipathy toward segmental governance, which is, after all, largely responsible for the "scattering of resources" he deplores in the passage quoted above. If there is a shortage of available resources, they must be concentrated not simply where they are needed most, but where they can be utilized to maximum effectiveness; that alone dictates a redefinition of educational priorities along lines closely attuned to industrial needs, permitting maximum cooperation with industrial power. Regional coordination is clearly a necessity if this kind of cooperation is to be effective; if, as Packard puts it, "the academic community and the business community of an adjacent area are to work together for the benefit of both." Since the dictum of "academic excellence" over "quantity of bodies" is part and parcel of this new set of priorities, it cannot be intended to promote "equality of opportunity"; if anything, it would make higher education more inaccessible than ever to the great majority of people.

The rhetoric of decentralizaton and community control has a certain appeal in minority communities which social managers are just beginning to exploit; indeed, the liberals on the Unruh committee would probably deny that there is necessarily any conflict between corporate needs and community needs. Couldn't regional governance be used to the mutual benefit of local industry and third world ghettos? The question remains, for the time

[4]The institutions referred to are Stanford, the University of California at Berkeley, and the California Institute of Technology.

being, mainly a hypothetical one, but it is interesting to observe the practical effect of one of Terman's major recommendations: that the engineering department at San Francisco State College be phased out because it is uneconomical. The city of San Francisco has four separate ghetto areas, all of which have very serious educational needs. The children of these ghettos have about one chance in a thousand of getting into one of the three schools designated by Terman as having "quality" engineering programs. But, as Terman himself observed in 1961, land values in San Francisco are far too high to be congenial to the rise of growth industries here, so engineering education cannot be expected to have any future in the city either. Clearly, in this instance the educational needs of San Francisco's ghetto inhabitants are in conflict with the business interests of California's growth industries.

Governor Reagan's tuition strategy, much as it seems like a radical departure from a long and ingrained tradition, is basically an attempt to bolster the educational status quo in California. Tuition at the state college and University level would function to protect their exclusiveness, while at the same time forcing more students onto the junior college track. The liberal alternative seems more enlightened and more attractive, but ultimately it would merely revamp the class stratification and institutionalized racism implicit in the Master Plan. By strengthening the private schools at the expense of the public ones and subjecting the public schools to a heightened degree of corporate manipulation, the Unruh committee plan would realign the educational system so as to better benefit the growth industries and the other corporate titans of the state. As for increasing access to the public four-year institutions, especially for the state's third world population, one can only wonder how this can be accomplished without major revisions in California's tax structure. Though it advocates expanding enrollment in the state colleges and the University, the Unruh committee fails to even suggest how this might be financed, leaving the recommendation with a hollow ring to it. In any event, while either strategy is a possible path for higher education in California in the seventies, both reflect the educational priorities of the men who own the state.

CHAPTER VIII

Guns on Campus:

PRELUDE TO THE S. F. STATE STUDENT STRIKE,

FALL 1968

THE DILEMMA OF SPECIAL ADMISSIONS

The limitations of the liberal ideology are never more evident than when liberals themselves come into positions of titular authority. That the Trustees and the Chancellor were willing to forgive Robert Smith for leading the "faculty revolt" in 1964 and appoint him to the Presidency of San Francisco State College in the summer of 1968 was a source of considerable amazement to the news media; by the time his brief administration had come to an abrupt end, many people were wondering why Smith had taken the job in the first place. Actually, the first question is answered easily enough: no one else was available. In a few short years San Francisco State had proved itself virtually ungovernable. The college presidency had changed hands five times in seven years, and even the initially promising administration of John Summerskill had turned out to be a dismal failure. Smith, however, brought more to the office than the simple good intentions of a Summerskill; he was an experienced and polished administrator who knew the campus thoroughly, understood its bewildering internal operations, and was liked and respected by the faculty. Though he had none of Summerskill's charisma, he had a far shrewder grasp of politics, knew the limitations of his office, and knew how to get the best mileage out of what little authority the system was willing to give him. If anyone could keep the lid on at S.F. State, he could—or so it seemed.

The actual precariousness of Smith's position became clear almost before he took office. Prior to his departure for Ethiopia, President Summerskill had made a number of promises the college was in no position to keep. The fall 1968 semester commenced with S.F. State operating at a $750,000 deficit; that left no money to launch the infant Black Studies Department. Worse, it made the special admissions program—the primary concession wrested from the administration during the May sit-in—all but dysfunctional. Over the summer an Educational Opportunity bill, designed to provide financial aid for special admittees and other "disadvantaged" students, had passed the state legislature only to be vetoed by Governor Reagan. Efforts by the college to solicit contributions from the local business community had failed miserably; San Francisco Mayor Joseph Alioto promised that $70,000 would be raised and came across with barely one-tenth that much. With resources so scarce, it was not surprising when the administration began to look for ways to hedge on its earlier commitments. In accepting applications for the 428 special admissions slots, it failed to make allowance for the normal 30 to 40 per cent "attrition rate" of students whose applications are accepted but who finally decide not to enroll or to go to school elsewhere. Accordingly, the number of third world students brought in under the program was really closer to three hundred. The other 128 slots were promptly budgeted out of existence, and at the beginning of the semester President Smith was obliged to announce that unless additional resources were made available the program would not continue past the end of the fall semester.

For the three hundred who were admitted, the institution was scarcely more generous. The chaos surrounding the establishment of the Black Studies Department effectively undermined the special curricula which had been drawn up for them, yet their financial problems were far greater. Most of the special admittees needed some kind of stipend or student aid in order to stay in school, a necessity which put them at the mercy of one of the most notoriously incompetent arms of the college bureaucracy.

For third world students who were unaccustomed to fighting their way through red tape, whose morale was already uncertain, and whose relationship to the college was still tenuous, the various insensitivities of the Financial Aids Office were even more destructive than they would have been to the average student. Financial Aids Director Helen Bedesem permitted a $70,000 bequest for financial aid to black students to slip through her fingers at a time when it could have made a difference in the survival of the special admissions program. Mrs. Bedesem turned down the bequest on the thesis that since it was earmarked for black students alone, it could not be legally accepted without violating federal anti-discrimination laws. Had she consulted with the Black Students' Union she might have been edified that the San Francisco State College Foundation could accept such a bequest. Unfortunately the Black Students' Union learned of the bequest only after it was too late to retrieve it. The rejection of the bequest is not without its own irony: by far the greatest proportion of money administered by the Financial Aids Office goes to white students.

The reason behind the imminent collapse of the special admissions program is not hard to trace. The Master Plan, in raising the entrance requirements of the state colleges and the University of California, had quite arbitrarily set a quota of 2 per cent of their total enrollments for whom the regular requirements might be waived. Not surprisingly, most of the "exceptional cases" involved athletic scholarships; the quota was never intended to deal with large numbers of students or to make the institutions more accessible to the community at large. By 1965, however, the inherent racism of the entrance requirements had manifested itself in a dramatic drop in minority enrollment at the state college level. That same year students in the S.F. State Tutorial Program had worked out a kind of response to the situation. Many of their best volunteer tutors were themselves high school students whose academic records failed to qualify them for college. The tutorial coordinators were able to argue quite persuasively that these students had earned a crack at a state college education; they proved that, outside the constricting framework of the public school system, they were capable of doing impressive and valuable academic work. The college agreed to admit thirty-five of these students as a part of the yearly 2 per cent quota; soon the BSU, reacting to the steadily dwindling number of black students on the campus, was demanding that their numbers be increased.

It should be emphasized that the emergence of the concept of "special admissions" as a way of dealing with racial imbalance did not take place in a vacuum; it was rapidly becoming part and parcel of a nationwide phenomenon. Like other institutions which had proven themselves to be functionally racist, America's colleges and universities were increasingly implicated in the black revolution; since they had always purported to play a progressive, enlightened role in dealing with social problems, the indictment was all the more damning. Under the aegis of the War on Poverty, the federal government had initiated the Educational Opportunity Program (EOP) for the purpose of removing some of the financial barriers to non-white attendence at the nation's colleges; it was introduced in California at the University of California's Berkeley campus in 1964. The problem with EOP was that it operated under a system of "matching funds." To qualify for a federal grant, local authorities had to raise an amount of money equal to what they expected to get. In institutions such as the California state colleges, where local authorities frequently lacked the resources or the inclination to provide the necessary support, the program tended to be seriously undercut. At more prosperous schools, problems of a different sort arose. Low income was only the most obvious barrier to college attendence; more subtle and pervasive was the cultural bias ingrained in the system of academic standards—in areas ranging from entrance requirements and curriculum to the more general ones of social convention and style of life. Thus, the EOP was not enough; it was necessary for an increasing number of institutions to follow the example of S.F. State and waive their entrance requirements for a select group of black students. Naturally these "exceptions" could never constitute more than a select group; even if they were willing to sacrifice their most basic educational assumptions and redefine themselves completely, few institutions could have mustered the resources to "open themselves up" to more than a tiny minority of those traditionally excluded. Yet the exceptions would be there and they would be visible, the more so for their conspicuousness, and the institution could use them, and the special accomodations it was making on their behalf, to justify itself to the black community.

The strategy of tokenism is calculated to deal with a demand on the Establishment not by removing its source but by lessening its impact. On the one hand, it seeks to lend the Establishment a shred of credibility; on the other, it weakens the unity of the group which is pressing the demands by promoting in its ranks a kind of regressive individualism—in effect, one member of the group is set against the other. Individual blacks are offered the option of benefiting from institutional tokenism at the expense of their fellows, who in turn are exhorted to follow their example: "Play the game well enough and you, too, might 'make it.'" Still, tokenism has its own law of diminishing returns. The institution's attempt at self-justification is at the same time an admission of culpability, which is in no way eradicated by simple confession. When it becomes necessary to waive entrance requirements for a few as a way of dealing with racial imbalance, the whole system of selection and retention of students is called into question. If selection standards are so much in conflct with the educational needs of the black community that such extraordinary exceptions have to be made to minimize the conflict, what is the point of keeping those standards at all—especially when the lot of the black community is not significantly improved by token gestures? Is it really so inaccurate to say that institutions which resort to such measures have adjudged themselves to be racist to the core? A few black people might accept the individualistic frame of reference which tokenism seeks to promote, but the rest are increasingly likely to see the contradiction of it and become more disenchanted than ever.

A less general, more immediate problem for the institution is what to do with the special admittees once they have gotten in. They are not assimilated into the academic community without considerable difficulty, for their arrival has been for the most part too abrupt to permit adequate preparation and there is reason to believe that, given time to prepare, the colleges still may not be capable of doing so. The black student who has "qualified" himself, or is in school on a scholarship, has accepted and adjusted to the academic mystique (at least outwardly; inwardly, the process of becoming "anglicized" is likely to be accompanied by an acute loss of identity). The special admittee is not nearly so deferential. He has less respect for the institution, is quicker to recognize its inadequacies and act accordingly—often in ways the institution cannot handle. Defenders of the institution might say the special admittee has been "so badly prepared as to be unable to handle the academic work"—but, as Michael Thelwell, a black professor at Cornell, has pointed out, "the psychological burdens are far greater than the academic ones." Often he must deal with latent or overt racism from white students and faculty; often he encounters insensitivity from college officials who are, for all their expertise, miserably equipped to deal with a ghetto youth right off the streets.

Simply by virtue of his own background, the special admittee's response to the racism of the institution is necessarily less equivocal and more militant than that of most other students. Admitted to the college as window dressing, he quickly becomes nothing less than a barometer of the institution's failures from within as well as without, a sensitive gauge of its most glaring internal weaknesses. At a private school he might react to the snobbish, rarified atmosphere and the irrelevant curriculum; at a two-year junior college it might be the manipulative counseling and testing apparatus and the overemphasis on vocational training; in a California state college it might be the debilitating shortage of resources and the unresponsive administrative apparatus. The wave of campus revolts that swept the nation during the 1968–69 school year can be attributed in no small part to the fact that special admissions programs had recently been established on many campuses. At Brandeis, a group of black students shocked the liberal administrators who had waived the entrance requirements for them by occupying a campus building in demand of an autonomous black studies program; at Cornell, special admittees reacted to disciplinary action against some of their members by the college administration and to crossburnings and threats from a segment of the white student body by arming themselves inside an occupied building, scandalizing the news media in the process. The College of San Mateo, a junior college in California, exploded in violence when the administration there tried to sabotage a College Readiness Program that was encouraging too many special admittees to stay off the vocational track and continue their college education. Similar incidents occurred at dozens of campuses, including several within the California state college system. Conditions within the structure of the institution would imperil a special admissions program; the program would, in turn, become a vehicle for attacking those conditions and politicizing the students within it.

In April, 1968, the Trustees of the California state colleges capitulated to pressure from below by raising their special admissions quota from 2 per cent to 4 per cent. Presumably, they did so with the impression that it would, while taking some of the pressure off themselves, at the same time reduce tensions on the campuses under their jurisdiction. In fact it simply exacerbated them; several hundred students came into the system under special admissions programs only to discover that the programs were ill-equipped to handle them. The Trustees had authorized the increased quotas, but the structure of the system itself prevented its successful implementation. The 300-odd students who entered S.F. State in the fall of 1968 found that they had been provided not with a "second chance at a college education," but with a renewed source of frustration and a long list of grievances. At the same time, they sensed that they were being used: the college was fishing for its reputation in the third world communities, and they were the bait.

MAYOR ALIOTO AND THE BLACK PANTHER PARTY

Pressure was accumulating from another source as well. During the first week of September, 1968, San Francisco Mayor Joseph Alioto returned from the Democratic National Convention in Chicago, where he had officially nominated Hubert Humphrey and narrowly missed being picked as the party's Vice Presidential candidate. When he left Chicago, the Democratic Party was in shambles, and the nation was reeling in the aftermath of the repression and violence with which the convention concluded. The Vietnam War, the black revolution, and the youth rebellion, coupled with the growing disintegration of certain crucial social institutions, had effectively destroyed the liberal-labor-ethnic consensus which had held the Democratic Party together since the New Deal. Fed up with both major parties, large numbers of white workers now threatened to defect to George Wallace's movement; simultaneously, the total failure of the welfare system and the economic decline of the inner cities were alienating the black population. Liberals and intellectuals were increasingly incensed over the failure of the Johnson administration to end the war; meanwhile, police were rapidly emerging as a powerful, independent, right-wing political force. If not "rising," as was often claimed, the crime rate was becoming more and more an index of political and social conflict, the court system overtly a political instrument. The clashes between demonstrators and police in Chicago merely repeated on a grand scale what had already been going on in dozens of cities.

When a liberal state is no longer capable of holding itself together through traditional means, it is forced to rely increasingly on repression. Official violence becomes progressively more pronounced; official institutions abandon their pretense of neutrality when dissident minorities—especially those which threaten to place the breakdown of "law and order" in a political context—are singled out for persecution. If the emergence of the Black Panther Party as a national phenomenon, and its rapid growth during the summer of 1968, served notice that the liberal state was already beginning to wear thin, the persecution of the party in the months that followed offered more than enough evidence that the policy of official repression was underway. Within six months after the Democratic Convention, virtually all the party's leadership were under indictment, in jail, in exile, or dead. Black Panther Party offices in dozens of cities were raided by police; countless members were being framed on charges of kidnapping, conspiracy, or murder. As the convention drew to a close, the final arguments were beginning in the murder trial of Huey Newton, the party's founder and Minister of Defense, in Oakland, California. The Newton trial had polarized the Bay

Area, where the Panther organization was perhaps stronger than anywhere else in the country. With the local power structure demanding a conviction and the black community threatening to explode if an acquittal was not forthcoming, the jury hit upon a compromise manslaughter verdict which so blatantly contradicted the evidence of the case that the political nature of the trial became clear. That night a pair of Oakland police, obviously incensed at the verdict, fired their guns repeatedly into the party's national office, which was fortunately unoccupied at the time. Two days before, a group of Panthers was assaulted in a New York courthouse by 150 off-duty police wielding blackjacks. These actions were mild, however, compared with the legally sanctioned ones that were to come.

Joseph Alioto's relationship with the Black Panther Party in San Francisco says a good deal about why the party was singled out for persecution. San Francisco is a labor town with several large minority voter-blocs and an educated and relatively enlightened white electorate. The traditional Democratic coalition, so precarious in other parts of the country, seemed to have a fair chance of survival there when Alioto, with the financial backing of the city's most powerful figures, was elected mayor in 1967. As he sought to preserve the "ethnic consensus," Alioto knew at the same time that it was political suicide not to stay in the good graces of the police. Police opposition was to literally wreck the administration of New York Mayor John Lindsay, with whom Alioto was frequently compared. The new mayor dealt with the latter problem by giving the San Francisco Police Department (SFPD) the green light to set up a special "Tactical Squad" for riot situations and by publicly backing the department to the hilt every time it came under fire or incidents of police misconduct occurred. At the same time he was working behind the scenes, without much success, to bring the department under his control. Alioto's strategy with respect to the ethnic minorities was, if anything, more sophisticated. His administration approached a number of militant street gangs, such as the Mission Rebels and the Young Men for Action, and bought them off with Office of Economic Opportunity (OEO) jobs and money gleaned from the business community. Tough as they were—the

Young Men for Action had terrified white San Francisco during the Hunter's Point riots of 1966—these gangs did not have a high level of political consciousness, and they were easy pickings for any politician smart enough to use them. The mayor's strategy faltered when he made similar overtures towards Black Panther Minister of Information Eldridge Cleaver on a local TV panel show, only to have Cleaver laugh in his face. Alioto reacted with fury; he began to refer to the Panthers as a "small-time Murder Incorporated" that advocated "shooting policemen." He even told a church group that their ten-point program for black liberation called for "robbing and raping."

Alioto soon discovered that, even if they refused to cooperate with his administration, the Panthers could be used in other ways. A rash of "police incidents," several of them involving members of the Tactical Squad, had occurred during the summer of 1968, provoking tremendous resentment and unrest in the community. Police got out of hand in July while quelling a disturbance that involved youths in the Haight-Ashbury district; a few weeks later two Tactical Squad members who had been guarding Vice President Humphrey literally ran amok in the Mission district, assaulting a number of chicano youths at random. Further embarrassment for the city came when another off-duty officer, apparently drunk, fired his pistol at a howling cat and accidentally shot a Chinese woman in the eye. Things came to a head a few weeks after the Huey Newton verdict, when a black bus driver named George Baskett was shot and killed by Michael O'Brien, an off-duty Tactical Squad member, in a little alley half a block from the Hall of Justice. Incredibly, the incident grew out of a minor traffic accident; soon O'Brien, who had been drinking, was waving his pistol at the crowd of black residents who had houses or apartments in the area, shouting, "I want to kill a nigger so goddamned bad I can taste it." None of the residents were aware that O'Brien was a police officer, and when Baskett attempted to disarm him the gun went off and Baskett was hit. According to witnesses, O'Brien then kicked his dying body, rolling Baskett over on his back.

The Tactical Squad quickly arrived on the scene, rescuing O'Brien from the angry crowd and arresting four of the witnesses on charges of conspiracy, assault with a deadly weapon, and assault to commit murder. Within four hours of Baskett's death the police department had adjudged it to be a case of justifiable homicide. The black community was furious, and eight days later the investigation was reopened. This time O'Brien was charged with murder, but a local judge promptly released him on his own recognizance. There was another outcry; the first judge was overruled, and bail was set at $24,000. It was promptly posted by local financier Louis Lurie, who said, "If this is a murder case, I'm the Pope of Rome." Shortly thereafter, the grand jury returned its indictment: not murder, but manslaughter. Just days before, Huey Newton, indicted for murder without benefit of eyewitness testimony or a murder weapon, had been denied bail pending appeal of his manslaughter conviction. Now O'Brien, who was defended at his trial by the famous criminal lawyer Jake Erlich, was to be acquitted a few months later by an all-white jury.

The O'Brien case touched off a storm of outrage in the black community even as it galvanized the position of the police department and its supporters. During the month of October, racial tensions in the city reached a high point. Police stations were bombed, fires were set, sporadic outbreaks of rioting occurred, and a wave of rebellions swept through the city's high schools. The polarization put Alioto in a difficult position: Jake Erlich expressed the sentiments of the law and order forces when he charged that O'Brien was being served up by the Mayor as a sacrifice to the black community. Though he continued to give the police his unqualified support, either by making excuses for them or by placing the blame on their victims, Alioto was forced to admit that the black community had "legitimate grievances." To resolve this dilemma, he turned increasingly on the Panthers, claiming they had "created the climate of violence" in which such incidents occurred and blaming them, through innuendo, for the rash of fires and bombings in the wake of Baskett's death. He tried repeatedly to isolate them from the equally angry, but less politicized elements in the black community, and at the same time used them to divert attention from the actions of the police.

Alioto was not simply using the Panthers as a convenient scapegoat. He was shrewd enough to recognize the threat of their rapid ideological development, which went beyond a simple refusal to be bought off. They had, recognizing it to be a sore spot, begun as an organization by attacking the police issue head-on; their image of disciplined, militant self-defense against an "occupying army" of law enforcement officers made them an immediate and formidable influence in the black ghetto. But the same nationalism that caused them to see the police as the military arm of a hostile and essentially foreign power enabled them to identify with colonized people throughout the world. They saw the black ghetto as "occupied territory" whose plight was one with that of chicanos, Latin Americans, Vietnamese, and other victims of American imperialism. Concluding that the key to black liberation was the overthrow of the capitalist system in the United States, they became outspoken advocates of socialism and in so doing made the race issue a class issue as well. As such, they threatened to harness the energies and anger of the black community and direct them into a coherent revolutionary movement which would not hesitate to ally with other third world groups, student radicals, "street people," and perhaps some day with the white working class. Such a perspective had to be quarantined.

THE REPRESSION COMES TO S. F. STATE

George Murray, the former Director of the S.F. State Tutorial Program, had been hired as a teaching assistant by the English department at the college when his involvement in the brawl in the *Gater* offices placed his job in peril. He finally managed to retain it, but by that time he had another strike against him—he had become Minister of Education of the Black Panther Party. The oldest son of a Baptist minister, Murray grew up in a family of thirteen children, whose pervasive experiences of poverty were humbly offset by deep religious convictions. He enrolled in San Francisco State College in the fall of 1965, managing to achieve excellent marks as a student in the English department, while at the same time helping to support his younger brothers and sisters. He began working in the Tutorial Program in the spring of 1966 and soon became its first black director; under his leadership, the program reached a peak in the number of students involved and the tutoring being done in the black community. Idealistic and outspoken, Murray had been bitterly disillusioned by the racial hypocrisy of Christianity and for a brief time turned to the Black Muslims for spiritual solace. Racial pride and a smoldering rage over the suffering of black people in America led him to devote more and more of his life to politics. Initially attracted to the early black nationalism espoused by the BSU, he soon came into contact with the Black Panthers and was profoundly influenced by their anti-colonial ideology and their aggressive style of politics. After joining the Panther organization in the Bay Area, Murray quickly emerged as a major party spokesman. In August of 1968, he traveled to Cuba to attend the conference of the Organization of Asian, African, and Latin American Solidarity, where he made a speech reaffirming the Panthers' faith in the concept of third world revolution. "Every time a Vietnamese guerilla knocks out a U.S. soldier, that means one less aggressor against those who fight for freedom in the U.S.," he told the conference. "Our freedom will come as soon as we create a few more Vietnams, Cubas, and Detroits." Later he added, "Our position regarding capitalism will not vary, because there is no room for the concept of private property in today's world."

The speech soon found its way into the San Francisco newspapers. The fall semester at Berkeley began with the announcement that Black Panther Eldridge Cleaver had been asked to deliver ten lectures in an experimental, student-initiated course, "Social Analysis 139X: Dehumanization and Regeneration in the American Social Order." State Superintendent of Public Instruction Max Rafferty, running on the Republican ticket for the U.S. Senate and looking about for issues, immediately denounced the Cleaver appointment, which he called "asinine and ridiculous." He was joined in his protests by Governor Reagan, who said it was an "affront and an insult to the people of California" and referred to Cleaver as "an advocate of racism and violence." For his part, Cleaver's response to this charge was characteristic: he suggested the Governor was "uptight" about the course because "one of the lectures will deal with the negative influences of

grade-B movies on the American mentality." The 139X controversy caused a fury up and down the state; the last week of October saw barricades and mass arrests on the Berkeley campus.
Long before that, the fury had spilled over into the state college
system when it was revealed that George Murray's contract had
been renewed by the S.F. State English department. "San Francisco State Puts an Admirer of Mao on the Teaching Staff," read
the banner headlines in the San Francisco *Examiner*, which proceeded to give some of the choicer excerpts from Murray's Ha-
vana speech. On September 26 the Board of Trustees met and
voted to formally request the college administration to transfer
Murray to non-teaching duties. Faculty representatives present at
the meeting were quick to express their opposition to the resolution, claiming that it violated the canons of due process and traditional faculty prerogatives in the area of hiring and firing of
professors. President Smith interpreted the resolution to mean
final discretion in the matter was his, and elected to ignore the
Trustees' request for the moment. "The public statements and
political philosophies of faculty members are not grounds for punitive action," he told an October 1st news conference, and added,
"The Trustees' concern apparently stems from Mr. Murray's actions
and statements outside the classroom. Reassignment to a non-
teaching position would require charges and an open hearing at
which an individual has the opportunity to defend himself. The
exact basis for the request that he be reassigned has not been
communicated to me in any written charges and his record at
this college does not warrant action at this time under our rules
and procedures." Smith did, however, leave the matter open by
alluding cryptically to an "investigation" of the Murray case which
was in progress; though details of the investigation remained a
mystery in the coming days, it seemed clear that Smith was stalling for time, looking for a way to dispose of the Murray controversy that would satisfy the Trustees while keeping tensions on
the campus at a minimum.

Students at S.F. State already had good cause to be resentful
of the Trustees. At the September 26th meeting, their Building
and Grounds Committee had given consideration to a $5 million
college union building proposal for the campus. A council of

eight students, three faculty members, and five administrators, all appointed by the Associated Students at the college, had begun work on the badly needed union building three years ago, and had already sunk $100,000 in student body funds into the initial design. Even at the outset of the project, the college bookstore and Commons were no longer adequate to accommodate the campus population; the Commons in particular had been built for two-thirds as many people as it actually had to serve. Student organizations had to be housed in a cluster of abandoned construction huts next to the Commons, and apart from the Gallery Lounge there were no real meeting areas, lounges, or places to relax and study. But the planners of the new union building had more than utility in mind; they wanted a building that students themselves could finance, plan, and design. In addition, they were trying to counteract the crackerbox architecture and the drab, prison-factory atmosphere of the other campus buildings. They hired Moshe Safdie, a prize-winning young Canadian architect who had designed the 1967 Montreal World Exposition, to come up with a design based on their specifications. Safdie's proposal was a breath-taking complex of polyhedral modular units which would form a crystal-like structure in the center of the campus. The Trustees' Building and Grounds Committee decided it was "ugly, impractical, and incompatible with existing campus architecture"—Safdie and the students were more than willing to concede the latter point. The Committee voted to recommend that the design be rejected by the full Board at its October meeting. "The Trustees," AS President Russell Bass told newsmen grimly, "are inciting students to riot." An incredulous Safdie said of the meeting, "I sat there not believing what I was hearing."

The students quickly learned that the Trustees had more unpleasantness in store for them. The Chancellor's office had drawn up a detailed proposal for revision of Title Five of the State Education Code. The revision dealt with the so-called "auxiliary organizations." Student government, food and book operations such as the S.F. State College Foundation, and outside conduits designed to supplement the college budget were to be placed under the control of the Chancellor's office. The office would regulate their managerial as well as fiscal operations, have veto power over any new programs they might try to establish, and assure that existing ones did not deviate from the "Trustees' or college policy." The proposal was clearly aimed, in part, at such student programs as the CIP, the Tutorial Program, and the Experimental College, as well as such peripheral activities as the S.F. State College Foundation's bail fund and its financial backing of the Black Studies Department. The BSU and the Third World Liberation Front saw that the effort to get their programs implemented within the structure of the institution was running out of time, and that they could no longer expect to work through the mechanism of student body government in the interim. Campus activists, who had been organizing in the community, working on special admissions, or developing new curricula in an atmosphere relatively free of outside interference, would now have to contend continually with a hostile Chancellor's office, making it virtually impossible for them to function effectively even if their programs were allowed to continue. The Trustees were scheduled to consider the Chancellor's proposal at their November meeting, and the students knew that, short of a massive and determined show of opposition from a majority of the eighteen state college campuses, they didn't have a prayer of a chance of stopping its passage.

The "crackdown" represented by Title Five was, in a sense, inevitable. Over the last few years the AS Programs, especially the Experimental College, had given S.F. State a national reputation; at the same time they had provided defenders of the institution with a handy pretext for discounting any serious criticisms of it. College administrators and "responsible" faculty members portrayed S.F. State as a bastion of freedom and experimentation, largely on the basis of the widespread acclaim of the student-initiated programs. Yet while proclaiming S.F. State's innovation and uniqueness, these same individuals had played, at best, a passive or even parasitic role in the development of the programs, and at worst a consciously obstructive one. As a result of national publicity accorded to him during the December 6th demonstrations and his reputed, though in fact quite ephemeral, contact with students in the AS Programs, John Summerskill had acquired an undeserved image as a "leader in the field of educational innovation" and, following from that, a comfortable job with the Ford Foundation. Marshall Windmiller had sought to justify the dismissal of John Gerassi—seemingly a serious breach of academic freedom—to readers of the *New York Review of Books* by alluding to the traditional atmosphere of permissiveness and creativity at S.F. State and by suggesting that it was for precisely this reason that Gerassi, faced with incontrovertible evidence that the institution was not nearly as repressive as he had claimed, had to "try to wreck" it. This pattern was repeated dozens of times by dozens of people, many of whom, like Chancellor Dumke, were highly conservative and in fact heartily opposed everything the Programs stood for.

It is certainly true that San Francisco State had played a vanguard role in providing models of student activism and "educational reform" for other campuses. But the final effect of this was as much to aid in the development of more sophisticated means of social control as it was to help create alternative visions of education. Significantly, ideas that had originated at S.F. State were quickly borrowed by heavily endowed, largely exclusive institutions before they had reached even a nominal fruition at S.F. State. While Nathan Hare's Black Studies Department foundered in red tape and a shortage of funds, Harvard and Yale drew up "Afro-American" curricula inspired by S.F. State's example, but put firmly under administrative control. With their more abundant resources and their elite-oriented student body, these institutions could assure rapid implementation and at the same time a healthy degree of respectability. Private liberal arts schools like Reed and Antioch could offer their students a maximum degree of participation in their education and a flexible, "relevant" curriculum, while S.F. State's Experimental College, which had first put forth in practical terms the notion that students had a right to determine their educational destiny, drifted farther and farther away from its initial goals of transforming the institution itself. Meanwhile, the State University of New York at Stoney Brook, an experimental "showcase" campus, developed an Experimental College format, consciously patterned after S.F. State's, for its own privileged student body; the program is both accredited and generously funded. In the context of such elitist institutions as these, the "Programs philosophy" is effectively sapped of whatever revolutionary potential it might possess. Black Studies becomes a mechanism for building up the "talented tenth" of the black bourgeois that the white Establishment so desperately needs in order to keep the other ninety per cent in line; "educational reform" is used to minimize the cultural estrangement of the sons and daughters of the rich by giving them a rarefied, super-humanized Utopia in which to live out their rebellious years, the better to shelter them from a brutalizing "real world" and to isolate them from their less privileged and equally alienated contemporaries. The Programs were, in short, tailor-made for an elite school bent on rationalizing the contradictions forced upon it by the changing social function of higher education. They were in no way appropriate for a tax-supported, tightly budgeted factory like S.F. State, the Chairman of whose Board of Trustees refers to it as a "major source of the four-year college-trained product." A California state college is not a lavish therapy center for the bored and alienated children of the affluent; it is a middle-echelon vocational center that strives for maximum output at minimum expense. As far as the Trustees were concerned, the move to cut S.F. State back down to size was long overdue. They were not concerned with the Programs' value to S.F. State as window-dressing, since the Programs allowed the college to indulge in the kind of pretensions and self-image which deviated from what the Master Plan had prescribed for it. Worse, the Programs made S.F. State increasingly difficult to control, while it served as a dangerous example to the other state colleges. Its faculty wanted to be treated like University faculty; its students wanted to be treated as something more than grist for the corporate mill.

The limitations of working within the Associated Students had already begun to manifest themselves when the black students decided to press for implementation of their program by the college. Now that the Trustees threatened to cut the ground out from under them, they had no choice but to do so, and the urgency of their situation had markedly increased. On October 24, the Trustees met in Fresno and drove the final nail into the coffin of Moshe Safdie's College Union Building design, defeating

it by an eight-to-eight vote. The opposition was led by Trustee
Charles Luckman, himself an architect, who contended that the
design was "incompatible," but it was really Trustee Dudley
Swim of Carmel Valley who delivered the clinching argument.
Swim said he had visited the existing facility on the S.F. State
campus, and it "looked like a pigsty . . . frankly, I'm not sure
those students *deserve* a new college union, if they can't keep
this one clean." The Union Building thus dispensed with, the
Board turned to the more perplexing problem of what to do
about George Murray. President Smith reassured the Trustees
that an investigation of the case was in progress and that he
would be able to report the results at their next meeting; unwittingly, he also managed somehow to give them the impression
that he would take some definite action before the end of the following week.

While the Trustees were convening in Fresno, the Instructional Policies Committee of the Academic Senate was meeting
back on the S.F. State campus. What ensued during the meeting
represented yet another battle in the protracted war between the
IPC and the Council of Academic Deans. The IPC voted formally
to allocate 11.3 faculty positions to the Black Studies Department for the spring semester. Vice President Garrity, who was
present at the meeting, promptly informed the committee off the
record that its decision would not be honored by the college administration. The college did not have the resources to pay for
eleven new teaching positions, Garrity said; in point of fact, the
new department would be lucky if it got three. This particular
disclosure flew directly in the face of all the assurances Garrity
had been giving Nathan Hare; and Hare, who had been watching
the meeting in silence, reacted to it by getting up from his chair
and storming out of the room.

THE SUSPENSION OF GEORGE MURRAY

On Monday, October 28, the Black Students' Union called a
rally on the campus. It was raining, so the rally was held inside
the Commons rather than on the Speaker's Platform. Among the
speakers were BSU Chairman Benny Stewart and George Mur-

ray; they announced that the BSU was calling a student strike for
November 6. Stewart told the crowd that it was time for the
black students on the campus to "get themselves together" and
declare where they stood; Murray, after reiterating the BSU-Black
Panther philosophy that black students had a right to armed
self-defense, explained why the strike was necessary:

> The Black Studies Department is no department at all. There
> are four and a half million black and brown people in California,
> and they all pay taxes to pay for the racist departments in this
> school, but none of those taxes go to black and brown people
> . . . The crackers still have the right to say how many black and
> brown people will come into this school and how many will not.

This is how the rally was described in Tuesday morning's San
Francisco *Chronicle*, by a reporter who had not even been present on the campus when the speeches were made:

> Black Panther Minister of Education George Murray yesterday
> called on black and brown students to bring guns to school and
> stage a strike on November 6.
> Murray, who stomped through the school yesterday to com-
> memorate the first anniversary of Huey Newton's gun battle with
> Oakland Police, stood on a table in the school cafeteria and
> shouted threats at the school's administration.
> "The only way to deal with a cracker like (S.F. State Presi-
> dent Robert) Smith," Murray said, "is to say we want 5000
> black people in here in February and if he won't give it to you,
> you chop his head off."

The previous week had been a rough one for San Francisco.
The city's high schools were racked by violence and disruption
and were threatening to close; student unrest had taken every
form from a massive and peaceful march on the Board of Education by over half the Polytechnic High School student body to a
hidden sniper firing at the principal of Galileo High School.
Blaming "outside agitators" for the disturbances, Superintendent
of Schools Robert Jenkins said he would not hesitate to use police to quell them and added, "Further protests and demonstra-

GUNS ON CAMPUS 215

tions will not be tolerated. We welcome suggestions, but students
are in no position to make demands." Plainclothesmen already
stood in the halls of a predominantly white high school in the
Sunset district, while the Tactical Squad was billeted in a predominantly third world high school in the outer Mission district.
Across the Bay, Berkeley students were occupying buildings and
erecting barricades in protest of the U.C. Regents' denial of credit to students taking the Eldridge Cleaver course. As a Richmond district police station in San Francisco was bombed and a
huge fire broke out in a public housing project, Mayor Alioto
stepped up his verbal attacks on the Black Panther Party. Fabricated though it was, the *Chronicle* report of Murray's speech
gave the Mayor new ammunition. "This is a wild and extremist
statement," he said. "Such exhortations to violence are part of
the reason for the tensions in this city." Alioto then announced
that he was, together with President Smith, investigating the possibility of filing a criminal complaint against Murray in lieu of
"administrative action [i.e., suspension] which might be used as
an excuse for further violence." After consulting with the District
Attorney, the state Attorney General, the U.S. Attorney and the
SFPD "red squad," however, Alioto was forced to concede that
there was no basis for criminal charges. No witnesses could be
found to corroborate the *Chronicle* story, and it became increasingly clear that any legal action brought against Murray would
not stand up in court.

The alternative—suspension of Murray by the college
administration—was a sticky issue. Since Murray's speech was
substantially no different in tone from literally dozens of speeches
he had made, on and off campus, during the past year, suspension of those grounds alone, especially without the benefit of
concrete evidence or an open hearing, would have seemed more
than a little arbitrary. However, national elections were less than
a week away, and "campus unrest" had been a crucial issue for
Republican candidates. Chancellor Dumke himself had no mean
stake in the issue, since his close ties to the Nixon camp were a
matter of common knowledge; there was even a rumor that he
was in line for an appointment to the post of Secretary of Health,
Education and Welfare in the event of a Republican victory.

Wednesday morning, Smith began to get telephone calls from Dumke and the Trustees, demanding that he dismiss Murray on the spot. The President was more than a little reluctant: "I thought the Murray-Cleaver dispute across the state was about two-thirds tied to the November elections, and I wasn't about to throw another catalyst into the city when it looked really threatening." Smith consulted Alioto, who advised him that nothing should be done for at least a week. Either because tensions in the city were too great to warrant immediate dismissal or because he wanted to thwart, or at least use for his own ends, the Republican strategy of deliberate provocation, Alioto persuaded Smith to resort to "established procedures of due process." That way, Murray's suspension could be handled on the Mayor's own time, and the entire procedure would have an air of legitimacy about it.

Wednesday afternoon, October 30, the Black Students' Union called a press conference to formally announce their strike plans. They were apparently aware of the furor among the college hierarchy over how best to dispose of Murray, but they decided not to make an issue of it; Benny Stewart, BSU Chairman, told the assembled newsmen that they would not let the "racist attacks" upon the Minister of Education divert them from the real issues. Of the nine "non-negotiable" demands that were read, four dealt with the establishment of a viable Black Studies Department, two with college admissions policies. The other three demanded that the proposed revisions in Title Five not be implemented; that Helen Bedesem be replaced by a financial aids officer more responsive to third world students; and that no reprisals be taken against black students, faculty, or administrators as a result of the strike.[1] The existing Black Studies program, Nathan Hare told newsmen, was a "polka-dot department"—all the courses offered under it were scattered throughout the existing academic departments, which retained power over hiring, retention, and tenure of professors and over the final form the courses would take. The BSU demanded that these courses be consolidated unter Hare's jurisdiction, that the new Black Studies department be authorized to grant B.A.'s, that as Chairman of the

[1]See Appendix I for full text of demands.

Department Hare receive a salary "suited to his qualifications," and that twenty full-time teaching positions be allocated to staff the department. The Black Studies Department would, in short, be fully autonomous, with control over its own personnel and curriculum, adequate resources, and the full status of a regular academic department. Demand number four called for the filling of the 128 unused special admissions slots for the spring 1969 semester, while demand number five—by far the most controversial—stated simply, "All third world students applying to San Francisco State in the fall, 1969, be admitted."

The Murray issue came to a head on Thursday, October 31. Smith had made an appointment to see Mayor Alioto that afternoon. At 9:30 in the morning he received a call from Chancellor Dumke, who asked him again what he was going to do. When Smith told him he was going to see the Mayor, Dumke was more than a little put out; he felt Smith was "dragging the Democrats into the thing," as Smith expressed it later. That afternoon Smith received written orders from the Chancellor's office to suspend Murray. The way in which he chose to capitulate is indicative of his political astuteness. Rather than suspending Murray right away, the President held a press conference late that afternoon, said the suspension order was "unprecedented," and asked to meet with Dumke on campus the next morning before taking action. Dumke predictably did not heed the request, but the next morning's papers were full of sensational headlines about Smith's "dramatic act of defiance." Late Friday afternoon, Smith called another press conference to announce that, inasmuch as Dumke had declined to meet with him, he had no choice but to suspend Murray for thirty days. His statement was short and terse, concluding with the observation, "I do not believe this abrupt manner of handling the situation contributes to the solution of a complex problem."

The BSU added a tenth demand: that the suspension of George Murray be lifted immediately.

Over the weekend the Third World Liberation Front pulled itself together and broadened the base of the strike, tightening its organizational structure in the process. After the chaos surrounding the May sit-in, the TWLF recognized that internal cohesion was an absolute necessity if it was to survive as an organization; it decided to restructure itself according to the principle of democratic centralism. Each of the third world groups, the BSU included, would send two representatives to a tightly disciplined central committee which would be responsible for formulating strategy and tactics and enforcing discipline in the ranks, and for carrying out the wishes of the full constituency. Five more demands were added to broaden the scope of the original ten, making them applicable to the five other third world organizations on campus. The demand for a Black Studies Department with twenty teaching positions was complemented by a demand for an entire School of Third World Studies, within which the Department would function, and the School would be allocated a total of fifty full-time teaching positions. The last demand, a recapitulation of the Murray issue, broadened it to embrace a concept of educational self-determination for third world people: "George Murray and any other faculty person chosen by non-white people as their teacher must be retained in their positions."

If there actually was a Republican strategy to disrupt the campus prior to Tuesday's elections, it failed. The campus was quiet both Monday and Tuesday, November 4 and 5, but tension was mounting.

CHAPTER IX

The War of the Flea:

THE INITIAL PHASE OF THE STUDENT STRIKE,

NOVEMBER 1968

HEIGHTENING THE CONTRADICTIONS

On the day before the strike was to begin, the Third World Liberation Front called a general meeting of its membership. The meeting was held, with some trepidation on the part of the college administration, in the Main Auditorium of the Creative Arts Building; it attracted over five hundred non-white students and a number of representatives of the various minority communities in the Bay Area. The tone of the gathering was both serious and spirited; the scheduled speakers had no trouble holding the attention of the audience, though they were often interrupted by militant outbursts of approval. After the fifteen TWLF demands were carefully elucidated, Stokely Carmichael was introduced by his old Howard professor, Nathan Hare. Carmichael, who was serving at the time as the Prime Minister of the Black Panther Party, briefly praised the uncompromising attitude that Dr. Hare had always taken with respect to black dignity. Then he spoke at length, meticulously explaining the revolutionary political perspective that was to guide the TWLF strike.

The central theme of Carmichael's presentation, much of which he drew from the theories of Mao Tse-tung, was that of "heightening the contradictions" of the system as a transitional program toward an eventual socialist revolution. In general, the theory of contradictions implies that an irreconcilable conflict of interests exists within any system or social order based on profit and exploitation. On the one hand, those who manage or control such a system are primarily concerned with maintaining their own wealth and power; on the other, they do so at the expense of the masses of people living under the system, whose fundamental needs are more often than not manipulated or ignored. To heighten the contradictions is to make them more obvious to a greater number of people, thereby strengthening the revolutionary opposition to the existing system. More specifically, the contradictions that needed to be dramatized through the S.F. State strike were those that had made it necessary in the first place. For over three years the black students had been patiently working to establish a Black Studies Department, yet it still did not exist. The college administration had agreed all along that Black Studies was a legitimate and urgently needed educational project, but it was never able to provide adequate resources to implement such a program. The crux of the problem was not merely bureaucratic sluggishness; it was much more fundamental than that. Put simply, the established priorities of the entire state college system were in sharp conflict with the educational needs and aspirations of the black community. Another evident contradiction could be seen in the S.F. State Educational Opportunity Program (EOP). Its very existence implicitly acknowledged that the admissions standards of the system were racist, and it had never received the authority or the resources to bring racial balance to the college. Having thus exposed itself as little more than a slick attempt to appease the racial minorities in San Francisco, the EOP was a constant source of controversy: third world students, many of them in the program, would demand that it be adequately equipped to deal with the problems of the denial of access to college to non-white people; administrators lamely responded that they lacked the necessary resources to accomplish such an end.

To heighten contradictions such as these, and to guard against cooption, Carmichael stressed the need to "focus the struggle on the general rather than the specific." For the most part, this was precisely what the TWLF demands were geared toward accomplishing. Rather than getting bogged down in bickering about specific quotas, as they had done in the past, the TWLF demanded open admissions for all third world students who wished to attend S.F. State. Rather than merely insisting that George Murray be rehired, they demanded that third world people be given sole power to hire and fire all faculty for the various ethnic programs. Moreover, a generalized focus was intrinsically linked to what Carmichael called "the process of internalizing the principles upon which our revolutionary activities must be based." Hence, the general demand for the authority to hire and fire faculty was a logical extension of the principle of self-determination, the right of third world people to determine their educational destiny. That, in turn, was translated into a policy of non-negotiability of the fifteen demands. These demands were not made gratuitously; they reflected the specific educational needs of third world people, and the refusal to negotiate them constituted more than a simple desire to avoid the moral taint associated with compromise. Rather, the TWLF sought to establish that racist institutions like S.F. State had no right to exercise power, even shared power, over third world people; that power belonged to the people themselves.

An uncompromising adherence to revolutionary principles, however, was not be be confused with the rigidity of militant tactics that was beginning to characterize student revolts around the country. Carmichael referred to the Columbia revolt as a particularly misleading model, especially where third world students were concerned. "You read about Mark Rudd," he said laconically. "Yeah, he's sho nuff bad. But he ain't got nothing to show for his badness." In point of fact, the entire student movement at Columbia had nothing to show for its badness. Having materialized seemingly out of nowhere, the rebellion had splashed into the news media due to its sensational and apocalyptic nature, only to sink into oblivion shortly thereafter. As a symbolic "seizure of power," "living the revolution" inside an occupied building was a gratifying emotional experience for the people involved, but it was, like other similar tactics of mass confrontation, predicated

upon the illusion of instant victory rather than a realistic assessment of what was necessary to win the struggle. Even the demands were lacking in vision, programmatic content, and conti-
nuity; granting them did little to change existing conditions, and
they were easily depicted as vague, directionless expressions of
resentment and dissatisfaction that some well-to-do young people
felt toward society. Indeed, the whole Columbia phenomenon
appeared to be more of a psychodrama than a serious attempt to
challenge an oppressive institution.

As an alternative to the seemingly disjointed pattern of the
Columbia revolt, Carmichael endorsed the Maoist concept of
"protracted struggle." The essence of this concept is that if a
movement or organization seriously intends to strive toward the
heightening of contradictions, then it must be prepared to wage a
long and arduous struggle to build a revolution. Symbolic acts of
protest and defiance of authority are hardly sufficient for such a
task, not when actual seizure of power is what is required. For
TWLF, "seizure of power" would become a major theme of the
strike, and they were not about to attempt it by occupying the
Administration Building or forcing the capitulation of the college
president. Concessions wrested from President Summerskill during the May sit-in had later proved all but meaningless; the
TWLF was well aware that President Smith would be no more
able to grant their demands than his predecessor had been. As
such, the strike would attempt to carry the struggle all the way
up the state college hierarchy: seizing power ultimately meant
taking it away from the Trustees, a goal that was represented in
the totality of the fifteen demands.

The understanding that such a transfer of power would not
come quickly or easily led the TWLF to adopt the "strategy of
the flea." The success of the strike required an effective and prolonged shutdown of the college. As a minority organization, the
TWLF obviously could not rely on the college community to
support their strike; hence, they needed a plan for disrupting the
college to such an extent that it would become nonfunctional on
a day-to-day basis. The reference to the flea was based on the fact
that the flea knows better than to confront the dog head-on. Instead, the flea prefers to nibble along at its own pace, often in-

visible, attacking the dog's more remote and vulnerable parts, unit it has broken the dog's resistance or worried it to extreme distraction. Benny Stewart, the Chairman of the Black Students' Union, spoke at the TWLF assembly after Stokely Carmichael had finished, explaining the strategy in this way:

> What does the flea do? He bites the dog, he slowly sucks the blood from it. That's the philosophy we've got to get into. We've got to wear them down. Something is always costing them. You can dig it—something is happening all the time. Toilets are stopped up. Pipes are broken. The water in the bathroom is just runnin' all over the place. The trash cans are on fire. People are running in and out of the classrooms, letting the students know that school is out for the day. Me? I don't know nothin' about it. I'm just on my way to take an exam. Dig? When the pigs come runnin' on the campus, ain't nothin' happening. Everyone has split, so the pig don't have no heads to bust. When he leaves, it starts all over again. On and on and on. We fight the racist administration on our own grounds, you see; not theirs.

THE FIRST DAYS OF THE STRIKE

The strategy of the flea was put into practice on November 6, the first day of the strike. During the morning, the campus was tense, anxious, and quiet. Class attendence was off a bit, but the only visible evidence of strike activity was some leafleting by white strike supporters. At noon, the white activists held a rally in front of the Commons; after the usual round of speeches, over four hundred white students marched on the President's office to find out what Robert Smith intended to do about granting the fifteen TWLF demands. President Smith met the students on the steps of the Administration Building and in an agitated manner attempted to dismiss the crowd. "I don't have time to talk to you now," he snapped, "there are things happening on this campus." While the white students had been holding their rally and marching on the President's office, mobile teams of third world students had quietly entered most of the buildings on the campus. They struck quickly and in unison, barging into classes to dismiss them, setting a number of small fires in trash cans, and generally disrupting the normal functions of the college. These guerilla tactics produced their desired effect: the campus was thrown into a state of chaos. Panic-stricken people began bombarding Smith's office with conflicting reports and wild rumors of violence and destruction. It was impossible to know exactly what was happening, but the alleged incidents, including some confirmed property damage, became numerous enough to induce President Smith to call in the police and close down the campus.

By the time the police arrived, the TWLF guerilla teams had disbanded, but the frantic confusion they had instigated showed no signs of subsiding. The white activists, who were as bewildered as everyone else about what had been going on, decided to regroup in the Gallery Lounge, where they tried to assess the day's events. Before they got very far, however, the building was surrounded by a cordon of police, who informed them that school was out for the day and they would have to leave the campus. At a later meeting, held off-campus and attended by some five hundred white strike supporters, an immediate antagonism developed between the SDS and the white student programs. The Program activists, who were as threatened as the TWLF by the proposed revisions in Title Five, saw the strike as necessary for their own survival and argued that white students should be shown that it was in their own self-interest to support it. SDS, on the other hand, took the position that the strike represented a principled struggle against racism, and to support it on any other grounds would itself be racist. This difference, though minor, was exacerbated by the bitter rivalry between the SDS and the Programs that dated all the way back to the 1966 cafeteria boycott. Fortunately, a schism never really developed, mainly because TWLF set up certain guidelines for white students to follow if they wished to participate in the strike. Among these were the promise not to raise any demands of their own, an adherence to the principle of third world self-determination, and an agreement to work within whatever strategy the TWLF devised. The white students readily accepted these conditions, which effectively curtailed their decision-making powers in the strike; in lieu of a decision-making body, they elected a broadly based "Communications Committee" to clear and coordinate white strike support activities with the TWLF Central Committee.

Thursday and Friday, November 7 and 8, saw an intensification of the guerilla tactics as the war of the flea began to pick up momentum. At a massive noon rally on Thursday, TWLF leaders explained why it was necessary for them to disrupt the college and why the demands were non-negotiable. Afterwards, over six hundred students marched on the Administration Building; when they were prevented from entering by campus police, they invaded an adjacent building, chanting strike slogans and turning out classes. A small home-made bomb exploded also on Thursday in the Education Building; there was little damage, and no one was hurt. By Friday, a *Daily Gater* survey indicated that daytime classroom attendence was as much as fifty per cent off. Mobile units of TWLF members escalated their disruption of the college; the police assigned to the campus were baffled by the hit-and-run tactics, and were unable to control the situation. Raiding parties invaded a number of departmental offices, pulling out phones and overturning furniture; the college administration reported that approximately fifty small fires were set during the day, and even President Smith had to put out a fire that was started in a restroom adjoining his office.

The mounting pressure paralyzed the educational process, and began to polarize the college community. As Smith began to rely more and more on police occupation, and suspended regular disciplinary procedures in order to punish disruptive students more quickly, forty-two members of the S.F. State faculty sympathetic to the striking students set up an Ad Hoc Faculty Committee. Led by economics professor William Stanton, a former state assemblyman who had been fired from his teaching post at San Jose State College for his civil rights activities, the Ad Hoc group was the first manifestation of a schism that would divide the college faculty for the duration of the strike. Ironically, the Ad Hoc Faculty based their initial appeals to their colleagues not upon the fifteen demands, but upon the fact that George Murray, a faculty member, had been undemocratically dismissed because of his political beliefs, a denial of due process brought on by "outside political interference."

A three-day weekend gave everyone an extra day to prepare for the coming week. When the college reopened on Tuesday, the police were present in such numbers as to resemble an occupying army. In his determination to keep the college functioning, President Smith had agreed to a police strategy to head off any possible disruptions by stationing units of combat-ready officers in all of the campus buildings, and billeting the entire Tactical Squad in the boiler room of the gym. A police command post was set up in a large parking area across the street from the campus, where a number of police units were held in reserve; a helicopter circled above the college for most of the day, observing the students' movements. After the TWLF leadership had sized up the situation, they decided to modify their tactics. The groups of classroom disrupters became "educational teams" who would politely ask the permission of the instructors to enter the respective classrooms and explain the strike issues to students. For their part, the white activists picketed the classroom buildings, went to their classes to discuss the strike, and distributed a great deal of literature. Meanwhile, the faculty went into emergency session, but about all they could accomplish after hours of acrimonious debate was to approve a motion calling for Chancellor Dumke's resignation for his conduct during the Murray affair. Resolutions supporting the strike and supporting President Smith were put off for the next day.

On Wednesday morning, November 13, the Ad Hoc Faculty went on strike; they picketed in front of the college for about an hour, then retired to the Main Auditorium to participate in what one student observer aptly described as a "parliamentary circus." The entire meeting was devoted to motions, substitute motions, amendments to the substitute motions, points of order, points of clarification, and points of information. Only one motion, which proved to be irrelevant, was passed; when lunchtime came around, Academic Senate Chairman Leo McClatchy found himself in doubt as to whether the meeting was empowered to recess itself, since there was no longer a quorum in the auditorium. At noon, while the faculty meeting was foregoing the rules in order to adjourn its morning session, the TWLF was holding a press conference in front of the small plywood hut that served as the BSU's campus office. George Murray, the principal spokesman for TWLF at the conference, told reporters that the strike was setting an important historical precedent: "This is the first time in this country that barriers have been dissolved between black, brown, and yellow people." Murray reemphasized that the strike would continue until all fifteen demands were met, and the press conference was over. Before the group assembled in front of the huts could disperse, however, the Tactical Squad marched across the quad and into the enclosed area between the Commons and the BSU office. Allegedly called into the area to investigate a report that a television cameraman had been roughed up by some black students, the Tactical Squad suddenly broke ranks as a large crowd of curious students followed on their heels. The third world students who had remained in front of the huts after the press conference were singled out for attack; Nesbit Crutchfield, a member of the BSU Central Committee, was beaten to the ground, as was Preston Webster, a black reporter who had stooped to help a black girl who had fallen into some bushes during the fracas. Two other black students were trapped, clubbed, and handcuffed. The students who witnessed the spectacle were appalled, especially when it became clear that only the black students were being singled out for attack. As their ranks swelled and they began to surge forward, one Tactical Squad officer pulled his gun and pointed it directly at them while his cohorts retreated with their prisoners.

A rally was immediately called at the Speaker's Platform, and some one thousand students, many of whom had just witnessed the Tactical Squad's raid on the BSU hut, gathered in a furious mood. Before anyone could speak, however, the police were sighted again, this time near the rear of the campus by the psychology building. The crowd swarmed angrily down towards the startled cops; the situation grew extremely tense as the two groups faced off, the students screaming obscenities and strike slogans. Just then the Ad Hoc Faculty, who had rushed out of the faculty dining room to see what was going on, marched up and interposed themselves between the students and the police, holding their picket signs high. The students greeted them with relieved cheers, and the police retreated to their vans and left the campus for the day.

After pausing briefly at another rally called by the TWLF, the

Ad Hoc Faculty marched back in the Main Auditorium, where the general faculty meeting was about to reconvene for its afternoon session. The police action had thrown the faculty into an uproar, and Professor Stanton tried to take advantage of the situation by making an impassioned plea for his colleagues to go on strike. The faculty wasn't that enraged, however; they settled for passing a resolution directing President Smith to suspend classes indefinitely. Meanwhile, the students had moved their rally up to the Administration Building, where they demanded an explanation from President Smith for the raid on the huts. Smith had been out to lunch when the incident occurred and was very upset by it. He tried to tell the students that this was "no way to run a campus," and was met with jeers; then he said that the police were on campus to "protect the safety of the students." That produced a long, antagonistic howl, and the brief audience was over. Later that afternoon President Smith held a press conference to announce that he was closing the campus "until we can open it on a more rational basis." Asked about the conduct of the police, he remarked cryptically, "Bringing in police as an effort to keep this campus open has not worked to my satisfaction." By the end of the day seven students had been arrested, and eleven were taken to the hospital for treatment of injuries.

THE REACTION OF THE STATE COLLEGE BOARD OF TRUSTEES

The announcement that S.F. State would be closed indefinitely touched off an immediate storm of public controversy. Assembly Speaker Jesse Unruh, the state's most powerful Democratic politician, fired off a telegram to Governor Reagan (via the news media) which read, "You should not sit idly by as Governor and permit San Francisco State College to close its doors. Such a posture would constitute a triumph for anarchy." The Governor, in a press conference held shortly after the college was shut down, called Smith's decision "an unprecedented act of irresponsibility," and demanded that "the college be reopened by any means necessary." When newsmen asked what he meant by "any means necessary," Reagan snapped, "It means that if it's necessary we'll call out the National Guard, and if that's not sufficient, call in federal troops!" Locally, Mayor Alioto, who had been in close contact with Smith since the strike began, blamed the crisis on Chancellor Dumke and the "absentee Trustees." Echoing most of S.F. State's liberal faculty, Alioto maintained that the strike would never have happened if President Smith had been given adequate time to dispose of George Murray in a more discreet manner—an assessment which missed completely the implications of the fifteen demands. The Mayor added that there was no need for the National Guard; San Francisco's law enforcement agencies were well equipped to handle the problem. What was needed, however, was for "outsiders" like Reagan to stop "interfering in local situations." For their part, the Chancellor and the Trustees refused to comment at any length on the situation at S.F. State; instead, an emergency meeting of the Board of Trustees was called for Monday, November 18, in Los Angeles.

When the California State College Board of Trustees was established in 1960, it was specifically modeled after the University of California Board of Regents. As a consequence, the gubernatorially appointed Trustees, like the Regents, are invariably scions of industry, agribusiness, banking, communications, real estate, transportation, and corporate law; as befits the second-class status of the state colleges under the Master Plan, they are somewhat less influential within the corporate elite than their counterparts at the University of California. Far from being a California phenomenon, this collusion of big business and higher education exists on a national basis. In the spring of 1969, a nationwide survey of college trustees, commissioned by the Association of Governing Boards of Universities and Colleges and the American Association for Higher Education, and conducted by the Educational Testing Service, illustrated what most student activists had known for some time. A carefully selected sample of 5,000 of the nation's 30,000 trustees yielded the fact that 96 per cent are white, 75 per cent are Protestant, and 73 per cent are businessmen over fifty. In addition, more than half of the trustees surveyed have net incomes of over $30,000 a year. Typical trustees' attitudes on civil liberties suggest that they are something less than enlightened despots: 70 per cent favor screening campus speakers, 40 per cent believe that student publications should be censored, 53 per cent support loyalty oaths for professors, and 27 per cent feel that faculty members don't have the right to express opinions. About half the trustees are registered Republicans, and a meager 15 per cent would call themselves liberal. With such attitudes and backgrounds, it is not surprising that trustees throughout the country have been completely unresponsive to the educational needs of non-white people, to the students' demands for a more flexible and relevant education, and to the protests against academia's overt complicity with the Vietnam War.

Except where they tend to be richer and more conservative in their attitudes, the sixteen California State College Trustees pretty much exemplify the national norms indicated in the survey. Occasionally a younger trustee will be "promoted" to the University of California Board of Regents, while the older Trustees are frequently men whose prestige among their fellow businessmen has begun to wane. For the most part, however, the individual Trustees derive their inferior position relative to the Regents from the character of their business enterprises, which are regional or local rather than national. As such, a sizeable majority on the Board has an extremely narrow educational outlook that reflects the economic interests and concerns of California's local business elites. The Chairman of the Board of Trustees is Theodore Meriam, former mayor of his home town of Chico, where he own a large department store and serves as vice president of a local savings and loan association. Other examples of arch-conservative Trustees with strong regional business ties are Daniel H. Ridder from Long Beach, who owns and publishes the town's only newspaper; and Karl L. Wente of Livermore, who owns Wente Farms, Wente Land and Cattle Company, Wente Brothers Winery, and is a director of the local Bank of America. Perhaps the most formidible right-wing influence on the Board is multimillionaire Charles I. Luckman, whose Los Angeles-based architectural firm has designed Cape Canaveral, strategic air command bases in Spain and Thailand, the Convair Missile Facility, and the Disneyland Hotel. Luckman, more representative of the national business elite, is also a trustee of Northwestern University, the California Institute of Technology, the University of Illinois, and Pepperdine College. The moderate-to-liberal minority on the Board is made up mostly of corporate lawyers, whose dealings with a number of different corporations and business enterprises tend to give them a broader and more rationalized concept of the function of higher education within the political economy of the state and the country. Board members James F. Thacher and Louis E. Heilbron are corporate lawyers from San Francisco, while William A. Norris is a senior partner in a prominent Los Angeles law firm. The lone non-white Trustee is Edward O. Lee, the black director of the East Bay Skills Center in Oakland, who also doubles as organized labor's sole representative on the Board.

For almost all of the Trustees, San Francisco State has always been a "troublesome" campus that exerted a "bad influence" on the other seventeen colleges in the system. State Superintendant of Public Instruction Max Rafferty, one of the five ex-officio members of the Board, once called S.F. State "an aviary for odd birds," while Trustee Dudley Swim is said to have suggested that it be "bulldozed into the ocean." In return, S.F. State's college community, especially the liberal faculty, constantly sniped at the Trustees because of their lack of "academic qualifications" and the "arbitrary decisions" they made that adversely affected the institution. When the student strike forced Robert Smith to officially close the college, and the Trustees called the emergency session, everyone knew that a showdown was imminent. Accordingly, each of the parties involved mobilized its forces. President Smith went to Los Angeles with most of his closest advisors, while the faculty voted to send the entire Academic Senate to represent them. The Trustees, for their part, readjusted their commitments so that all of them would be present, as did Chancellor Dumke and Governor Reagan. A number of student observers and Associated Students representatives also attended the meeting, but the TWLF sent no official spokesman, preferring to remain in the background for the time being.

The meeting was held in a small auditorium located on the seventh floor of the Wilshire Boulevard superstructure that houses the mammoth central bureaucracy of the State College System. Security precautions for the session were unusually strict; police in riot gear were ominously positioned both inside and outside the building where they checked the credentials of those who wished to attend the gathering. Many people were turned away due to the limited number of seats available to observers. The first part of the morning session was devoted to the opening statements of the major combatants; the statements were delivered from a small podium directly facing the huge table where the Trustees sat. Chancellor Dumke, who spoke first, quickly went on the offensive. "I have urged President Smith to reopen the college immediately," he declared, "and have pledged him all the support that is at our disposal to accomplish this end. I have also made it clear to President Smith that the demands of some groups at San Francisco State College are far in excess of the resources available to him." Dumke went on to propose that "maximum security" be maintained during the reopening and that "prompt proceedings" be initiated against "those responsible for the disruption of the educational process" with the aid of investigators from the State Attorney General's office. Smith responded by patiently trying to explain that his closing of the campus hadn't been an arbitrary or unwarranted act. "The confrontation was turning from malicious mischief to violence," he said, "and large numbers of police on campus had only served to aggravate the situation." He called off classes after the faculty, the black administrators, and the academic deans had recommended it, and he intended to reopen the college "just as soon as we can do so in a normal and positive manner." However, what S.F. State needed most at this juncture was not "ultimatums," but "additional resources" to adequately cope with the "pressing needs of our minority students."

President Smith was followed to the stand by Academic Senate Chairman Leo McClatchy. After assuring the Trustees that Robert Smith "IS our president and the president we want," Professor McClatchy went on to stress that both the faculty and the administration couldn't "operate an institution of higher learning unless we come to terms with the deep causes underlying the dangerous unrest that has come to our campus." To resolve the immediate crisis, he outlined the faculty request that the Black Studies Department and a School of Ethnic Studies be provided with adequate resources to launch their programs and that George Murray be reinstated so that the "normal disciplinary procedures of the college" could dispense with his case. Rather than deal with the issues that McClatchy raised, the Trustees preferred to question his right to speak for the S.F. State faculty. And when three conservative members of the thirty-five-man Academic Senate gleefully broke ranks to acknowledge that they didn't subscribe to McClatchy's assessment of the situation, the Trustees readily concluded that the Chairman of the Academic Senate represented no one but himself, and curtly dimissed his presentation.

The next ploy of the Trustees was to refocus their attack on President Smith, and bait him about the proposed Black Studies Department. Trustee Dudley Swim, the Chairman of the Board of National Airlines and a director of the Del Monte Corporation, charged that Black Studies was "inherently racist" because only "Negro instructors" would teach it. Smith, who had only a shallow grasp of the black studies concept, made an inept attempt to apologize for the program's primary appeal to black students and teachers; he stated that the faculty might be all black "at first," but that wouldn't be necessarily so in the long run. Trustee Charles Luckman quickly continued the attack. "If it is true that not only the professors but also the students would be all black," he said, "then you're talking about segregation. And segregation is anathema to me and my fellow Trustees." "What assurances do we have that the program won't be used as a forum for black power propaganda?" added Trustee Louis Heilbron before Smith could even respond to Luckman's accusation. At this point, President Smith was momentarily bailed out by Edward Lee, the Board's only black Trustee. "I can understand the reluctance of some of the Trustees to have black folks consulted," he said drily, "because what might be propaganda to one person is education to another." The lop-sided debate continued for some time, with Smith and his collegues hard-pressed to appease the hostility of the Trustees. Finally, Governor Reagan demanded of President Smith that the BSU have no part in the Black Studies Department if it were to be instituted. "I've traveled up and down this state talking to responsible Negro leaders," Reagan said loftily, "and I know I speak for 98 per cent of the Negro community which wants no part of the Black Students' Union when I condemn them for their tactics of violence and disruption." The Governor then went on to say that as far as he was concerned, black studies was not the issue: "What we're here to determine is the reopening of that school . . . and to rid the campus of those who cause disruption."

During the noon recess, the Trustees retired into executive session amid rumors that Robert Smith was about to be removed as President of S.F. State. The rumors remained just that, though, and by the time the afternoon session started, it was apparent that Smith would probably keep his job for the time being. The first item on the agenda was a statement from Lowell Clucas, an S.F. State student who represented an anti-strike student group on campus called the Committee for an Academic Environment (CAE). Clucas had so impressed the Trustees that the Chancellor's public relations man had set up a special news conference for him during the lunch break, and Trustee Dudley Swim had gotten the afternoon agenda juggled so that the CAE representative could lead off the session. Even though he admitted that there were only thirty-five students in the CAE, Clucas was presented to the press, and then to the Trustees, as the spokesman for the "silent majority of students at S.F. State." He played the role to perfection, earnestly telling the press and then the Trustees that it was imperative for the college to be reopened so that the students could continue with their education. The Trustees smiled their approval; Dudley Swim effusively congratulated Clucas after he finished reading his prepared statement, while Governor Reagan chatted and posed for pictures with him after the meeting.

The next students who spoke, however, were not so enthusiastically received by the Trustees, even though they hardly represented a radical student point of view. Russell Bass, S.F. State student body president, told them that there had been no "program of education" taking place at San Francisco State College since the strike began, and that it would be impossible for students to return to class "as long as the problems which created the tensions on campus are present." Rather than worrying so much about reopening the college, Bass suggested that it might be better if they attempted to "supply the necessary resources and funds that San Francisco State must have if we are to provide equal and relevant education for third world students." As with Professor McClatchy, the Trustees found it more convenient to dispose of the President of the Associated Students by labeling him "irresponsible" and "unrepresentative" of student opinion at the college. The last student allowed to speak was Victor Lee, the student body president at San Jose State College who was also the president of the California State College Student Presidents Association (CCSPA), an organization which officially represented all of the students in the state college system at the Trustees' meetings. Lee outlined what he perceived to be "the sickness" of the state college system, specifically citing its callousness toward minority groups, its "toleration of outside political intervention" in its affairs, and its perpetuation of "a superfluous, outmoded concept of curriculum." Maintaining that students were being provoked into open rebellion against the system, the CCSPA leader concluded with a plea for campus autonomy and mutual moderation: "If you open the campus by any means necessary," he said, referring to one of Governor Reagan's public statements, "you will simply be no more right than those who say that they will close that campus by any means necessary." The Trustees were even less pleased with these remarks than they were with those of Russell Bass. Board Chairman Theodore Meriam took strong exception to the charge that there was outside political interference in the affairs of the state colleges, and Louis Heilbron called Lee's statement "the most disrespectful and disappointing speech I've ever heard from a student."

Having disposed of their obligation to hear the opinions of a few students, the Trustees finally got down to the real business of the day—getting S.F. State reopened as soon as possible. Toward this end, Governor Reagan and Charles Luckman had collaborated on drawing up a resolution, which Luckman now put to the Board in the form of a motion. The resolution, in three parts, directed President Smith to "reopen the college immediately"; it also specified that "immediate disciplinary action" be taken against anyone who "interrupted the educational process," and that there could be "no negotiation, arbitration, or concession of student grievances" until order was restored on campus. In the discussion that followed, the opposition to Luckman's resolution— what little there was—was led by Trustee William Norris. The Trustees, he argued, were not giving Robert Smith a "free enough rein." "We're playing a charade for the public," Norris charged. "If we don't like the job President Smith is doing we should replace him, but we shouldn't try to do his job for him." With a subtle appeal to the business sense of his fellow Trustees, he continued, "You don't delegate responsibility to a man and then withhold from him the authority to carry out that responsibility. That's not the way to run a factory!" President Smith concurred with Norris' assessment of the resolution, though he cringed a bit at the factory analogy. Most distressing to him was the "no negotiations" clause, which handcuffed him in any attempt to resolve the issues of the strike. When the Trustees held that "negotiations under duress" would be a violation of "public responsibility," Smith, in a rare moment of candor, commented that in the three days prior to George Murray's suspension, he had been under considerable "duress" from Trustees demanding that he dismiss Murray immediately. Many of the Academic Senate members sitting directly behind President Smith laughed uneasily at this barb, but the Trustees showed no trace of amusement. A vote was soon thereafter called for, and Luckman's resolution passed overwhelmingly, bringing the meeting to an abrupt end. President Smith was given until Wednesday, November 20, to reopen the college.

THE CONVOCATIONS

It was quickly to become apparent that the Trustees had given Robert Smith just enough rope to hang himself. On the day before the deadline for reopening the college, President Smith addressed a general faculty meeting called to discuss the results of the Trustees' meeting. This "state of the campus" presentation was also carried over closed-circuit television for the benefit of the students who were on campus in spite of the fact that no classes were being held. In a desperate attempt to "normalize" the situation on campus, Smith called for a "ninety-day cooling off period" to see "if we can reassess our priorities and muster the resources . . . to complete the programs we need." Blaming a "dispersal of priorities" within the state college system for the "lack of adequate minority programs," he estimated that it would take as much as "two million dollars" to eliminate the S.F. State deficit and "launch new programs." Since the Trustees had refused to provide the college with any new resources to accomplish this task, President Smith suggested that "we must turn more to the community for additional resources and assistance," but this also included, "if necessary, the law enforcement agencies," should the TWLF continue with "disruptive tactics." Finally, the beleagured President maintained that one of the "basic problems" facing the college was a "breakdown of communications." A ninety-day cooling off period would not only restore peace and tranquillity to the campus, it could also "rebuild an atmosphere of trust and harmony with the college community." Almost as an afterthought, Smith concluded his speech by announcing that S.F. State's regular instructional program would resume on the following day.

Even before the striking students could respond to President Smith's statement, the faculty flatly rejected its implications by voting not to teach their classes. Immediately after Smith had finished speaking, a call for a vote of confidence in the President's leadership was met with a chorus of boos from the faculty gathering. Only a few weeks before, he had had the enthusiastic support and admiration of almost the entire faculty; now Smith's apparent abdication to the Trustees' ultimatums irreparably undercut his authority and prestige on campus. A sizable majority of the faculty at the meeting realized that a ninety-day cooling off period was about as unrealistic as the suggestion that the San Francisco community be asked to come up with the resources necessary to implement the TWLF programs. Attempts to raise money in the community had failed dismally in the past, even with Mayor Alioto's official support; the Trustees' refusal to deal with the underlying issues that provoked the strike, much less provide resources to alleviate the college's pressing problems, made the possibility of a cooling off period ludicrous at best. In

addition, the faculty was chafing over the degrading treatment
that their representatives had been subjected to at the Trustees'
meeting. Thus, rather than meekly acquiescing to the Trustees'
mandate to—as they saw it—resume teaching as if nothing had
happened or would happen, the faculty voted to defy the Trustees
by holding a "convocation" instead of a regular schedule of
classes.

The convocation, as the faculty resolution put it, was to "bring
together representatives of the college administration, the faculty,
and the Third World Liberation Front" to "discuss in a rational
manner what is possible" with regard to "resolving the present
crisis." It was an enticing faculty gambit: the model had been
used before, and while it had not done anything to resolve pressing issues, the 1967 War Crisis Convocation had succeeded in
completely disorienting the student antiwar movement at San
Francisco State. Structurally, such convocations could do little
else, especially when no decision-making apparatus was included
in the scheme. Hence, the TWLF Central Committee expressed
serious doubt as to whether a convocation could be productive in
any way; many third world leaders feared that it was a stall tactic, or even an attempt to confuse and coopt strike supporters.
Nevertheless, they agreed to participate if all classes were called
off and if the focal point of the discussions would be the fifteen
demands. These terms were readily acceptable to the faculty, but
President Smith had already made other plans. After his speech
to the faculty, Smith had called a press conference to announce
that the regular schedule of classes would resume on the next
day. Later that evening at an emergency Academic Senate meeting, the President stubbornly refused to reconsider his position,
in spite of the pleas of some of his closest academic associates.
Faced with the choice of either siding with the faculty or the
Trustees, Smith chose to carry out the wishes of the Trustees;
however, in a flaccid attempt to appease his former collegues, he
agreed to participate in the convocation, calling it the "best way
to start reopening the campus."

On Wednesday morning, November 20, an overflow audience
gathered both in the Main Auditorium and the various classrooms
serviced by closed-circuit television in anticipation of the opening

of the convocation. The TWLF had only that same morning been informed that President Smith had ordered classes to be held, even against the expressed wishes of the faculty; they hastily called a meeting in the wings of the auditorium to decide whether or not to participate in the convocation. After a lengthy assessment of the situation, during which President Smith and other members of the college administration sat quietly on the auditorium stage, the TWLF Central Committee narrowly voted to join the day's discussions, even though the agreement they had made with the faculty had been violated. Over an hour behind schedule, the TWLF representatives finally took their places on stage, but before the actual discussion of the fifteen demands was initiated, BSU spokesman Jack Alexis launched into a scathing indictment of Robert Smith. Citing his failure to respond positively to third world educational needs, his acquiescence to the Trustees' bullying in Los Angeles, and most of all, his refusal to support the convocation by calling off classes as the faculty had requested, Alexis concluded that the President's own actions demonstrated that he was nothing more than a "lackey of the Trustees." So devastating was Alexis's attack that at one point Smith stormed off the stage, only to return after consulting with his staff.

Actually, very few classes were being held on campus, partly because most of the faculty had voted not to teach and partly because most of the students were more interested in the convocation. Still, after reading an explanation of each of the fifteen demands, the TWLF representatives continued to hammer away at Smith, driving a wedge between him and the rest of the college community. This provided the context in which the discussion of the demands took place, and gave the TWLF the initiative throughout the morning session. Smith was isolated from any potential support and forced on the defensive; he had not only to explain his reopening of the college, but also the posture of the institution, the state college system, and the Trustees—who proved to be his greatest liability. Thus, BSU representative Nesbit Crutchfield could charge toward the end of the morning: "All Smith wants to do is talk about why he reopened the college against everyone's wishes except the Trustees' or why there has to be pigs on campus. There's already been too much focus on the effects of the problems and not the causes." Then he said directly to Smith, "If you don't deal with the issues, you won't deal with anything. That's not a threat; it's a promise!" For his part, President Smith tried, without much success, to restablish what he saw as the appropriate approach to the issues. "I look at these problems from the perspective of a social liberal," he said in reference to the fifteen demands. "I agree with the needs but I disagree that it is necessary to revolutionize the entire institution. Change can come peacefully." Yet while recognizing the legitimacy of the third world students' grievances, Smith could not grant the demands that reflected the needs he agreed with. Instead, all he could suggest was that, "We need a large amount of autonomy to do what is needed." To which Crutchfield replied, "If you think we need autonomy, then why do you persist in siding with the Trustees? They won't even deal with our demands because they are businessmen who want to keep the lid on the cesspool of the ghetto since they profit off it. These demands aren't just for us, they're for all of our people."

If anything, the afternoon session of the convocation went even better for the TWLF forces. Two black administrators, Dean of Student Activities Elmer Cooper and Dean of Undergraduate Studies Joseph White, joined the third world students on stage. Cooper immediately continued the attack on the Trustees:

> The Trustees are worried about a Black Studies Department having an all-black faculty. They didn't mention that there are departments with all-white faculties. These people are scared of giving black people control over their own destinies. Does the college plan to do something about institutional racism or is it just going to fire black power advocates? I haven't seen anybody fired for being a racist.

Smith's response was apologetic. "Among the mistakes I've made as president," he admitted, "was not establishing an interracial group to investigate racism." Vice President Glenn Smith, the administration's financial expert, eventually presented the college's most persistent explanation for its inability to grant the demands. He somberly detailed the college's fiscal situation, concluding, "These are the facts of life. San Francisco State is already $750,000 in debt." Without the necessary resources, it was impossible to adequately fund "minority programs" until "at least the fall of 1969." Dean Joseph White responded that a number of the demands—rehiring George Murray, granting amnesty to the strikers, firing Financial Aids Director Helen Bedesem, and granting the TWLF full control over their programs—required no financial resources to be implemented. In addition, the problem had more to do with the "priorities of the institution" than simply a lack of funds. As White saw it:

> The machinery of the college is controlled by the Trustees. It is not set up to deal with third world demands, it is set up to deal with white reality. We will never return to normal. You can forget about that. More education has gone on since the strike started than in the six years I went to school here. Either the machinery begins to deal with our needs, or it doesn't function at all. It's as simple as that.

With the afternoon session drawing to a close, LASO spokesman Roger Alvarado announced that the Third World Liberation Front would not participate in another convocation unless all classes were cancelled. Reemphasizing that the TWLF had acted in "good faith" by honoring its part of the agreement made with the faculty, Alvarado stressed that it was now President Smith's turn to demonstrate that he was "serious" about wanting to "resolve the issues." Smith could do this by simply "calling off classes," thus showing that he was "responsive to the large majority of students and faculty on this campus." The President, in turn, was equivocal, indicating that he would consult with "all parties" involved and then make his decision. Jack Alexis then wrapped up the discussion with the following assessment of the basic problems confronting the college:

> The power to grant the fifteen demands is not on this campus. We must educate everyone at San Francisco State to that fundamental reality so we can move on the people who hold the power. I hope that at the end of these convocations even President Smith will recognize the necessity of joining us in fighting the Trustees.

Later that evening, the Academic Senate held another emergency meeting and again voted to ask President Smith to cancel classes. He refused, maintaining that the most he was able to do under the circumstances was to give individuals the choice of going to class or to the convocation. When asked if he took the TWLF threat to pull out of the convocation seriously, Smith could only say that he "hoped" they would "understand" his precarious position and continue to participate in the discussions. This proved to be wishful thinking, especially since it seemed apparent that he was keeping the college open in order to comply with the Trustees' orders. On Thursday morning, November 21, the third session of the convocation came to a grinding halt before it ever really got started. The TWLF representatives surprisingly showed up on stage, where President Smith and his colleagues anxiously waited, but BSU leader Leroy Goodwin immediately voiced their primary concern. "Will classes be discontinued for the duration of this convocation?" he asked loudly. "I cannot allow a sizable and important minority to dictate that the entire school process be stopped," Smith began. But before he could elaborate on his position, Goodwin snapped at him, "Answer yes or no!" The S.F. State President ignored the black student's ultimatum and attempted, instead, to further explain his policy. The TWLF delegation was not listening, however; they all walked off stage, holding their clenched fists in the air and chanting. "On strike! Shut it down!"

Most of the students attending the convocation took up the strike chant and followed the TWLF leaders out of the auditorium. At a rally that was called hastily after the mass walkout, Nesbit Crutchfield derisively told a huge crowd of over two thousand strike supporters, "We asked President Smith whether or not he was going to call off classes, and it took him twenty minutes to say no. It won't take all of us here half that long to shut them down, once we get moving!" Shortly after Crutchfield finished speaking the mass of strikers streamed out across the central campus toward the classroom buildings at the south end of the college. The crowd first swarmed into the Behavioral and Social Science Building, shouting slogans, beating on trash cans and looking for the few classes still being held. A number of plainclothes police officers were stationed in the building; their attempts to arrest and handcuff some of the students making noise in the building resulted in a couple of brawls. At one point, a plainclothesman who was trying to escape from the area with a struggling prisoner fired his revolver over the heads of some other students who threatened to rescue his captive. By the time a phalanx of riot-ready police marched up to the building, the student raiding parties had dispersed, and an uneasy peace returned to the campus for the remainder of the day.

Unable to find a way to keep the college open and peaceful at the same time, President Smith reluctantly agreed, at a Thursday night Academic Senate meeting, to call off classes Friday afternoon in order that departmental meetings could be held. These meetings would hopefully provide some basis for possibly reconvening the convocation the following week; in any event, they would forestall the outbreak of more confrontation on Friday—or so it was thought. Friday morning, however, some of the plainclothesmen who had been involved in Thursday's melee were spotted casually drinking coffee in the cafeteria. A crowd of taunting students quickly gathered around them; the frightened officers bolted from their seats, ran out of the cafeteria and up towards the library with a throng of students loudly pursuing them. The chase ended when the plainclothesmen reached the safety of the library's interior, and most of the students who had stalked them drifted back to the Commons. The Tactical Squad, however, having been alerted about the incident via walkie-talkie, came pouring out of their boiler room hideaway in the gym, and charged across the campus toward the library. They reached their destination just as several students were pushing their way out of the library to see what the commotion was, and a number of other students were frantically trying to get into the library to avoid the on-rushing formation of police. This resulted in a frenzied congestion on the library steps, into which crashed the Tactical Squad, flailing students with their long riot sticks. No one was arrested, but several students were beaten to the ground and trampled; after the injured were taken to the health center, small groups of students stood around angrily talking about the attack and pointing to the blood stains on the library steps.

The beatings provoked a storm of indignation on campus. At an emergency meeting called right after the departmental gatherings, the faculty voted overwhelmingly to hold another convocation. No classes would be conducted while the convocation was in session; and, at the urging of the TWLF, the faculty further demanded that all police be removed from the campus. President Smith, again caught squarely in the middle between his faculty and the Trustees, this time decided to accede to the wishes of the faculty. Over the weekend, a committee made up of faculty and TWLF representatives worked out the details for the second convocation. The format would practically remain the same; all discussion was still centered on the fifteen demands. As an added attraction, KQED, San Francisco's educational television station, agreed to televise all of the proceedings live. Meanwhile the Trustees, obviously miffed by Smith's capitulation to the sentiments of his faculty, placed S.F. State on the top of the agenda for their next scheduled meeting. Coincidentally, that meeting was to take place on the same day that the new convocation was to begin.

On Monday, November 25, the convocation got off to a late afternoon start, while the Trustees began to gather for their committee meetings in Los Angeles. The general Trustees' meeting wouldn't start until Tuesday, and for that occasion, Robert Smith had been ordered to make a personal appearance. "The problems are great and the time is late," President Smith told Monday's convocation audience after detailing the pressures that the Chancellor and the Trustees were putting on him to reopen the campus again. But such talk only further convinced the TWLF that Smith and his administrative assistants were only straw men. "It is inevitable that we will have to fight the Trustees before our demands are met," stated BSU spokesman Jerry Varnado. Implicit in this remark was the realization that the convocation could not possibly resolve the issues of the strike, an attitude that was shared by Governor Reagan—though for entirely different reasons. "The convocation should not be taking place," Reagan told a Monday afternoon press conference. "The talks are a further vacillation on the part of President Smith and are not in any way meaningful. The situation is disgraceful!" Not to be outdone, State Superintendant of Public Instruction Max Rafferty chimed in, "If I were President of San Francisco State, there would be a lot less students, a lot less faculty, and a lot more law and order!" Unwittingly, Rafferty's quip would prove to be a prophecy of things to come.

By Tuesday morning it was becoming increasingly clear that there wasn't much mileage left in the convocations. All the "meaningful dialogue" in the world wouldn't grant the fifteen demands, and the TWLF, having pretty much exhausted the talkathon's propaganda potential, began to grow impatient. Monday afternoon's session had ended abruptly when Jerry Varnado, one of the BSU's less temperate leaders, suddenly called President Smith a "pig." Professor Juan Martinez told Tuesday's audience, "This convocation is a move of desperation; it is irrelevant to us because it avoids taking action on the demands." Dr. Nathan Hare was even more explicit in his assessment: "The purpose of this convocation is to stall for time and attempt to coopt our movement," he stated angrily. "All it does is allow Ronald Reagan and his Sacramento canine corps time to decide how to move against us." At the same time, the Trustees had gone into closed session to decide the fate of Robert Smith and San Francisco State College. During the lunch break, President Smith, who had been harshly interrogated all morning, calmly said to a group of Trustees as he finished eating his meal, "Gentlemen, I witl save you a lot of trouble here—I resign." Later that afternoon, Smith formally made his resignation public. He cited his "inability to reconcile effectively the conflicts between the Trustees and Chancellor, the faculty groups on campus, the militant student groups, and the political forces of the state," as well as "the desperate limitations in financial resources cast against the commitments made in the college prior to my assumption of the role of president," as the "major factors" in his decision.

About the same time that Robert Smith was informing the Trustees that he was stepping down as S.F. State's President, the Tuesday afternoon session of the convocation was beginning. Or rather ending, for TWLF spokesman Roger Alvarado immediately announced that the convocation was over. A number of suspension notices, issued by the college administration, had been received without prior warning by most of the Third World Liberation Front's prominent leaders. Alvarado read his own notice to the stunned audience, and then asked rhetorically: "Is this what Smith means by establishing an atmosphere of good faith? Is this what the administration means by finding a way to deal with the problems in a rational manner?" Further pointing out that the suspensions were a direct violation of the amnesty demand, Alvarado finally charged that this attack on the TWLF leadership was an underhanded attempt to break the strike. When he had finished speaking, the TWLF delegation walked off the stage. The convocations were over for good—almost three hours before anyone at the college knew that Robert Smith had resigned.

CHAPTER X

The Emperor's New Clothes:

ACTING PRESIDENT HAYAKAWA

TAKES A "HARD LINE"

THE MIND OF S. I. HAYAKAWA

Central to the problems of violence on campus is the existence of a large number of young men and women [who] practically take pride in being outside the main stream of the culture, of being against the Establishment, against authority . . . How did they get alienated? Well, besides the usual psychologically neurotic [sic] reasons there is something else that's going on. I think they are taught this alienation by their professors. Especially in the liberal arts departments, the humanities, English, philosophy; sometimes the social sciences. There's a kind of cult of alienation among intellectuals, in the literary fashion such as you find in the *New York Review of Books* and the *Partisan Review*. They sneer at the world the way it's run by politicians, businessmen, and generals. Knowing themselves to be much smarter than the politicians, businessmen, and generals, they feel it's a dreadful world which they ought to be running instead.

The first great enunciator of this theory was Plato, who believed that philosophers should be kings—notice that he himself was a philosopher. The contemporary literary critics and philosophers feel the same way.

Supposing you're an alienated intellectual . . . You have no

power, no influence in Washington or Sacramento. But you can
influence your students. You can use phrases like—well, a phrase
I just picked up from a professor of English in San Diego, "the
illegitimacy of contemporary authority." It becomes a moral duty
to oppose that illegitimate authority. The middle-aged professor
passes this on to his young students; the young students are more
likely to act upon it . . .

Now, professors tend to give A's to students who are alienated.
And as the students get A's, they get appointed graduate assistants.
They soon become professors themselves, and pass their alienation
on to a new generation of students. Before you know it, you have
whole departments which are basically sources of resistance to the
culture as a whole.

All this upsets me very, very much. The universities and the
colleges should be centers for the dissemination of the values of
our culture, and the passing on of those values. But, damn it,
with enough half-assed Platos in our University departments, they
are trying to make them centers of sedition and destruction.

—S. I. Hayakawa to the U. S. Commission on the Causes and
  Prevention of Violence

T he author of the above state-
ment, one of the more remarkable figures in American higher
education, was appointed Acting President of S.F. State within a
few hours of Robert Smith's resignation. The statement is as revealing a character note as anyone could hope to provide. Its al-
lusions to the *New York Review of Books* and the "cult of alienation" suggest a familiarity with the academic mentality that
could only come from an insider; at the same time, the blatant
anti-intellectualism and mistrust of independent critical thought
indicate that if our speaker is in the academic community, he is
not of it—he is not at home there. He sees through the pretensions of academia but expresses his disapproval in such a way as
to suggest that it is not the pretense which bothers him, but its
intellectual basis: the petty *hauteur* of the intellectual snob is
rejected in favor of the not-so-petty *hauteur* of the "politicians,
businessmen, and generals" whose authority is accepted so
unquestioningly that none but a disgruntled college professor
could ever want to challenge it. The punctured self-esteem of a
small and relatively isolated social group is thus held responsible

for a social conflict which is, in fact, serious enough to threaten the foundations of American higher education.

Before assuming the Presidency of S.F. State, S.I. Hayakawa was commonly referred to in the news media as an "internationally renowned semanticist," a title which would stick even when he was in the public eye for other reasons. The title is an ambiguous one, to say the least. Few scholars have ever taken general semantics seriously as an academic discipline; it can best be characterized as an outgrowth of the conflict-resolution theories of the 1930's, when there was considerable appeal to its comfortable assumption that all social discontent could be attributed to a breakdown in communication, being the result of faulty verbal mechanics rather than disparate human experience. Whatever appeal it may have had then has been effectively preempted by the advent of electronic communication and the more sensational theories of Marshall McLuhan. The semanticist's ambiguity has another source as well: Hayakawa is less of an original thinker than a popularizer of other people's work. His widely read book, *Language in Thought and Action,* is basically a distillation of semantic theory for purposes of mass consumption. Its shallowness notwithstanding, the book established Hayakawa's reputation, and he has not done a great deal of academic work since its initial publication during World War II. His true calling in recent years has been that of a "public scholar" and seasoned traveler of the lecture circuit, providing Rotary Clubs, Junior Chambers of Commerce, and other such organizations with a reassuring stereotype of the intellectual. His theories, while couched in an aura of academic respectability, tend to do little more than to give some credence to a lot of popular cliches: the sanctity of the ballot box, the reconcilability of social conflict, the mistrust of ideologies or systematic views of the world, and the need to "see both sides of every question."

As a public scholar, Hayakawa is more than willing to recognize the limitations of scholarship, as his remarks about alienated intellectuals attest—or his observations in *Language in Thought and Action* about the perils of "thinking too much." The most impressive of his credentials, however, is his personal history. The son of a Japanese immigrant who worked as a houseboy,

Hayakawa held a number of menial jobs in his youth, managed to put himself through college, earned three degrees and eventually went on to become a recognized authority in his chosen field. In attitude as well as experience, he is the kind of latter-day Horatio Alger figure who made his way up the ladder through obedience, hard work, and putting his faith in the system. As such, the traditional American myths of equal opportunity, individual initiative and achievement, the self-made man, and social mobility through education are precious realities to him. At a time when non-white minorities are angrily protesting against the economic and social conditions to which they are subject, Hayakawa's platitudes about social justice and opportunity for all take on a special meaning for his lecture-circuit audiences. There are not many "third world spokesmen" left who wax so enthusiastic in their praise of the American system.

This is not to say that Hayakawa regards himself as a spokesman for Japanese-Americans. On the contrary, his belief in his own success effectively precludes such a role. When he first came to San Francisco in 1946, he declined an invitation to speak before a Nisei group on the grounds that he didn't believe in ethnic organizations. Apparently impervious to the fact that the entire Nisei population on the West Coast had recently been incarcerated in concentration camps for the duration of the war—a fate he himself escaped only because he happened to be in the Midwest at the time—Hayakawa told the group that he felt ethnic distinctions were of no consequence in egalitarian America, and therefore should be disregarded. This sort of faith in American racial tolerance is accompanied by an equally fervent faith in the benevolence of the American university, the institution to which Hayakawa owes most of his success. The university gave him prestige, fame, status, and security, opening doors to which orientals seldom had access. Ironically, this very loyalty to the university as an institution is accompanied by an almost total estrangement from the academic profession. Hayakawa arrived at S.F. State in 1956, fully expecting to be accorded a welcome commensurate with his formidable reputation; he was more than a little put out by the coolness of the English department *littera-teurs*, who were about as much in awe of his scholarly prowess as

they would have been of that of a famed alchemist. His contact
with the academic community remained ephemeral in the years
that followed: he taught only part-time, was unsuccessful in his
efforts to set up a semantics curriculum, lectured from the same
notes year after year, and often missed his classes. In addition,
he rarely departed from his regular syllabus, and established a
reputation among his students for being extremely defensive
when confronted with criticism or voiced disagreement.

It was not until the spectre of student unrest rose to haunt
American college campuses that S. I. Hayakawa began to take an
interest in university problems. Outspoken in his criticism of the
Berkeley Free Speech Movement in 1964, a pivotal event in his
intellectual history, he grew increasingly alarmed as a viable student movement began to emerge at S.F. Stage, and threw himself
into campus politics totally following the disruptions of November and December, 1967. He quickly became the mentor of a
group called the Faculty Renaissance Committee, forged in opposition to the student activists but mainly preoccupied with attacking the Academic Senate, traditional stronghold of the faculty
liberals. The Faculty Renaissance tended to draw its members
from two primary groups, both of which were directly threatened
by the prospect of institutional unrest or instability. The first was
made up of tenured faculty, some deans and department heads
like history department Chairman Ray Kelch; all of these individuals tended to be thoroughly engrained in the academic hierarchy of the college. The second group of professors came from
nonacademic departments such as physical education, business,
and design and industry; it tended to be less respectable in its
academic credentials, hence less mobile professionally. Lacking
any real academic tradition to fall back upon, the professors from
the nonacademic departments attempted to bolster their status by
maintaining a rigid authoritarianism and an unremitting hostility
toward student activism or educational innovation. Prominent
among their ranks on the Renaissance Committee were Richard
Westkaemper, Dean of the Division of Health, Recreation, and
Physical Education; Howard Waldron of the Department of Design and Industry; Carl Larson, the marketing professor responsible for setting up Students to Keep the Campus Open during the

War Crisis Convocation; and George Derugin, a world business professor who received his Ph.D. in economic sciences from the University of Berlin in 1942. The choice of Hayakawa as the theoretician and intellectual spokesman for the group was a natural one. With his national reputation, he could command the kind of respect accorded to a scholar who is free to choose the institution where he will teach; moreover, he could give the Renaissance Committee's views an audience far beyond the confines of the campus.

Hayakawa's association with the most prominent right-wing faculty group on the S.F. State campus is not without its irony. Politically, he describes himself as a "liberal democrat," though he is closer to the social democratic tradition of the 1930's than the corporate liberals of today. There is a good deal about him to suggest the bohemians of another era: his impulsiveness, his casual dress, his penchant for flippant remarks, the mild obscenities which sprinkle his public statements. He cultivates, quite deliberately, an eccentric image which effectively counteracts that of the pompous academician or the stolid, predictable bureaucrat. He takes an obvious relish in drawing attention to himself. During World War II, Hayakawa developed a spiritual affinity for Chicago's South Side, reminiscent of the New York bohemians who commuted regularly between Greenwich Village and Harlem. He wrote a jazz column for the Chicago *Defender*, became friendly with Mahalia Jackson and Duke Ellington. Arriving in the Bay Area, he became active in a local consumer cooperative, but had a falling out with its membership in 1966 over a decision to remove Dow Chemical products from its shelves. Today, he cites Norman Thomas as an example of a "responsible radical" whose ideas came to be accepted by a ultimately benign and flexible Establishment. In certain respects, Hayakawa resembles a political Rip Van Winkle, uttering the cliches of yesterday's progressives as if they were daringly contemporary and original insights; invariably, this anomaly leads him to side with the forces of reaction while posing as a mainstream liberal. In any event, few of today's liberals would feel comfortable with his spirited defense of Mayor Daley after the Chicago Convention, or his crudely patronizing attitude toward black people.

THE FIRST DAYS OF THE HAYAKAWA ADMINISTRATION

What projected Hayakawa most totally into the presidental picture at S.F. State was a speech he delivered on November 15 which was, at the Board of Trustees meeting three days later, echoed so exactly by Governor Reagan as to suggest a psychic communion between the two. The occasion for Hayakawa's remarks was an emergency meeting of the college faculty. Two days before, the first serious student-police clash of the strike had forced President Smith to close down the campus indefinitely; now the faculty was engaged in one of its typical soul-searching sessions, and Hayakawa rose to the occasion. "If we are to call San Francisco State College racist," he asked rhetorically, "what term do we have left to describe the government of Rhodesia?" Suggesting that it was "intellectually slovenly" to use the term so injudiciously, Hayakawa continued:

> Black students are again disrupting the campus. A significant number of whites, including faculty members, condone and even defend this maneuver. In other words, there are many whites who do not apply the same standards of morality and behavior to blacks that they apply to whites. This is an attitude of moral condescension which every self-respecting Negro has a right to resent . . . and does resent. Let me say on behalf of the silent majority of Negro students who are advancing themselves and their race without recourse to violence and intimidation that they want to be treated as equals.

There was, perhaps, only one other public figure in the state of California arrogant enough to openly declare himself a spokesman for an oppressed minority group to which he did not belong. On November 18 he told the state college Trustees:

> I know I speak for ninty-eight per cent of the Negro community which wants no part of the Black Students' Union when I condemn that group's tactics of violence and disruption.

Having this kind of remarkable rapport with the Governor of the California, it is hardly surprising that Hayakawa should have

been selected by the Trustees to bring law and order back to
S.F. State. Unfortunately, the manner in which the selection
occurred did nothing to restore the credibility of established authorities and procedures, since it bypassed the duly constituted
Presidential Selection Committee of the faculty, of which Hayakawa himself was a member. In light of the Trustees' "open the
campus" policy, the first official act of the new administration
also raised a few eyebrows; it consisted of declaring school closed
for the Thanksgiving holidays one day early.

Hayakawa's strategy for reopening the school began to take
shape over the long weekend. It was clear that he had no real
base of support on campus, either from the faculty or the students; the Renaissance Committee had never been a potent force
in faculty politics, and the student Committee for an Academic
Environment, which emerged during the November Trustees'
meeting, represented no more than a few dozen. Accordingly,
there was nowhere for Acting President Hayakawa to go for his
mandate but off-campus, and he did so with alacrity. From the
beginning, public relations was to be a major weapon of his administration. From his old friend from Chicago, W. Clement
Stone, a multimillionaire insurance magnate and advocate of "positive mental attitude,"* Hayakawa received $100,000 and the ser-
vices of Stone's San Francisco public relations man, Mike Teilman. Teilman's schemes included demonstrating Hayakawa's
rapport with black people by bringing Mahalia Jackson to the
campus, piping music over the public address system when demonstrations were in progress, and having the Acting President plant
flowers for the benefit of the TV cameras. His biggest stroke of
inspiration, however, was the blue armbands that supporters of the
new regime would wear—ostensibly to demonstrate their overwhelming numbers when compared with strike supporters.

On Saturday, November 30, Hayakawa held the first in a
memorable series of press conferences to announce the institution of what newspapers like to call a "hard line" policy.

---

*"With positive mental attitude," says Stone, "you can accomplish anything you set
out to do. You can restore order to a college or become President of the United States."
Stone also contributed $200,000 to Richard Nixon's presidential campaign.

His opening statement began with the announcement that a "state of emergency" had been declared on campus. The Speaker's Platform was off-limits; sound amplification equipment was forbidden without his expressed permission; and faculty who failed to show up for their classes Monday morning would be promptly suspended—as would students who disrupted the "orderly processes of campus life." Finally, justice would be meted out to all such miscreants within a period of seventy-two hours. The purpose of the latter provision, Hayakawa explained, was not to eliminate due process but simply to "accelerate" it. Naturally, implementation of the new policy would require massive use of police; that posed some problems since many faculty and students persisted in entertaining a "terrible prejudice against policemen." The prejudice was, however, based on misconceptions which could be easily corrected. Hayakawa explained:

> The innocents who object to police on campus are, it seems to me, profoundly misled by their warm sympathies, by their imperfect acquaintance with American traditions of law enforcement, and by their inflamed literary imaginations. It is unfortunate but true that sometimes American law enforcement officers do overreact and behave like Cossacks or storm troopers. But the *raison d'etre* of American police and of storm troopers is entirely different. The function of storm troopers, like Cossacks, is to suppress dissent and to diminish individual liberties. The function of American police, who operate on an entirely different kind of legal base, is to protect dissent and to secure us from those who would interfere with our liberties and endanger our lives. Therefore, when Cossacks are brutal it is because they are well-trained. But when American police are brutal it is because they are not well-trained enough.

In conclusion, Hayakawa predicted that as students and police enjoyed prolonged contact with one another, they would get to know each other as human beings and mutual antagonisms would disappear.

Matters of security thus dispensed with, the Acting President turned to the more "substantive issues." The strike, he said, was "largely unnecessary—almost comically inappropriate—America is not a racist society in principle and only partially a racist society in fact." The problem with the TWLF's fifteen demands was that they "add[ed] up to so little when the society is willing to grant so much . . . There is abundant money available to grant far more than the BSU or the Third World have demanded. All that is needed to get it is evidence that it will be used wisely. But the BSU and Third World have not completed their homework and have not given that evidence." Advising strike leaders to "discuss their desires and hopes and plans with the many people in our faculty who know something about the scholarly and technical problems involved," Hayakawa suggested that they "draw up big plans for involving realistic curriculum goals, teacher training programs, imaginative research projects." To the black students who had been trying for three years to do just that, only to be met with continual resistance or vacillation from the faculty and administration, this last remark was particularly offensive. The insult was not assuaged by Hayakawa's assertion, a few minutes later, that "self-determination is not given, it is earned . . . [It] comes from having enough money to be your own boss or from having the intelligence and creativity so that others are willing to entrust great projects to you." "Let me tell the members of the BSU that I am on their side," he concluded grandiloquently. "I want to be counted as an ally."

Finally, Acting President Hayakawa brought his opening press statement to a close with the announcement that students and faculty returning to campus on Monday morning would find something special in store for them: the Committee for an Academic Environment would be there to distribute blue armbands, the purpose of which would be to symbolize support for "Racial Equality, Social Justice, Non-Violence, and the Resumption of Education." Hayakawa urged all students and faculty to wear the armbands proudly, saying, "What we have to gain is the college itself." With that, the floor was thrown open for questions.

During the exchange that followed, the buoyant atmosphere Hayakawa had sought to create in his opening statement was punctured by two separate incidents. The first was an incredible blunder on his part; the second, a case of spurned affections.

After fielding several questions, Hayakawa was stopped by a black reporter from a local "soul music" station. Apparently perceiving a note of hostility in the reporter's question, Hayakawa froze, then demanded that he show his press credentials. After another moment of icy silence, the reporter snapped, "I don't see you asking white men for their credentials."

The Acting President turned red. "You don't look like a reporter to me," he muttered apologetically.

"Well I am," announced the reporter, waving his press card. Hayakawa hurriedly went on to the next question.

The second incident arose when Kay Boyle of the creative writing faculty accused Hayakawa of misrepresenting the content of a faculty referendum which had passed overwhelmingly in the aftermath of the first Trustees' meeting in November. The referendum had been intended as a vote of confidence for President Smith; however, in his opening statement Hayakawa had claimed it also gave him a mandate from the faculty to reopen the school immediately. When Miss Boyle angrily objected that that had not been the resolution's intent, Acting President Hayakawa gave her a condescending smile and said she had probably misinterpreted it. As the press conference was breaking up, Hayakawa, cognizant of the lingering presence of the television cameramen and no doubt distressed that they had witnessed a bitter exchange between him and so prominent a member of his faculty, walked up to Miss Boyle and started to put his arm around her. The novelist stared at him coldly. "Don't touch me," she said, turning her back on him.

At the outset, at least, Mike Teilman's public relations efforts did not meet with a great deal of success. The blue armband scheme in particular backfired horribly; throughout the first weeks of December, it would be difficult to find more than a hundred students on campus who would wear them, and the "silent majority" they were supposed to bring into the open remained as silent as ever. But Hayakawa had an intuitive genius for public relations which far outdistanced that of the professionals who surrounded him. (Aside from Teilman, these included Harvey Yorke, a former U.S. Air Force lieutenant colonel who served as the college's Public Information Officer, and a public relations expert from the Chancellor's office.) It was an apparently completely spontaneous act on his part, rather than the image-building efforts of his public relations men, that projected him into the national limelight and turned him into a contemporary folk hero of epic proportions. Ironically, it was also an act for which anyone else would have been arrested.

At eight o'clock Monday morning, December 2, with 600 police stationed just off the campus, a crowd of pickets gathered at the entrance to the school at 19th and Holloway, where a sound truck implored people not to go to class. Though it was not parked on campus property, the sound truck could be easily heard as far away as the Administration Building where Hayakawa was sitting in his office. The Acting President—as he was later to describe it—"blew his stack." Sporting a blue and white tam-o-shanter, carrying a stack of mimeographed copies of his "emergency regulations" and a number of blue ribbons under his arm, he stormed out of his office and up to the campus entrance, with several plainclothesmen and a battery of television cameramen close on his heels. Leaping onto the sound truck, he began tugging at the wires in an attempt to cut off the power. A crowd quickly gathered. Several students tried to restrain him, whereupon he engaged them in a shoving match and shouted repeatedly, "Don't touch me, I'm the President of this college!" The tam-o-shanter fell from his head as he tossed his leaflets and blue armbands in all directions. Standing in the crowd watching the fracas was Kay Boyle, who pointed at the wildly gesticulating administrator on the sound truck and shouted "Hayakawa-Eichmann! Hayakawa-Eichmann!" The Acting President glared down on her. "You're fired," he said emphatically. Later in the day Hayakawa was to deny that he had fired Miss Boyle, claiming he had merely called her a "fool."

A modicum of sanity was restored when the Tactical Squad appeared from behind a building and hustled the President back to his office, returning a few minutes later to break up the picket line. The crowd had dispersed, however; no one was left but the owner of the sound truck, who was arrested for operating it without a permit.

Students who witnessed the sound truck incident were incredulous; they found themselves seriously wondering whether the new President was mentally unbalanced. But to a nationwide television audience that watched it on the six o'clock news that night, it was a welcome respite from the usual steady, monotonous diet of official impotence and inflexibility in the face of violence, disruption, and civil turmoil. It was like an extravagant fantasy being played out on a living stage: the student "anarchists" were getting a taste of their own medicine, from a cocky little man whose deportment was every bit as outrageous as their own. Here was no faceless, spiritless bureaucrat or anonymous phalanx of police, trying vainly to restore order, but a genuine individualist who threw caution to the winds, took the law into his own hands, and dared to commit that one rash, impulsive act which would sweep away all dissident or discordant elements which threatened an already disintegrating way of life. Hayakawa's meteoric rise to prominence was a true creation of the politics of despair, a historical accident which placed him beyond criticism, beyond the law, almost beyond reality. For all the blunders he was to make in the coming weeks, his image would remain intact; even when the strength of the strike would force him into defensive postures or compel him to go back on his assurances that everything was firmly under control, he would be forgiven—he was still the "tough no-nonsense little guy who takes a hard line." As Hayakawa himself was to admit later:

> That was the luckiest thing that ever happened to me—that sound truck incident. It just suddenly, you know, placed the kind of power in my hands that I don't know how I would have gotten if I had wanted it.

By midday the theatrical atmosphere of the morning's events was utterly gone. Police were everywhere in evidence; when a guitar-strumming humanities student named George Gorner walked past their lines singing plaintively, "The Blue Meanies are here," it was a simple statement of fact. Just past noon, a crowd of about 1500 students gathered in the central campus area to test Hayakawa's ban on rallies. While George Murray, shouting through a bullhorn to make himself heard, talked about

seizure of power and armed self-defense, two hundred San Francisco police and California Highway Patrol officers lined up to
the right of the Science Building. Three policemen started towards the Speaker's Platform, thought better of it, and returned
to their troops. Gradually the crowd started toward the Administration Building, chanting for Hayakawa to come out and show
himself. Those at the head of the crowd got as far as the office
door before the appearance of the Tactical Squad turned them
back. The crowd remained mobile and fluid, moving on one
building after another and veering away to another part of the
campus as police lines appeared to head them off. For their part,
the police seemed equally unwilling to initiate any major confrontations. This cat-and-mouse game continued for the better part
of an hour, while tensions slowly mounted and the loud-speakers
on the Administration Building roof, just installed at Hayakawa's
request, blared away endlessly: "Go to your classes. Go to the
library. Leave the campus."

It was only as the crowd was attempting to leave campus,
moving up the corridor between the Administration and the Behavioral Science buildings, that the month's first serious violence
occurred. As the strikers approached 19th and Holloway, a
scuffle broke out between them and a small contingent of blue
armband-wearing "jocks," giving the Tactical Squad a pretext to
attempt an immediate dispersal. Clubs drawn, the officers came
up behind the crowd and drove it into the intersection with more
than the usual force, drawing a line across the entrance to the
campus. The crowd retaliated by picking up small rocks from
around the streetcar tracks and throwing them at the police lines,
appreciably slowing traffic on 19th Avenue. It was then that the
Tactical Squad broke ranks. Students were driven out of the intersection and onto the lawn of the Ecumenical House, a campus
ministry across the street from the college, where several of
them—including a cameraman who had been photographing the
police maneuvers—were trapped and beaten by individual police.
Several others were caught in the intersection: one student who
was dragged to a paddy wagon with a billy cub against his throat
was beaten by eight Tactical Squad members during a nightmarish ride to the Parkmered Police Station; he sustained long-

term injuries to his kidneys, testicles, and spermatic cord. After being held for thirty-six hours without the benefit of medical attention or a phone call, he was charged with obscenity and obstructing a public sidewalk. Both charges were later dropped by the District Attorney when the student refused to plead guilty to even one count. Monday's events came to a close with Acting President Hayakawa's press conference, where he announced that five strike leaders had been suspended. They included Jerry Varnado, Roger Alvarado, Tony Miranda of TWLF, and Hari Dillon and John Levin of Progressive Labor.

Perhaps because of the minor property damage which had occurred while the crowd was in the central campus area the day before, the police had a new strategy for Tuesday morning: they would prevent any congregation of people whatsoever from assembling on the campus. At nine o'clock in the morning the Tactical Squad charged a group of about fifty white students who were peacefully picketing in front of the Behavioral Science building, scattering them in all directions. Ten persons were arrested in pursuit, several of them on the central campus lawn, where they were clubbed to the ground. SDS leader Howie Forman made it all the way to the Commons, where he hoped to lose himself in the morning breakfast crowd. Three Tactical Squad members followed him in and, oblivious at first to the people all around them, used his jacket to pin his arms behind his back while they kicked and clubbed him when he offered any resistance. The crowd was horrified; some rose to their feet, others screamed obscenities, whereupon the officers, aided by reinforcements who had just charged through the door, turned on them. Bystanders were singled out at random; a cafeteria worker had his shirt torn off his back as police clubbed him repeatedly over the head and dragged him out of the Commons, blood streaming down his face. Another officer swung his riot stick at a bystander, missed him, and hit the central serving table hard enough to splinter his club.

Ten minutes later an enraged crowd began to converge on the Administration Building, shouting its anger. Within minutes, the police were chasing them across the campus and through the maze of construction huts that housed various student organiza-

tions on the south side of the Commons. Flimsy barricades were
thrown up in front of the cafeteria; two fires were started in trash
cans nearby. Tempers flared when a group of athletes attempted
to dismantle the barricades, but the furor subsided when the law
enforcement officers unexpectedly retreated for the time being.

For the noon rally, the Black Students' Union had invited in
four black "community leaders": Dr. Carleton Goodlett, publisher
of the *Sun-Reporter* newspaper, the Rev. Cecil Williams of the
Glide Methodist church, Berkeley City Councilman Ron Dellums,
and State Assemblyman Willie Brown. The rally drew a huge
crowd, noisy and defiant; when it was over, about 2,500 strikers
moved toward the Behavioral Science Building. Twenty-five police initially moved in to seal off the door, whereupon the crowd,
repeating the tactics of the previous day, veered off in the direction of the Science Building. This time, though, they were attacked by the Tactical Squad before they got very far. A police
flying wedge formation split the crowd in two and drove it back
toward the central campus area, where heavy fighting occurred
for nearly half an hour. A phalanx of highway patrolmen moved
up from behind the Commons, linking up with the Tactical
Squad and the SFPD's regular units to form an unbroken line
stretching across the front of the Commons, past the gymnasium,
and all the way up to the Science Building. One side of the central campus area was thus entirely sealed off.

At least six individuals who failed to leave the vicinity of the
Behavioral Science Building when the Tactical Squad charged
were injured or arrested. Don McAllister, a hulking black student who would later be charged with attempted murder (police
claimed he threw a rock), was jumped by four officers whose riot
sticks opened a huge gash on his head, causing him to bleed pro-
fusely. A white-coated doctor from the Medical Committee for
Human Rights, which had decided to maintain a medical team
on campus to treat the injured and to act as a deterrent to violence, feared that McAllister would go into shock and asked the
police for permission to administer first aid. For his trouble, he
was beaten himself, though he managed to avoid serious injury.
Throughout the strike the white-coated medics were singled out
for police attack as frequently as were the photographers. Three

other witnesses to McAllister's arrest were themselves arrested, one of them beaten and then charged with assault with a deadly weapon. Finally, a creative writing professor named George Price, who was on his way to his office in the Behavioral Science Building, was jostled from behind, bumped into a Tactical Squad officer, and was roughly dragged away to the paddy wagon for resisting arrest.

Soon, the tightly packed crowd on the central lawn, which had swelled to 5,000, surged once again towards the Behavioral Science Building. Students threw anything they could get their hands on—rocks, pieces of brick, sticks, handfuls of mud—that would stop the business and accounting classes they knew were going on inside. Within a matter of seconds at least four windows had been shattered. As the crowd began to move across the corridor toward the Administration Building a police wedge drove them back down in the direction of the library. Suddenly the Tactical Squad, having been redeployed near the far end of the Behavioral Science Building, raced across the campus at double-time and plunged into the right flank of the crowd as it backed up onto the library steps. Caught in a crossfire, the students could do nothing but try to scramble up the stairs and into the building.

The charge on the library steps produced the most intense and brutal action of the strike. Students and bystanders alike were scattered in all directions, stumbling out of the way of police lines advancing on them from two directions. Some tried to stay and fight; others were caught in the police charge and were clubbed indiscriminately. Fallen students who were too badly hurt to get up and walk away were dragged around the side of the building and thrown into paddy wagons. Gradually the police cleared the steps and sealed off the entrance to the library, sending out skirmish lines to the left, right, and center. As the tumult waned, one student could be seen lying with his face in a pool of blood. A doctor from the Medical Committee for Human Rights tried to get to the fallen student to administer first aid and was rebuffed by police. Another student, pummeled in the rib cage as he had turned to walk into the library, had made his way up to the second floor before he collapsed. He lay there unconscious for over an hour while attempts were made to contact a doctor;

unfortunately, police would allow neither the white-coated medics nor the doctor from the campus health center to get by the front door. Finally four police officers went upstairs, placed him under arrest, and carried him out on a stretcher, after which he was taken to General Hospital. X-rays revealed three broken ribs, but it was not until four hours later that a doctor in residence learned of his case and ordered a spleen test. That night his spleen was removed; had the operation not been performed, he would not have lived through the morning. One of the misdemeanor charges against him, inciting to riot, was dropped during his trial, while the other, interfering with an officer, produced a jury hung eleven-to-one in favor of acquittal.

Not surprisingly, it was Acting President Hayakawa who provided, at his afternoon press conference, the appropriate climax to the day's events. After praising the police for their "restraint and professionalism," Hayakawa, draped in a floral lei, was asked how he liked being S.F State's President. "This has been the most exciting day of my life," he said breathlessly, "since my tenth birthday, when I rode on a roller coaster for the first time!"

THE STRIKE GAINS COMMUNITY AND FACULTY SUPPORT

"Bloody Tuesday" finally shook the San Francisco State faculty out of its doldrums. A hard core of 100 to 125 professors had been lending their support to the student strike for the better part of November, some to the point of risking their jobs by refusing to teach their classes. Now, the long-dormant campus local of the American Federation of Teachers (AFT) was stung to action as well. Irked by the irregularities surrounding Hayakawa's appointment, enraged over his high-handed attitude toward the will of the college community, chafing under the "emergency regulations," and openly fearful at the rapidly escalating level of campus violence, the AFT called an emergency meeting that same Tuesday night. Before the meeting was over, the 300-odd members of the union, many of them Ad Hoc Faculty who had been striking for some time, voted overwhelmingly to request strike sanctions from the San Francisco Central Labor Council. At the same time, they stipulated that if any faculty member was suspended or dismissed under Hayakawa's "state of emergency," they would go out immediately, strike sanctions or no strike sanctions.

The four black leaders who had spoken at the noon rally, now thoroughly convinced of the strike's importance to the black community, were if anything more shaken by the day's events than the teachers. Carleton Goodlett called a meeting of the most prominent members of the black community, to be held the next morning in the *Sun-Reporter* building. Among the two hundred in attendance were teachers, social workers, doctors, lawyers, the heads of the local NAACP and the Baptist Ministers' Union, representatives from a number of ghetto social action groups, and virtually every elected or appointed black public official in the Bay Area. Graciously, Acting President Hayakawa also accepted Goodlett's invitation to appear and address the group.

When the meeting got underway on Wednesday morning, December 4, Dr. Goodlett began by introducing Hayakawa and saying that the Acting President would explain his plans for resolving the crisis at S.F. State. This promise was not kept; instead, Hayakawa regaled his astonished audience for forty-five minutes with tales of his youthful tribulations as a busboy and a washer of toilet bowls, at one point asserting that he knew black people because he had slept in their homes on the south side of Chicago. The relevance of all this to the matter at hand was never clear, but members of the audience who had dealings with patronizing white people recognized the pattern easily enough: Hayakawa was showing his credentials, at the same time giving them a heavy dose of his Horatio Alger philosophy. Those community leaders who were not bored by the autobiographical dissertation found it profoundly insulting. They tried repeatedly to get the Acting President to return to the point; Hayakawa did not appreciate their efforts. He addressed one black woman as "baby"; she didn't like it and neither did the men in the room. A question about the fifteen demands provoked another rambling discourse in which Hayakawa patiently explained that, under the state's Master Plan for Higher Education, the junior colleges were supposed to accommodate poor blacks and others of their social station. One man snapped that if the state colleges were good enough for the white people's kids, they were good enough for his own. Another asked Hayakawa if he would withdraw police from the campus and close the school in order to deal with the demands. The Acting President said bluntly, "No, I will not," calling the request "irrational."

The meeting was degenerating rapidly. When Hayakawa informed the group several times that they were "acting like children," a black professor from the University of California at Berkeley got to her feet and objected. Using his best classroom decorum, Hayakawa imperiously told her to sit down. Several of the men in the room angrily reminded the famous semanticist that he was talking to a lady, to which Hayakawa responded, a bit obscurely, "I didn't put you into slavery, the white man did!"

Finally Ron Dellums stood up, called Hayakawa a "puppet," and suggested to the rest of the group that they were wasting their time talking to him. The Acting President walked over to his attaché case, pulled out a sheaf of telegrams, and waved them over his head, saying, "This is my strength and my power. The vast majority of the people support me." In his left hand he held what he claimed was the only critical telegram he had received. A black woman interjected, "Man, you're lying. I sent a telegram and that's not it." The meeting stopped just short of coming to blows when Hayakawa gathered his papers together and stormed out of the room, shouting, "You're all irrational people!"

Sympathetic as they were to the BSU demands, the community leaders had been reluctant to openly applaud the strike, given its tactical militancy and their own respectable positions in the local social structure. Now, Hayakawa had practically driven them into the strikers' arms. They appeared by the dozen on the Speaker's Platform at noon, some of them raising clenched fists and chanting with the students. Tearful black women vowed to "die to keep our kids living." Carleton Goodlett went so far as to remind the crowd of its "constitutional right to bear arms," adding, "We will not tolerate the use of police against our fine young manhood and young womanhood!" The militancy of the speeches enthralled the strikers, most of whom were unaware of what had gone on that morning and were amazed to hear such strong statements emanating from "responsible Negro leaders." Toward the end of the rally, five faculty members also spoke, openly defying Hayakawa to discipline them for flaunting his emergency regulations. A little before two o'clock, a march around the campus began, the huge crowd of about 6,000 strikers and their off-campus supporters making a closed circle around the perimeter of the central campus area. Police lines were nowhere in sight, though individual officers with walkie-talkies stood on the roof of every building in the immediate vicinity. Meanwhile, Acting President Hayakawa's voice came blasting over the public address system: "Attention everybody! This is an order to disperse. It is time to disperse. There are no innocent bystanders. The police have been summoned. If you are found on campus in the next few minutes you can no longer be considered an innocent bystander."

The marchers, who remained peaceful, continued their chanting.

"Don't be a damn fool!" bawled the loudspeaker, with a surprising lack of formality. "The police are coming. Get out of the way!"

"Tell 'em we're here, you idiot!" someone yelled.

At 2:15 police formations appeared between the Speaker's Platform and the Commons, then between the library and the bookstore. One by one, the entrances to the campus were being sealed off. A group of jocks gathered in front of the men's gym and cheered, "Push 'em back, push 'em back, waaaay back!" They were unsuccessful in drawing strikers out of the line of march and into a confrontation. TWLF leaders and community spokesmen maintained discipline. Finally the police announced that the march was an "unlawful assembly," and, coaxed on by the community leaders, the long line moved off the campus at 19th and Holloway, chanting "We'll be back!" as it passed the Administration Building.

Thursday, December 6, two busloads of community people arrived on the campus for the noon rally; they were representatives from the Chinese, Japanese, Filipino, and chicano communities as well as from the Fillmore and Hunter's Point districts. Before the rally Carleton Goodlett told newsmen that he and other community leaders would, if necessary, throw themselves in front of the police lines to protect students from attack. The crowd at the noon gathering was not nearly so passive as Wednesday's; as the rally ended it moved toward the Administration Building, chanting, "We want the puppet!" Police officers outside Hayakawa's office door drew their guns as the students entered the building, driving them back in confusion. The windows of the Behavioral Science building yielded before a hail of rocks, bottles, and clods of dirt. Goodlett attempted to draw students back down towards the Speaker's Platform by getting himself arrested; he put himself in the path of a police line advancing from behind the men's gym. The arrest was witnessed by a crowd of about 400; the rest found themselves gradually split off from one another as police lines swept across the campus again and again. Among the close to one thousand police deployed on campus were the SFPD motorcycle and patrol units, the Tactical Squad, the California Highway Patrol, and auxiliary forces from a number of Bay Area communities that had been called to the scene under a "mutual aid" agreement. Police lines crisscrossed the campus, with groups of students standing on either side of them straining to see what was going on elsewhere on the lawn or moving hurriedly out of the way as new lines advanced. There were twenty-five arrests and at least an equal number of injuries during the melee, including a broken leg and a fractured skull sustained by two students; most of these occurred in the middle of the campus as the fringes of the crowd were isolated by the sweeping police formations. Finally the size of the crowd that had managed to stay in the central campus area was reduced to about a thousand, and police wedges succeeded in driving it off campus and into the intersection of 19th and Holloway. There the strikers brought traffic to a halt and immobilized two streetcars before a group of forty highway patrolmen drove them up Holloway street away from the campus.

Massive use of police had clearly done nothing to break the strike, which was gathering momentum as community support increased. Friday's rally drew a huge, peaceful crowd, including a large contingent from off-campus. Police did not attempt to break it up; instead, Hayakawa offered a carrot. A statement was released to the press, then read over the public address system in the middle of the rally, announcing a "dramatic breakthrough": six of the demands had been granted, including the establishment of a Black Studies Department. The "concessions," however, represented nothing that had not already been promised time and time again by previous administrations; and they did not even include the demands of the entire TWLF, but concentrated instead on the black students' grievances. While the crowd chanted, "Bullshit! Bullshit!", the BSU told newsmen that it could not even begin to discuss the implementation of the demands as long as classes were in session and police remained on campus. The TWLF Central Committee released a formal statement rejecting the "compromise" the following day. The noon rally concluded with 4,000 persons leaving the campus, some to regroup later in front of San Francisco City Hall to demonstrate against police occupation of the campus.

Over the weekend it became clear that the strike was beginning to have an impact in places other than the third world ghettoes of the city. The AFT had officially lodged its request for strike sanctions, causing a bewildering situation to develop on the local political scene. Sanctions were not an absolute prerequisite for a faculty strike, but they meant that all AFL-CIO unions would have to honor the AFT picket lines and, San Francisco being a "labor town," the longshoremen and teamsters probably would as well. To get sanctions, a union must first draw up a list of grievances around which to negotiate; this the AFT leadership did, dredging up a number of "bread and butter" demands (salaries, workload, fringe benefits, grievance procedures, etc.) around which it had been vainly trying to organize the S.F. State faculty for almost a decade. These grievances were all the Central Labor Council was interested in talking about, since the union bureaucrats couldn't have cared less about the student strike and weren't about to risk antagonizing the rank and file by lending their endorsement to a struggle with such obvious racial connotations. As a matter of fact, George Johns, the Labor Council's executive secretary, probably would have preferred to see the teacher's union vanish without a trace, were it not for a dilemma he shared with labor leaders around the country: union membership had not been growing in recent years, and with the advent of automation it would probably go into sharp decline. With the power and influence of the labor establishment on the wane, there was literally nowhere else to turn but to the largely unorganized public service employees, who were growing increasingly restive as the government bureaucracies for which they worked proved less and less able to hold themselves together. A strike by state college faculty was, in short, something the Labor Council could not afford to disregard, especially since one of the things the teachers were trying to establish was their right to strike and to bargain collectively with the Trustees. If sanctions were refused, there was a real danger of alienating other public service employees' unions with whom the Labor Council was trying to build bridges.

At the same time, the Labor Council was being pressured by another source as well. Mayor Alioto, to whom Johns was very close politically, was doing everything he could to prevent a faculty walkout. Alioto had lost his man on campus with the resignation of President Smith, but he was not about to quit; girding his loins for his coming challenge to Governor Reagan in the 1970 elections, the Mayor was anxious to prove himself more capable of bringing the embroilment at S.F. State under control than any of the splenetic "hard-line" policies advanced by Reagan and endorsed by a majority of the Board of Trustees. The Governor having succeeded in making campus unrest a major concern of the state electorate, Alioto was searching for a firm place to stand on the issue which would, at the same time, set him clearly apart from his Republican opponent. He persuaded George Johns to hold off granting sanctions. Instead, a meeting was called on Sunday, December 8, at the San Francisco Labor Temple, where assorted civic, religious, and labor leaders, liberal politicians, and representatives of the Mayor's office gathered to discuss the possibility of "mediating" the dispute. Also in attendance at the meeting were a pair of prominent mediators Alioto had flown in from the East, Ronald Haughton and Samuel Jackson; Haughton's credentials included having negotiated a settlement between striking California farm workers and the DiGiorgio Corporation, while Jackson was a black Republican associated with the American Arbitration Association. Although the mediation scheme was in no small part a stalling tactic on the part of the Labor Council and Mayor Alioto, the AFT was—for the public, at least—willing to go along with it.

There was only one problem: no one really wanted to talk to the teacher's union. Several days after he arrived in San Francisco, Haughton received a telegram from Theodore Meriam, Chairman of the Board of Trustees. While informing Haughton that the Trustees appreciated his "interest and concern," the telegram reminded him that the issue at hand was under their jurisdiction alone and they did not appreciate any attempt by outsiders to "intrude" in the affairs of the state college system—especially when Acting President Hayakawa was "clearly making substantial progress" in his efforts to resolve the crisis.

Whatever moral support he may have been getting from the Trustees, the strain upon the fledgling administrator was clearly beginning to show. Heavy rains fell on the campus Monday and Tuesday, making outdoor demonstrations impossible, but Hayakawa had other worries. Besides the outpouring of community support for the striking students and the threat of a formal walk-out by at least part of the faculty, there was increasing evidence that classroom attendance had fallen off sharply. Worse, many professors were defying a presidential edict by teaching their classes off the campus. At a Sunday press conference, Hayakawa had begun by announcing that "outside radicals" were converging on campus "from as far away as Paris," adding that many of the student demonstrators were "hopped up on drugs" (as evidence, he cited their "perceptible overexcitability and irrationality"); he then went on to repeat an assertion that he had been making all week: that most classes were going on as usual, that attendance was "excellent," and that "a vast majority of students are voting with their behinds—they are going to class and sitting down." The Acting President's smugness was short-lived, however. On Tuesday night, December 10, he made a scheduled appearance on KQED, San Francisco's non-commercial television station, on its popular nightly hour-long news broadcast. The program began with fifteen minutes of news on breaking developments at S.F. State: the situation of the AFT and the mediation efforts was reported in detail; mention was made of the fact that several churches had, under pressure from their parishoners, withdrawn permission from a number of professors who had been using their facilities for off-campus classes; finally, there was a synopsis of a report on classroom attendance by Dean Pentony of the School of Behavioral and Social Sciences, who estimated that it had been as much as 50 per cent off during the first week of December.

Hayakawa, who had apparently not known about the report, was reduced to a mixture of uncertainty and rage. Almost before the anchorman had had a chance to ask the first question, he accused the assembled reporters of "ganging up" on him. "You've been consulting with my enemies," he cried. "You're repeating accusations about me . . . I regard this as a completely hostile group. You're trying to corner me with all this hostile information from hostile sources . . ." Several attempts were made to placate him; one reporter advised the Acting President to "think for a minute about the impression of paranoia you may be giving the audience." It was, however, to no avail; after a few minutes of shouting back and forth, the enraged semanticist had stormed out of the studio, leaving the newsmen in the middle of a live broadcast with astonished looks on their faces.

Actually, the attendance figures should have come as no surprise to Hayakawa. There are rarely more than 6,000 people on the campus at any one time; if up to 5,000 of them are on the central lawn either clashing with the police or observing the clashes, then it is clear that very little instruction is going on inside the buildings. By Thursday, Hayakawa had found an explanation for the figures which may have satisfied some people. Pointing out that attendance was virtually normal in such departments as business, physical education, and design and industry, the Acting President observed, "The more volatile people are found in the humanities and the creative arts, and it is only natural that they should participate in the strike to a greater degree."

Wednesday, December 11, the AFT set up an "informational picket line" in front of the Administration Building. Police did

not interfere; evidently they were under orders from Mayor
Alioto to leave the faculty pickets alone. They were zealous
enough in dealing with students, however. Even small congrega-
tions of people were broken up as a police detachment occupied
the Speaker's Platform in the morning to prevent any noon rally
from taking place. Brandishing outstanding warrants signed by
Acting President Hayakawa, officers chased three TWLF
leaders—Jack Alexis, Bridges Randall, and Tony Miranda—across
the campus, dragging them down and placing them under arrest
in full view of the AFT pickets, who remained unmolested. The
teachers were horrified, but they could do little else but emotionally reassert to whomever would listen that, whatever formal
name they gave their action, they were on strike and nothing
would change the fact. "We can't teach on our knees!" exclaimed Eric Solomon of the English department.

Thursday the AFT legally obtained the administration's permission to use the Speaker's Platform to explain their position.
The question of sanctions was still very much in doubt, given the
fluidity of the local political situation, the vacillation of the Labor
Council, and the finagling of Mayor Alioto. Still, a formal strike
vote seemed imminent. Student and community spokesmen also
addressed the rally; among the announcements made was that the
Officers for Justice, a black policemen's organization in San
Francisco, had endorsed the fifteen demands and requested that
they not be assigned to S.F. State. After a peaceful march around
the central lawn, the crowd began to file through the corridor
between the Behavioral Sciences and the Administration
buildings—"death alley," the students now called it—when it was
attacked by police. The violence that ensued was as bad as anything which had occurred during the previous week. Tensions
had been extremely high for the past two days, and the uncer-
tainties surrounding the teacher's strike had done a good deal to
sap the enthusiasm that had built up over the sudden outpouring
of community support seven days ago. People came to the campus on Friday, December 13, expecting things to get worse. A
major rally had been called for noon, and it was an open question whether or not police would allow it to take place. Nevertheless, a large crowd began to gather on the central lawn at 11:30,

growing uneasy as a familiar voice began blasting out of the loudspeakers on the Administration Building roof. This was not an order to disperse, however; it was a totally unexpected announcement—Christmas vacation, which had not been sched- uled to begin until December 23rd, was to start a week early. There would be no classes next week; Hayakawa was closing down the school. There was a moment of silence from the crowd. Then, as the significance of what they had just heard began to sink in, the strikers erupted into applause, chanting and shouting their jubilation. They paused only to laugh with derision as Haya- kawa concluded his announcement with the words, "Merry Christmas."

What followed amounted to a victory rally. Nathan Hare told the cheering crowd, "Reagan is watching us, Hayakawa is watch- ing us, the world is watching us—and we're looking good." A representative of a local Painter's Union said he had fought dur- ing his own youth for the right of workers to strike and he looked forward to the day when students enjoyed that same right. Joseph White, the Dean of Undergraduate Studies, told the stu- dents to use the three-week vacation to "renew your inner re- solve." Roger Alvarado suggested they should also "go back to the neighborhoods and educate our people" on the importance of the campus struggle. Kay Boyle, on her way to Paris, promised to convey to the students at the Sorbonne "your fearlessness, your determination, and your pride." And George Gorner, the strike's troubador who had been arrested twice for singing to the police, was called up to the Platform, sang for ten minutes (all of his lyrics were improvised), and was applauded wildly. After the rally, there was the usual march around the quad, and the strik- ers noticed that their numbers were larger than they had been at any time during the past two weeks. As the long column filed off the campus, singing and chanting, the police were no- where in sight. The six-week-old strike had reached a high point.

Hayakawa's decision to close the campus was no magnanimous gesture. Though classes at S.F. State had been scheduled to con- tinue through December 20, the city's public schools were begin- ning their vacation on December 16. Throughout the past week the situation in the public schools had been highly volatile: there were scattered incidents of violence in most of the high schools, a one-day walkout by students at Lincoln High School, and a brief outbreak of rioting at the City College of San Francisco. TWLF had designated December 16 as "Third World Community Day"; the prospect that high school students might celebrate their release from captivity by converging on the campus was not one which the college administration could afford to ignore. It might have been expected that the Trustees would be infuriated by this abrupt departure from their decision of three weeks before to keep the college functioning whatever the cost. Such was not the case, however; in a statement which must have sounded terribly amusing to Robert Smith, Theodore Meriam told reporters, "The threat of undue physical violence did not warrant keeping the campus open."

THE NEGOTIATIONS THAT NEVER BEGAN

The next three weeks produced the most elaborate political charade of the S.F. State strike. On Monday, December 16, the Trustees overcame their initial recalcitrance and announced that they would be willing to meet with mediators and/or the AFT for the purpose of informal discussions. This was done despite some dark imprecations from Governor Reagan, who said repeatedly that he didn't think there was anything to discuss. In any event, Ronald Haughton was elated by the Trustees' apparent change of heart. A meeting was scheduled for December 19, with representatives of the AFT, the Labor Council, and the Hayakawa administration invited to attend. An invitation was also extended to Theodore Meriam, but the Chairman of the Board of Trustees was occupied with more pressing matters; his department store in Chico was in the midst of its Christmas rush. In his place, the Trustees sent their attorney, Norman Epstein, and Mansel Keene, an underling from the Chancellor's office. The college administration was represented by Dean Daniel Feder and by Frank Dollard of the Faculty Renaissance, whom Hayakawa had just appointed as his "Executive Vice President." George Johns represented the Labor Council. In addition to its attorney, Victor Van Bourg, the AFT sent along an eight-man "negotiating team" headed by a gregarious philosophy professor,

Art Bierman. As a general rule Bierman was to do most of the talking while the other seven members of the team waited in the wings; long a common figure in San Francisco liberal-labor circles, he was probably the only one in the union who really knew George Johns's politics from the inside.

From the beginning, the absurdity of the talks was clear. The AFT came prepared to enter into formal negotiations; the Trustees' representatives were under strict orders to do nothing more than "discuss." The AFT would ask Keene for a clarification of the Trustees' intent; he would respond by saying, "We are here to get this thing under way," or something equally vague. A second meeting on December 27 found the AFT asking for the Trustees' response to their specific strike issues. Keene, after a good deal of equivocation, said that two of the teachers' demands had already been granted. The AFT asked for a written agreement on those demands for openers, but Keene was not about to sign anything. As the talks came closer to an impasse, George Johns realized that the Labor Council would probably have to grant sanctions before very much longer. He began casting about for ways of keeping the student strike separate from the faculty strike, frequently accusing the Trustees of, in effect, sabotaging his efforts to arrive at an amicable agreement. At one point, Johns referred to the student strike as a "slop-over" from the faculty demands. Most observers couldn't help but think it was the other way around.

The AFT, meanwhile, was preparing itself for the strike by attempting to lay the groundwork for some political alliances. Together with Mayor Alioto and several other local Democratic Party politicians, the union leadership concocted a "home rule" proposal for S.F. State that would remove the college from statewide control and place it under the jurisdiction of a locally appointed Board of Trustees. Gary Hawkins, the boyish, inoffensive head of the S.F. State AFT chapter, told newsmen that "home rule" would eliminate the "overcentralization of authority" which was chiefly responsible for the college's ills. "The Trustees," he said, "are men of good will trying to do an impossible job." At the same time, the union was preparing to launch a public relations campaign essentially aimed at discrediting

Governor Reagan. Art Bierman drafted a full-page newspaper ad which sought to combine an explanation of the AFT's position with a blatant appeal to San Francisco provincialism. "Don't Let Mr. Reagan Turn San Francisco State into an Orange County of the North," the banner headline read, referring to the right-wing stronghold in Southern California which provided the Governor with his major base of support.

By the time their representatives were prepared to meet with the AFT for the third time, the "men of good will" had finally decided where they stood. Mansel Keene let the cat out of the bag at the January 3 meeting when he admitted, "We are not willing to negotiate anything . . . I am not under a mandate to negotiate. I'm not even free to recommend." With that, the negotiations which had never begun were all but over. Knowing them to be doomed from the start, the AFT had nevertheless played along as a way of exposing the Trustees' intransigence, making sure that strike sanctions would be forthcoming, and hopefully gaining a measure of public support for their own position. All other parties to the talks had either been stalling for time or hoping that some miraculous breakthrough would occur.

Sunday, January 5, found Governor Reagan engaged in his favorite pastime, preparing the voters of the state for a campus Armageddon. "San Francisco State should be kept open," he said with a straight face, "at the point of a bayonet, if necessary."

Sunday also saw Mayor Alioto huddling with Police Chief Thomas Cahill and Acting President Hayakawa to make preparations for the reopening of the campus the following day. Alioto promised to provide 600 police to be deployed on and around campus, but said he was sorry that the negotiations had broken down; policing S.F. State during the strike had already cost San Francisco $186,000. His entreaty had a hollow ring to it, however. Time and again, Governor Reagan had expressed a willingness to send in the National Guard, which could be deployed at the college at federal expense. All he needed was for local authorities to request it—something Alioto was not about to do. The last thing in the world the Mayor wanted was to have to admit that his administration was unable to control the local situation and would have to be bailed out by the Governor's office. Instead, Alioto made liberal use of the California Highway Patrol and a mutual aid agreement which, under the California Disaster Act, allowed Chief Cahill to bring in outside police at his own discretion, drawing from all of the coastal counties from Monterey Bay to the Oregon border. Invoking the Disaster Act was costly, but it kept Reagan from getting any more political capital out of the S.F. State crisis.

Sunday night the AFT met and voted unanimously to begin its strike at eight o'clock on Monday morning, January 6.

The last word belonged to Hayakawa. He announced that the state of emergency remained in effect, and the central campus area was still off-limits. "Specifically," he warned, "rallies, parades, be-ins, hootenannies, hoe-downs, shivarees, and other public events likely to disturb the studious in their reading and reflection are hereby forbidden on the central campus." If anyone wanted to hold an outdoor meeting, the Acting President concluded, they could obtain the permission of the physical education department and use the football field.

The student strike was entering its third month.

CHAPTER XI

Solidarity Forever:

THE FACULTY STRIKE BROADENS THE CRISIS,

JANUARY, 1969

THE AFT AND THE IDEOLOGY OF PROFESSIONALISM

With the onset of the seven-week-long walkout by the American Federation of Teachers, Local 1352, the struggle for San Francisco State College ceased to be a simple "campus revolt" and became something else, more subtle, more complex, as paradoxical as it was sweeping in its implications. The AFT action was the first teachers' strike in the history of California public higher education; ironically, it owed its inspiration and its very existence to the TWLF strike. Even taken by itself, however, it consistently failed to fit the mold of a conventional labor-management dispute, in spite of all the efforts of the union leadership to put it there. It was able to weather a series of court injunctions which were intended to break it, but not the treacherous "support" of the local labor hierarchy which had sanctioned it. It broadened the base of support for the student strike dramatically, at the same time placing upon it some crippling and ultimately fatal limitations. It attempted to set rather modest precedents: union recognition, the right of state college faculty to bargain collectively and to strike for redress of grievances. Those precedents were not firmly established, but the historical precedents that were set, and the issues that were raised in the process, went far beyond anything that was suggested in the union's official list of grievances. Perhaps unwittingly, the AFT had exposed the critical gap between the traditional role of college professors and the new realities being forced upon them by the changing functions of higher education.

Up until World War I, there were essentially two very distinct categories of colleges and universities in the United States. One was the vocational schools which specialized in agricultural and mechanical instruction, as well as teacher training; they were usually public land grant colleges that accepted a wide range of students, though not in large numbers. The others were the well-known private schools like Harvard, Amherst, Yale, and Williams; these elite educational institutions catered to the sons and daughters of the upper-middle and upper classes. When graduates of the elite schools decided to become professors or college administrators, they would then participate in the task of developing and sustaining standards of taste, scholarship, and conduct befitting the social elite who attended their institutions. In contrast, the teachers and administrators at the vocational schools usually devoted themselves to strictly practical tasks. In salary as well as style, they aspired to, but provided only a pallid imitation of, the lofty professionalism of their colleagues in the elite schools.

Since World War I, and especially with the advent of mass technology, the traditional modes of higher education have been fundamentally altered. The class and social functions of the schools have been superseded in importance by their vocational functions, blurring the once distinct prerogatives associated with the two types of institutions. Both have become preoccupied with turning out that large body of skilled workers needed at every level of the employment pyramid—an undertaking whose spiraling costs are borne more and more by the state and federal governments. The elite strongholds like Harvard, Columbia, and Stanford have evolved into "multiversities" which rely increasingly on public rather than private monies for their sustenance; the land grant and "vocational" schools have expanded in size and scope to the point where they occupy a larger and larger part of their state budgets. As the public funds are allocated to subsidize the job training costs of private industry, the college professor assumes the role of the civil servant or public service employee whose destiny is directly tied to government spending of one sort or another. Scholarly prowess is no longer the primary index of his professional standing; rather, the terms of his employment are dictated by a pair of considerations, weighted against each other, which lie outside the purview of the academic profession. The first is the available supply of tax dollars; the second, the estimates by the managers of education, mainly businessmen, as to the size and composition of the required skilled labor force.

While the status of academicians has been changing to that of public employees, their definition of themselves as professionals has become more rigid. Academic standards, especially at the graduate level, have taken on new refinements, while the academic disciplines are becoming even more compartmentalized and obscure. Both of these developments may be viewed as a desperate attempt by college professors to defend their deteriorating professional status, and hence economic security, by invoking traditions not really applicable to workers in an educational bureaucracy. This apparent contradiction—the effort to revive an outmoded ideology of professionalism—is their direct response to government intrusion into the functions and purposes of higher education. It is no coincidence that the concept of "academic freedom" only begins to emerge as the rallying cry of scholars and intellectuals when the government, mildly during World War I and finally without restraint during the McCarthy years, began to meddle in the internal affairs of the colleges and universities around the country. But where the concept of academic freedom asserts, in theory, that professors, as professionals, have the right to regulate their own job market by setting standards of competence for themselves and criteria for participation within their professional community, in practice the concept has been largely ineffectual as a bulwark against outside interference. This is so because it is largely a defensive mechanism, more an expression of wishful thinking or a profound cultural lag than a realistic assessment of the political situation on American campuses.

The founding of an AFT chapter at San Francisco State College in 1960 (they then spread to other state college campuses) was an attempt to define, tentatively, the professional allegiances and status of state college professors in light of a new economic and political reality—the Master Plan. The process of faculty unionization—which proceeded very slowly—was also part of an overall strategy of the American labor movement to recruit new members from the growing ranks of public service employees. The idea of an association of college faculty connected with organized labor met with very little enthusiasm at the time; most professors considered it demeaning to their professional aspirations and status. Most AFT professors, however, also saw themselves as professionals, and hoped that a trade union approach could effectively reconcile the ideology of academic professionalism with a political strategy to bolster the faculty's threatened position in the new state college structure. Hence, their concept of a faculty union was inherently elitist in nature, based on the intellectual skills of its members rather than on the total economic needs of the system in which they were immersed. In essence, they opted for a trade or craft union strategy in attempting to organize the faculty, rather than an industrial union perspective, which would have tied their interests and concerns more closely to the other constituencies in the state college system—namely, the students and the non-faculty employees. This led to a circumscribed and self-centered outlook that tended to deal with the faculty as if they existed in a world all of their own. As such, the major goal of the AFT would always be to equalize the professional status and the competitive position of the state college faculty relative to other faculty, especially those in the University of California system.

During the early 1960's, when the state colleges were being reorganized under the newly instituted Master Plan, the AFT was a feeble voice in the wilderness. As the only faculty group that was vocally critical of the New Order, most of S.F. State's eighty-odd AFT members were viewed as academic pariahs by their fellow professors. Nevertheless, they continued to condemn the Master Plan for subtly relegating the state colleges to second-class status; moreover, they saw the newly created office of the Chancellor and the Board of Trustees as serious obstacles to their long-range desire for collective bargaining rights. Being a recently established union, the AFT also found the going difficult in recruiting new members. They were constantly confronted with an entrenched faculty bias against labor unions, which were considered unprofessional for professors, and by the fear on the part of tenured faculty that their positions in the academic hierarchy would be threatened by a powerful union. Finally, there was a deep mistrust of the AFL-CIO, to which the AFT belonged, by conservative faculty who saw it as corrupt and by left-wing faculty who thought it had "sold out."

Still, the overall tendencies of the state college system seemed to work to the AFT's advantage. Given the arbitrary power relationships that affected the state college faculty in salary, lack of contract, workload, and personnel matters, a strong union offered perhaps the only means of consistent protection for individual faculty members against the depersonalized encroachments of a centralized system. Collective bargaining, if achieved, promised to clarify lines of authority within a top-heavy bureaucracy and to give the faculty a potent means of asserting themselves in a unified fashion. Many of the union's early promoters thought that it was only a matter of time before the AFT would be the most powerful faculty organization in the entire state college system. But as time passed and the union failed to develop as quickly as many had prophesied it would, the optimism grew less and less.

Buell Gallagher, a renowned liberal educator from New York, was brought in as the first Chancellor of the state college system in 1961. Though the fledgling AFT was naturally predisposed against the office of Chancellor, they did attempt to give Gallagher some support, especially when he was subjected to a vicious right-wing smear campaign. Seven months after he had begun his job, Gallagher resigned, citing the smear campaign and an inability to work effectively with the Trustees as the reasons for his action. After some political maneuvering, Glenn Dumke, the former S.F. State President and a co-author of the Master Plan, was appointed as Gallagher's replacement—over the protests of the AFT and a good number of other faculty organizations. In 1964, Dumke again became the focal point of a heated protest during the infamous 1.8 per cent faculty pay cut controversy. The pay cut violated a verbal understanding that had gone along with the hiring of most of the state college faculty, but when several AFT stalwarts took the matter to court, they lost their cases on the grounds that since the understanding had not been in writing, they had no legal contract with their employers.

In 1966, the election of Ronald Reagan had the overall effect of heightening the political tensions on California's campuses. The tuition scare, initiated by the new Governor, stirred up a good deal of resentment among the students, but it was the AFT that initially tried to harness the discontent. They called for a student-faculty march on Sacramento, without bothering to consult with any students; then they tried to manipulate its structure and political content for their own recruitment and propaganda purposes. Most of the skullduggery was initiated by the statewide hierarchy of the union, not the college membership; when the students caught on to what was happening, they went to the faculty AFT and threatened to sabotage the march. Most of the state college AFT, including the S.F. State local, sided with the students, and an open schism was averted when a number of march policies were reversed. Nevertheless, the incident served notice to a number of the more politically active students that the AFT wasn't exactly adverse to using students for their own ends.

Shortly after the march on Sacramento the AFT, in conjunction with the Association of California State College Professors (ACSCP), its rival organization in the state college system, conducted a statewide poll. A majority of the state college professors who participated favored collective bargaining, but they also favored the ACSCP rather than the AFT as their bargaining agent. (At S.F. State, the AFT also lost, but only after a runoff election.) After the poll, the ACSCP failed to take advantage of its mandate to establish a collective bargaining procedure for the state colleges. However, it was a known fact that the Trustees, not to mention the Reagan administration, were dead set against giving the faculty in the public education system collective bargaining rights.

By 1967, the state college AFT chapters had switched their attention to the faculty work load, which happened to be one of the heaviest in the entire nation. At S.F. State, about 600 faculty members signed an AFT-ACSCP pledge not to teach more than nine units of classes in the 1968 spring semester; but by spring-time the pledges were mysteriously forgotten and business contin-ued as usual. About the same time, President John Summerskill was being raked over the coals by the Trustees for his failure to avert the December 6 demonstrations. The AFT issued a militant call for a full faculty strike in support of Summerskill; when the rest of the faculty failed to respond enthusiastically, the union members quietly rejected a proposal that they strike on their own, and then let the whole idea pass into oblivion. When John Summerskill was finally fired by the Trustees at the height of the May sit-in, the AFT didn't even bother to protest; it was all but reconciled to its impotence in the face of the Trustees.

The fall of 1968 found the AFT working on a merger with the ACSCP around the issue of a nine-unit teaching load for state college faculty. The merger seemed likely, with only the details yet to be worked out when the TWLF began its strike on No-vember 6. The AFT officially remained aloof from the student strike at first, though a large minority of its membership was ac-tive in the prostrike Ad Hoc Faculty Committee. After almost six weeks, with the students' struggle showing no signs of abetting and with the college in a state of complete chaos, the AFT drew up its own list of demands and threatened to strike if the Trust-ees refused to negotiate with them. On January 6, almost a de-cade after it was founded, the S.F. State AFT local officially went out on strike. It was the first such strike by a faculty organ-ization in the history of California higher education.

TENSIONS BETWEEN THE AFT AND THE TWLF

The AFT demands,[1] which had the effect of giving the faculty strike its own validity, were broken down into three separate sec-tions. The first was directed to the S.F. State college administra-tion and dealt with issues that were supposedly to be resolved at the local level; these included the whole range of faculty griev-ances from personnel and workload decisions to the allocation of office space and parking permits. The second section was di-

[1]See Appendix II for the full text of the AFT demands.

rected to the Trustees; it included demands that any agreements made between the faculty and the local administration be binding, and that the resources required to increase the number of overall faculty positions in the college be provided. Finally, the last section, addressed to the Governor and the state legislature, stipulated that there be no faculty salary cut as a result of the imposition of a nine-unit teaching load in the state college system and that enough monies be allocated to allow the college to implement any concessions made to the faculty or the students. All of the demands were, of course, negotiable, since a fundamental tactic of the AFT strategy was to force the Trustees in particular into negotiations, thereby securing recognition of the AFT as a legal bargaining agent. In this manner, they hoped to establish the precedent of collective bargaining, making it applicable to the faculty of the entire state college system.

Underlying this rather elaborate set of demands, as well as the notion of collective bargaining, was the principle of shared or countervailing power arrangements that had been used successfully in the accomodation of the American labor movement. In fact, the AFT's entire strike strategy, including its reliance on behind the scene negotiating, was taken part and parcel from organized labor's bag of tricks; to a great extent, the faculty union took its cues from the San Francisco Labor Council. In this instance, however, the Trustees were in no mood to play the game; they viewed the strike as an illegal action taken against the state of California by a group of dissident public employees. Within the context of the state college system, the AFT was after a slice of the Trustees' authority so that they could influence decisions on the issues they perceived to be within the faculty's self-interest. Popular faculty strike slogans calling for "campus autonomy" and "home rule" indicated the crux of the conflict. The AFT simply wanted the faculty in general to have more control over the affairs of the college, while the Trustees were totally opposed to relinquishing their power in favor of a more decentralized arrangement.

In deference to the TWLF strike, the AFT's demands also embraced some of the outstanding student grievances. They called for the approval of Moshe Safdie's plan for a new S.F.

State Student Union Building and the rejection of the proposed changes in Title Five of the state Education Code. Most important, though, was the equivocal way in which they handled the fifteen demands. Rather than directly supporting them, and hence jeopardizing their chances of obtaining strike sanctions, all that was mentioned was that the "Black Students' Union and the Third World Liberation Front grievances must be resolved and implementation assured." The most obvious implication here was that the AFT wouldn't end their strike unless there was a resolution of the student strike—something that remained to be seen. Yet once beyond this, it became clear that the AFT, while paying homage to TWLF self-determination, hadn't really taken a firm position on the TWLF demands. Part of this was due to the fact that the AFT was first and foremost concerned about reducing the level of violence of the student strike, but a good deal of it was also due to the differing perspectives of the two forces.

Nowhere were these dual perspectives more evident than in the nature of the two sets of demands. Some AFT members actually believed that their demands were more revolutionary than those of the third world students, a contention that had more to do with novelty than with insight. In an immediate sense, the AFT demands did pose a greater threat to the system, mainly because they were geared to appeal to the specific interests of the Trustees' most disgruntled employees—the state college faculty. But the overall intent of the AFT demands was to restore equilibrium to the system. This was not because of the AFT's motives; their sincerity and concern for the welfare of the students and even the college were genuine enough. Rather, it was indicative of the diluted nature of their ideology. The AFT sought to share power with the Trustees; the TWLF sought to seize power from the Trustees. The AFT took the calculated position that their demands were all negotiable, hoping to expose the intransigence of the Trustees and maintain the blessings of the San Francisco labor hierarchy; the TWLF demands were non-negotiable, they would not compromise their needs any more than they would accommodate racism. Finally, the basic objective of the AFT demands was to achieve economic and professional equality for state college faculty, on a par with the position of the faculty of the University of California. In effect, they wanted to become first-class citizens in California's academic community. On the other hand, the demands of the third world students weren't oriented toward achieving equal status for their constituency; they sought to establish more far-reaching precedents. "We don't want educational equality," emphasized TWLF leader Roger Alvarado, "we want self-determination." Given these differences between the AFT and the TWLF, it is not difficult to understand why the joint student-faculty strike at S.F. State faced some serious problems of coordination and mutual trust. Luckily, aside from the fact that both parties were striking, there were some formidable common enemies: the Trustees, Acting President Hayakawa, the police, Governor Reagan—all of whom inadvertently contributed to strike solidarity. Beyond that, however, the two groups still faced a number of divisive obstacles.

The initial dispute between the TWLF and the AFT came prior to the reopening of the college in January; it involved the question of tactics. A meeting was called over the Christmas holidays to discuss the possible coordination of strike activities if the AFT voted to go out. At the meeting, AFT representatives outlined the procedures they had already agreed upon in anticipation of a faculty strike. They planned to ring the campus with pickets, and request of everyone that their lines be honored. In this way, or so they thought, the campus would be virtually deserted and the violence that had often characterized the first two months of the student strike could be averted. There would be no on-campus rallies, no classroom disruption, and no confrontations with the police; instead, there would simply be a great deal of peaceful picketing. The TWLF leaders generally thought that the AFT plan was completely inflexible and were not very enthusiastic about it. They pointed out that by trying to make the strike into a proper and respectable protest, the AFT was sacrificing tactical mobility and initiative. If the administration and the police knew exactly what the strikers intended to do, when they intended to do it, and where they intended to do it, then they would be in a much better position to dictate the conditions under which the strike could continue. This would, in effect, allow them to stop the strike's momentum—something the "strategy of the flea" intrinsically avoided. For their part, however, the AFT faculty couldn't even conceive of imitating the guerilla tactics that had been effectively used by the students. Hence, all that could be agreed upon was that students would be encouraged to help man the picket lines, but that the TWLF would resort to other tactics whenever they deemed it appropriate.

On Monday, January 6, the first day of the long-awaited faculty walkout, the number of pickets was so massive that the campus looked virtually deserted by comparison. Over three thousand strike supporters marched on a line that at times stretched nearly all the way around the mile-long campus perimeter. Class attendance figures had plummeted down to around twenty per cent, where they would remain for the rest of the month; many nonstriking instructors who were nevertheless sympathetic to the student strike continued to meet their classes off-campus despite Acting President Hayakawa's edict forbidding this. By noon, the buoyant morale of the strikers was further bolstered by the announcement that the San Francisco Central Labor Council had granted the AFT strike sanctions. Though there were five arrests during the day, no injuries were reported; the day's picketing had been spirited but peaceful. At his now traditional late afternoon press conference, Hayakawa was visibly annoyed by the day's turn of events. He had spent most of the morning unsuccessfully trying to convince the Labor Council to withhold strike sanctions, and appealing to the labor bureaucrats' class consciousness by referring to the college as a "working-class" school. Now the Acting President, indignantly claiming that he came to S.F. State in order to "be in touch with the lower classes," had some harsh words for Labor Council Executive Secretary George Johns, among others. Moreover, he spuriously threatened to bring in "volunteer teachers" to break the AFT strike, maintaining that he had "at least fifty offers" already. Simultaneously, Chancellor Glenn Dumke had called his own news conference to publicly warn the striking faculty members that if they stayed away from their classes for five days they would be fired. This was due to a stipulation in the California Education Code which specified that any teacher absent from his classes for five days without official authorization would be considered to have "automatically resigned."

The next day, the number of pickets tapered off somewhat to a respectable two thousand or so, but the line was still proving successful in limiting classroom attendance. Still, trouble was beginning to brew between the AFT and the TWLF. George Johns had issued a statement maintaining that the Labor Council had granted the sanctions to the AFT "with the clear understanding that we do not regard student problems as labor strike issues." Since the Council would be intricately involved in any further AFT negotiations, it could conceivably influence the AFT to settle without the students getting any satisfaction on their demands. This would be an especially bitter pill for the TWLF to swallow, given the debt that the faculty strike owed the students. Chafing from their suspicions, the TWLF put out a leaflet reaffirming the primacy of the student strike and their own position of leadership. In addition, they were critical of the faculty union's willingness to allow the Labor Council to issue statements that were detrimental to continuing student-faculty cooperation.

As if to demonstrate their disapproval of the AFT dealings with San Francisco's labor hierarchy, and to reassert their independence from the striking faculty, about five hundred third world and white students broke away from the main picket line around noon on Tuesday. They marched down to the Administration Building, where they formed their own line and began boisterously chanting strike slogans. When an announcement from Hayakawa's loud speaker system warned the students that they were violating the ban on campus gatherings, the strikers defiantly chanted even louder. A few AFT picket captains rushed down to the disturbance and pleaded with the students, imploring them to return to the main picket line before the police were called in large numbers. The students ignored the professors' entreaty and continued to make as much noise as possible. Finally, some two hundred riot police marched onto campus; they formed a wedge and slowly eased the students back up to the 19th and Holloway intersection. Acting President Hayakawa was quick to see the significance of the students' diversion from AFT strategy, and lost no time trying to exploit it. After referring to the AFT as a "militant minority" that had "hitchhiked" on the student strike "for a vicious power grab," the semanticist told his Tuesday afternoon press conference that it was obvious that the AFT was "losing control" of the picket line to the "student trouble-makers." He also suggested that, if given the opportunity, the AFT wouldn't hesitate to "sell out" the student strike.

ACTION ON THE PICKET LINE

By Wednesday, January 8, with the novelty of the picket line starting to wear thin, the students decided to revitalize their struggle by "tightening up the line," rather than bolting it as they had done the day before. This tactic involved making it very hard for nonstrikers to get on the campus, and led to a number of individual confrontations, most always verbal, between striking and nonstriking students. One such clash took place when a young black woman, who was a special admissions student at the college, deliberately stepped in front of a white drama student on her way to class.

"Where you going, sister?" asked the black student. The drama student didn't answer; instead, she tried to go around her interrogator and through the picket line without being noticed. "I said where you going?" repeated the black student emphatically as she moved in front of her target again. When there was still no answer, whe moved to just inches from the white girl's face. "Are you a scab?" she inquired loudly. "Are you breaking our strike?" The drama student, now beside herself with fear and embarrassment, was unable to speak or to get around her tormentor. Finally, she just broke down and started weeping. "Cry, damn it, cry!" shouted the young black woman, "because you don't have enough sense to care about other people's lives." By this time a crowd of curious students had gathered around the two, and the picket line had halted where they stood. A cop stationed at the 19th and Holloway entrance to the school spotted the congestion and moved in closer to see what was going on; he quickly separated the two women and then escorted the drama student through the picket line. But by the time the officer got back to his post, the black student had circled around the crowd and come up in front of the young white woman for a second time. "I just wanted you to know how angry we are with you white middle-class chicks," she taunted. "This system has had it. It's falling apart and you'll go with it if you don't start thinking about someone beside yourself."

"Please let me go," was all the white girl could manage to say. The cop, who must have been watching, again intervened, this time warning the black student that she could be arrested. He walked the visibly shaken drama student farther onto the campus; the black girl watched them go and then returned to the picket line, where her friends greeted her with a black power salute. "Right on, sister," they said approvingly.

The badgering of nonstriking students trying to cross the picket line at 19th and Holloway indirectly touched off the first serious student-police battle of the new year. Early Wednesday afternoon, January 8, the police demanded that the strikers clear a path in front of the entrance to the campus in order to allow a free flow of traffic to and from the classroom buildings. The students ignored the order and continued to bunch together in front of the entrance, harassing any strike-breaker that attempted to get on campus. Then, without warning, about fifty Tactical Squad officers swung around the front of the Administration Building and drove their wedge formation into the ranks of the startled students, forcing them to retreat into the intersection. A handful of students was trapped in the scramble to escape the oncoming cops; they were gratuitously clubbed, roughed up, and arrested. About four hundred students escaped into the intersection, where a number of them retaliated by showering the police formation, which had halted at the curb, with rocks, bottles, and obscenities.

Suddenly, from out of nowhere it seemed, some two dozen mounted police came galloping down 19th Avenue from the south; they broke through the left flank of the students occupying the intersection, and scattered them in every direction. The mounted skirmishers, brandishing four-foot-long riot sticks, wheeled to the right and started up Holloway after the main contingent of fleeing students. Most of the students instantly realized that it was impossible to outrun the horses, so they sought sanctuary in the nearest front yard that bordered on Holloway; once behind a fence or a tree, they watched in safety while the sweep continued up the street. Quite a few students failed to make it to safety; many were knocked down in the street by the rampaging horsemen. All told, seven students were arrested and thirteen injured in the sweep.

Wednesday also saw an escalation of legal attacks against the strike at San Francisco State College. Governor Reagan led things off by sternly announcing that he had ordered the Department of Finance to stop the pay checks of any instructor reported to be striking or even not teaching his classes on campus. The Governor then officially opened the 1969 session of the California legislature by calling for "tougher laws" to deal with "campus anarchists." In the State Assembly, California's lower legislative house, no less than twenty-five "campus crackdown" bills, as the press enjoyed calling them, were submitted for consideration. Most of these were geared toward making any kind of campus disruption a criminal felony. In San Francisco, an injunction was issued against the AFT strike. Filed by the offices of the California Attorney General on behalf of S.I. Hayakawa, the injunction, which was granted by a local superior court judge, enjoined the AFT from striking or picketing at S.F. State. Acting President Hayakawa was delighted about the injunction and optimistic about the immediate future. During his regular afternoon session with the press, the smiling semanticist predicted, "Peace is closer than ever. The striking faculty will be fired in a few days," he continued, "and my new disciplinary procedures will dispense with the dissident students."

To most observers, however, the immediate future not only at S.F. State, but also throughout the entire state college system, looked as if it would be even more turbulent than ever. The uprisings at San Francisco State were bound to have an impact on the other state college campuses, given the nature of the issues involved and the attention that both strikes had attracted. On Wednesday, January 8, the inevitable happened—major rebellions broke out at San Jose State College and San Fernando Valley State College. At San Jose State, close to three hundred AFT professors, about one fourth of all the faculty employed at the college, went out on strike for essentially the same demands that the S.F. State AFT had made. The San Jose AFT local along with the San Francisco local were considered to be the two strongest AFT chapters in the state college system. As the next step in the AFT's overall strategy to close down a number of major campuses in the state college system, the fate of the San Jose State strike would be a crucial factor in the AFT's drive to force the Trustees to concede collective bargaining rights to the state college faculty. At San Fernando Valley State, a mass arrest of 320 students succeeded in crippling campus' student rebellion, which was also led by third world students, and involved demands similar to those of the TWLF at S. F. State. The revolt had lasted only two days, which greatly disappointed S. F. State's striking students. Like the striking professors, the TWLF and their supporters realized that beyond shutting down San Francisco State College, a number of other colleges in the system would also have to be paralyzed by rebellions if the momentum of the struggle was to spread to other campuses, and thus gain a new lease on life.

Meanwhile, S.F. State student strike supporters continued to dutifully march on the picket line, though many were also beginning to indulge in a variety of mischievous tactics on the side. Stink bombs dropped into the ventilation system of the Science Building and the Library were so putrid that the occupants had to leave the buildings for over two hours while they were aired out. Large numbers of bent nails began to materialize in the faculty parking lots, where the rate of flat tires had skyrocketed. Even the toilets weren't spared, nor were the non-union maintenance men who had to go from one building to the next unplugging them. More violence erupted at the 19th and Holloway entrance to the campus on Thursday afternoon when a police lieutenant sprayed mace into the eyes of two leashed dogs that were growling at him. The spraying enraged a number of students, who quickly surrounded the officer only in turn to be themselves encircled by a couple of squads of club-wielding police. As usual, the students got the worst of the encounter; five were arrested and seven others injured, three of whom had to have their bloodied heads sewed up. One of the dogs that had been maced was blind on arrival at a veterinary clinic. On Friday, the striking students came up with a new tactic—the "book-in." Small groups of students would go into the library and check out as many as they could carry; then they would immediately return them. This proved to be a welcome respite from walking for hours on a picket line, and by Friday afternoon, the library was so jammed with recently returned books that the head librarian estimated it would take over a week to reshelve them.

While the student strikers were coming up with new schemes to further sabotage the already dysfunctional institution, the AFT was engaged in a war of nerves with the college authorities. Late Thursday morning, January 9, the striking faculty marched onto the picket line boisterously singing "Solidarity Forever," which had become the unofficial anthem of their walkout. The AFT professors, some three hundred strong, had just voted unanimously to defy the court injunction and continue the strike. For the remainder of the day, they waited expectantly for the arrests to begin, but by early evening nobody from the AFT had been apprehended. The college administration had no explanation for why the injunction hadn't been enforced. By Friday, the focus of attention became whether or not those faculty members who had been striking would be fired, since it was the fifth day they had been away from their classes. Everyone from Governor Reagan to Chancellor Dumke to Acting President Hayakawa had vowed that all striking faculty members would be sacked when the five-day automatic resignation deadline came around. On the other hand, the statewide AFT had threatened to call a general teachers' strike in all of California's public schools if the S.F. State professors were fired. After a day of rumors and confusion, no one had apparently been fired. When pressed, the college administration finally admitted that since twenty-two department heads had refused to provide Hayakawa with figures on the classroom attendance of the professors in their respective departments, it was virtually impossible to tell who was teaching and who was not. In addition, a large majority of the S.F. State faculty had refused to sign a personal statement swearing that they had been teaching their scheduled classes on campus; the Chairman of the Academic Senate likened it to a "loyalty oath," and was severely critical of Hayakawa for having sent it out to the faculty.

It was wet and cold throughout the second school week in January, and the strike settled into something of a routine for students and faculty. The only incidents that occurred on the main picket line, where a token force of four to five hundred strikers with umbrellas and raincoats kept a monotonous vigil, took place when the police broke into the lines to arrest students who had warrants out against them. This was part of a general strategy of harassment and intimidation directed exclusively at the TWLF leadership, most of whom were arrested at least four times during the course of the strike. On Monday, January 13, Roger Alvarado and Tony Miranda were picked off the picket line and booked on four misdemeanors each; their total bail came to an exorbitant $5,000. On Tuesday, the police went after Bridges Randall of the BSU, who managed to evade them for close to an hour by hiding in the middle of a large cluster of students who tried to protect him. When the police finally did nab Randall, however, they were far from gentle. He was roughed up, as were several of the students around him. One student, William Larson, was worked over by four or five cops while his friends watched in horror, futilely screaming obscenities; another, SDS leader Bruce Hartford, was viciously choked by a police officer who placed his riot stick up under Hartford's chin and then dragged him over to a police van. By Wednesday, January 15, the San Francisco Human Rights Commission, which was watchdogging the campus action for Mayor Alioto, recommended to the Mayor that he make the police stop serving warrants to strike leaders on the picket line.

After having apparently won two tactical victories involving the court injunction and the five-day resignation rule, the AFT settled back to wait for Hayakawa and the Trustees' next ploy. On Monday, January 15, their picket lines were graced by some unexpected company in the person of ex-President Robert Smith and several other prominent faculty liberals. Though Smith and his colleagues were by no means joining the strike, they did feel obligated to demonstrate their opposition to the court injunction and the policies of Acting President Hayakawa. Another development during the early part of the week was that garbage was beginning to pile up all over the campus. The strike sanctions, while not proving to be a major factor in the strike, were at least as annoying as the students' stink bombs and book-ins. Besides the garbage problem, the cafeteria was completely shut down, as were all food services in the dorms. By Wednesday, January 15, the accumulation of trash had become serious enough to impel the college administration to shanghai some non-union grounds-keepers for a garbage detail.

THE TURNING POINT OF THE STRIKE

The Trustees' strategy for dealing with the AFT challenge became evident on Thursday, January 16, when twenty-six San Jose State AFT professors were fired for missing five days of school. Through bypassing the S.F. State AFT, the Trustees began to implement a rather shrewd policy of containment, singling out the more vulnerable San Jose professors for retribution, and as a warning to the other rebellious state college faculty. Since its inception, the San Jose strike had run up against a number of insurmountable obstacles. Student participation in the strike had been haphazard at best. White student activists had backed the striking professors at first, but more in sympathy with the S.F. State students than in support of the AFT demands, which meant virtually nothing to them. On the other hand, the strong black and brown students' organizations saw nothing whatsoever in the AFT strike to benefit them, especially since their own demands and programs had already been agreed to by the college administration. Non-AFT faculty were very hostile to the strike, accusing the union of engaging in a power play which could bring nothing but trouble to the college. The college administration was very adept at maximizing the inconsistencies in the AFT's position and playing them off against the interests of the other campus groups. Hence, San Jose State's striking faculty quickly found themselves isolated from the rest of the college community, and their base of support off-campus was almost nonexistent. Even the union's own membership became quickly disillusioned with the whole venture, many of them returning to class before the five-day limit was up. The union's position was undercut even further when twenty-six professors were singled out for firing, ostensibly because they were the only ones the administration was certain had violated the five-day rule. The AFT protested loudly, to the point of threatening a statewide walkout, but it was an empty threat: the firings had delivered the psychological *coup de grace* to the strikers' morale. Though the twenty-six would eventually be rehired for the spring semester, the strike was still an unqualified disaster for the AFT's statewide strike hopes.

On Monday, January 20, the TWLF announced that it would hold a rally at the Speaker's Platform the following Thursday, in defiance of Acting President Hayakawa's ban on campus gatherings. The decision stemmed from a growing apprehension of most third world leaders that the strike was losing its momentum. In spite of the fact that classroom attendance had been fixed at a mere twenty per cent for the entire month, the enthusiasm of the strikers was discernibly waning. The monotony of having little else to do day after day but walk the picket line had discouraged many strikers from coming out to the campus at all. Only three or four hundred students could be counted on to join the line consistently, where only two weeks before there had been close to three thousand manning the lines. Beyond the boredom of the picket lines, the sustained nature of the strike—it was now in its twelfth week—was beginning to take its toll as well. Mental and physical fatigue were common among the striking students, and, especially with the failure of the San Jose State walkout, an end to the struggle was nowhere in sight. The continual presence of large numbers of policemen on campus, almost since the strike began, was having a debilitating psychological effect on strike supporters: it was like living under the thumb of an occupying army that created an atmosphere of oppression wherever it went. The daily pattern of confrontations, or just having to watch the robot-like columns of riot police march back and forth across the campus, produced a pervasive sense of helplessness among the strikers. It was as difficult to ignore as it was to accept. With the number of students involved in strike activities dwindling, TWLF leaders felt it imperative that they do

something that would reestablish contact with their base of supporters and perhaps bolster morale in the process. A rally seemed
like the most obvious way to do it. It could refocus attention on
the issues and remind people of the fact that the strike would be
continued into the spring semester if necessary.

Several new developments occurred during the three-day build-
up for the Thursday rally. On Tuesday, January 21, a number
of San Francisco third world community leaders, including Carleton Goodlett and John Ramirez of a Mexican-American Political
Alliance, walked out of a Trustees meeting in Sacramento after
the Board members had refused to discuss the fifteen TWLF
demands with them. That same day, the newly formed Third
World Liberation Front at U.C. Berkeley launched a strike to
back up their demands for a Third World College. The Berkeley
strike would be a see-saw affair lasting a total of fifty-two days; as
with S.F. State, police would be used liberally in an effort to
break it. On Wednesday, January 22, the AFT sponsored a
one-day walkout of faculty throughout the state college system to
protest the San Jose firings. The response to the walkout was
dismal. Picket lines formed at only eight of the eighteen state
college campuses, and even at those eight they made little impact
on actual classroom attendance. Wednesday afternoon, the Trustees officially appointed a five-man committee to begin "discussions" with the S.F. State AFT; San Franciscan Louis Heilbron
was selected to head the group. The formation of the committee
came less than two weeks after the Board Chairman Theodore
Meriam had cancelled all meetings with the AFT and the Labor
Council at the behest of Governor Reagan.

On the morning of January 23, students began to arrive at the
campus early in anticipation of the noon rally. The TWLF, fear-
ing that police would try to prevent them from reaching the
Speaker's Platform if everybody marched down from the picket
line at once, had the strike supporters divide up into groups of
twenty to fifty and station themselves at various points all around
the campus. The atmosphere was tense and expectant as the
different contingents began to move stealthily into position. No
police were occupying the central campus area, though large
numbers of them had been spotted behind the Science Building

and in a parking lot beside the Library. At about ten minutes after twelve the signal was given; students chanting strike slogans and waving clenched fists swarmed onto the central campus from all directions. Within minutes a crowd numbering close to a thousand had congregated around the Speaker's Platform, while perhaps an equal number watched from a safer vantage point. The AFT had declined to attend the rally as an organization; some of its members were there, but most of them remained at their picket stations.

The students had no loudspeaker system, so the speeches had to be amplified by bullhorns, which didn't carry very far. Consequently, the first couple of minutes were spent trying to get people to move in closer so they could hear. After about five minutes—no one had really had a chance to begin speaking—the crowd was given an order to disperse by the loudspeakers on the Administration Building roof. The mass of students responded by roaring, "Strike! Strike! Strike!" It was at this point that police moved out onto the central campus. About 150 highway patrolmen massed in front of the Library, while an equal number of San Francisco police lined up in front of the Science Building. As the order to disperse was read for a second time, the two massive police lines rolled swiftly up from behind the crowd still clustered around the Speaker's Platform. Watching the huge police formation converge upon them, the students began shouting defiantly: "Power to the People!"

As the two police lines closed in, the TWLF leaders urged people to pull even closer together, anticipating that the cops would try to split their ranks with a flying wedge as they had done in the past. But the police had devised a different strategy for this occasion: the last two rows of each of the two formations suddenly changed directions and began double-timing around either flank of the contracted crowd, executing a faultless encircling maneuver. Many of the students didn't even realize what was happening; they were too preoccupied with what was going on in front of them, on the platform. As the noose began to close, about a hundred students situated near the rear of the platform saw that they were being trapped; they bolted for freedom, momentarily preventing the two police lines from joining up with one another. The police, however, used their clubs aggressively to close the circle, and very few additional students were able to escape. Once the maneuver was complete, there was little resistance from the bewildered strikers who had been caught inside the circle. The police had just scored their biggest tactical victory of the strike.

It took over three hours to haul all of the arrested students down to the Hall of Justice, where they spent a harrowing night being booked and waiting to be released. Everyone was charged with three misdemeanors: illegal assembly, failure to disperse, and disturbing the peace. Bail was set at $500 for each of the first offenders; TWLF strike leaders, almost all of whom had been arrested, received an additional charge of inciting to riot and had their bail set at $5000. During the evening, the 200 women who had been arrested were routed with high-pressure water hoses when they protested the fact that one of their number had been slapped into solitary confinement. Conditions in the jail were abominable: there was extreme overcrowding due to the large number of prisoners from S.F. State; no food was served until Friday morning, almost eighteen hours after the arrests; very few of the captives were allowed to make the one phone call they were supposedly entitled to; sleeping accomodations were so scarce that most of the strikers had to sleep on the cement floor, covered only with old newspapers. Thirty-five hours after they had been hauled off the campus, the last of the 450 arrested strikers were finally released from jail.

The students reacted to the mass arrest with a show of defiance and bravado, but few were unaware of the dampening effect it promised to have on the continuation of the strike. Close to 700 strike supporters had now been arrested on campus; their options were restricted by the charges against them, the punitive nature of the trials they faced, and the prospect of having to serve stiff jail sentences. The last week of January saw the campus very nearly deserted. The three-month strike had hopelessly disrupted final examinations, so much so that the Academic Senate was obliged to institute a pass-no report grading option for the fall semester. Any student could request a simple "pass" from his professor, or a denial of credit which had no bearing on his grade point average if the professor felt he had not earned a passing grade; no one could be penalized academically for not attending class. Also during the final week of the semester, the TWLF gamely called for another rally. An injunction was issued to prohibit it, however, and the police were present in such numbers to enforce it that the TWLF decided that it would be better for the 500-odd students who showed up to simply picket peacefully rather then risk another mass arrest. With the future of both the student and faculty strikes in limbo, the fall semester ended quietly on Friday, January 31.

CHAPTER XII

War of Attrition:

THE CONCLUSION OF THE

STUDENT AND FACULTY STRIKES,

FEBRUARY–APRIL, 1969

New semesters at San Francisco State College traditionally begin with the President's official "welcoming address" to the faculty a few days before the resumption of classes. The event is usually well-attended, although it has no real significance beyond its serving as a "get-acquainted session" for faculty and administrators. The opening faculty meeting of the spring 1969 semester, however, was to take place under extraordinary circumstances. The new President had all but ignored faculty opinion since taking command of the college two months before, and the faculty, its ranks bitterly divided by the strike, was in no mood for a unity rally. Accordingly, Acting President Hayakawa's announcement that he would renew old ties with his former colleagues by addressing their first meeting on Friday, February 16, produced a mixed reaction. The Faculty Renaissance Committee mobilized its forces for an all-out show of support. The AFT, which was still officially on strike, decided that a picket line in front of the Main Auditorium would be appropriate. Most of the liberal and "moderate" professors, who constituted a majority of the faculty and supported neither the strike nor the college administration, simply stayed away from the meeting. Finally, the newly formed Black Faculty Union, led by Dr. Nathan Hare, resolved to disrupt it.

Only about 300 of S.F. State's 1300 faculty were on hand for the Friday assembly. As Acting President Hayakawa, having been formally introduced, began to address the sparsely attended gathering, the Black Faculty Union, perhaps some fifteen in all, stood up in the rear of the auditorium and began chanting, "Down with the puppet!" The rest of the audience, most of them ardent Hayakawa admirers, were appropriately enraged; they, in turn, wheeled around and began shouting and shaking their fists at the demonstrators. The tumult heightened as Hare led a delegation of protesters up to the stage, where a crimson-faced Hayakawa was yelling into the microphone that his free speech rights were being violated.

"Nathan Hare, you get the hell out of here!" he shouted as the black professors and teaching assistants lined up in front of him.

Hare replied with an infuriating and supremely confident grin. "We're not going anywhere," he said, as his cohorts continued to chant strike slogans. Finally the Tactical Squad, which had been stationed offstage in anticipation of just such emergencies, materialized from behind the curtain and placed Hare and three others in custody for "disturbing the peace." Hayakawa then continued with his welcoming address, but it was distinctly anticlimactic. Within days he suspended Nathan Hare for a month and vowed that the black professor would never serve as Chairman of the S.F. State Black Studies Department.

The disruption of Hayakawa's welcoming address provided striking students and faculty with a moment of comic relief, but it did not alter the mood of confusion and apprehension which marked the beginning of the new semester. Reports that the AFT was negotiating again had placed the future of the faculty strike in doubt; still, the union leadership insisted that the professors would not return to work until TWLF grievances were resolved, and it urged students to register for classes taught by AFT members as a way of protection against their possible firing or the flunking of striking students. For their part, the student strikers had already decided to re-enroll for the spring semester, the better to maintain their political leverage within the institution and further impede the "educational process." In addition to signing up for AFT classes, however, they also flooded those to be taught

by such notorious strike opponents as John Bunzel, the old nemesis of the Black Studies Department. Involved here was more
than a desire to simply repay old debts. All students had to show
up for the initial sessions of their classes in order not to be
dropped from the enrollment lists; given that, the strikers
couldn't even attempt to resume their classroom boycott until
after the first week of the semester. As an alternative, they
hit upon the idea of disrupting from the inside by preventing
classes taught by Bunzel and others of his persuasion from getting off the ground. These infiltration tactics proved successful in
some cases, but their overall effectiveness was short-lived, and
the TWLF did not appear to have any other tricks up its sleeve
for the moment.

HAYAKAWA'S SPRING OFFENSIVE

If the strike leaders didn't have a highly visible strategy for
the spring semester, Acting President Hayakawa did. Vowing to
"outwear the opposition," the former semanticist began a whole
series of administrative actions aimed at isolating TWLF supporters and crippling the student strike. This "spring offensive," as
it was sardonically referred to, was planned and executed with
such dexterity that it immediately placed strikers in a highly defensive position. No sooner would they respond to one crisis
foisted upon them by the college administration than another one
would materialize in an equally vulnerable area. True to his
word, Hayakawa kept the pressure on, but this time he utilized a
much better variety of weapons than simply reliance on massive
police power. His tactical flexibility was enhanced by the fact
that he was even less reluctant to risk alienating faculty and students by tampering with the established machinery of the college
than he was by provoking bloody police confrontations. In point
of fact. Hayakawa knew very little about how the college operated, and he was not about to trouble himself with finding out.

The first manifestation of the Acting President's new strategy
of attrition fell under the purview of student discipline. As long
ago as December, Hayakawa had tried to initiate mass suspensions and expulsions of strikers by appointing a marketing pro-

fessor named Edwin Duerr, stalwart of the Faculty Renaissance Committee, to the hastily created position of Internal Affairs Coordinator. Duerr had undertaken the sticky task of initiating disciplinary procedures when he began to run into stiff opposition from the Academic Senate. The problem was the composition of the disciplinary panels: the Senate, echoed by the Associated Students, wanted the panels to include both students and faculty, to be chosen by their duly constituted representatives—namely, the Academic Senate and the Associated Students. This was completely unacceptable to Hayakawa and Duerr, both of whom felt that neither body was in any way representative of the "vast majority of faculty and students." The deadlock was broken in early February, when Duerr announced that the administration was proceeding on its own. Students would be barred from sitting on the panels, as would all but the nonstriking teachers. The Academic Senate narrowed the range of prospective candidates even further by urging all faculty who still respected the Senate's authority not to serve on the panels. That left things in the hands of Hayakawa's most ardent supporters; students concluded that the disciplinary hearings were a "kangaroo court" and refused to cooperate with them in any way. Many strikers were tried "in absentia" and punished with suspension or probation. Though they were soon overshadowed by the trials in the civil courts, the hearings were, for a time, one of the administration's most effective harassment tactics.

Hayakawa's charge that the Associated Students was unrepresentative was first levied during his inept attempt to promote the Committee for an Academic Environment as the spokesman for the "silent majority" of students. When the CAE failed to muster much enthusiasm for a recall campaign aimed at unseating AS President Russell Bass, and when its effort to provide Hayakawa with visible student support through its "blue armband campaign" proved equally disastrous, the Acting President was forced to take matters into his own hands. He accused the AS incumbents or rigging their own election and using student body funds to "buy guns"—two charges which were, needless to say, never substantiated; at the same time, he was working behind the scenes with the state Attorney General's office, preparing a court action against the student body government. On Monday, February 18, the Attorney General confiscated all student body funds and ordered Russell Bass and the other AS officers to vacate their posts. The $410,000 in AS assets were placed in the vaults of the Bank of America, which was awarded a "receivership" by the Superior Court judge who authorized the action. Every person or organization that relied on the AS for financial assistance, including all of the pro-strike student programs and over a hundred student employees, was cut off without a dime. Meanwhile, the AS was forced to defend itself in court against trumped-up charges of "misallocation of funds"; these courtroom battles dragged on until long after the strike was over, by which time a new development occurred to make their outcome all but irrelevant. Less than a month after the receivership was imposed, the Trustees belatedly pushed through their revisions in Title Five of the State Education Code, making student control of their own monies a thing of the past in the state college system. At S.F. State, it was literally the end of an era: no longer would the Associated Students be able to launch or even support the community and educational programs that had given the college its national reputation.

While the student body government was being effectively dismantled, the administration strategy was revealing itself on two other fronts. The first involved the two student body newspapers, both of which had been outspoken in their support of the strike. Forced to halt their publication temporarily as a result of the fund freeze, the *Daily Gater* and *Open Process* now found themselves the objects of a formal suspension order, to remain in effect until Hayakawa could establish a new, "all-college" Board of Publications. The old Board had functioned under the auspices of the now-defunct Associated Students; the Acting President claimed that, under its jurisdiction, the two papers had been "unrepresentative of two-thirds of the student body." The *Daily Gater* eventually severed all official ties with the college and came out irregularly as an independent campus newspaper, but *Open Process,* which had already weathered two suspensions, was unable to resume publication. Accused of trying to muzzle the student newspapers because they were critical of his administration, Hayakawa responded blandly, "I'm not trying to interfere with freedom of the press; I'm trying to establish it."

During the abortive Convocation, President Smith had bemoaned the lack of outside financial assistance necessary to implement the TWLF demands or to help maintain the student-initiated Programs on campus. The situation grew bleaker in late February as TWLF announced that Hayakawa had sabotaged the second installment of a Carnegie Foundation grant that would have amounted to more than $100,000. Actually, it was not that the Acting President did not want the money to come to S.F. State; rather, the dispute was over who would control the funds and what use they would be put to. The students had demanded that either Elmer Cooper or Joseph White administer the grant so as to assure that the money would go into the programs that had been responsible for attracting it in the first place—the Ethnic Studies Institute, the Black Studies Program, and the Experimental College. But the choice of the two black administrators was completely unacceptable to Hayakawa, who was not about to turn over that much money to the very forces he had been battling against for three months. Since he had to sign the grant in order for it to be awarded, Hayakawa insisted that, in return for its signature, he would reserve the right to determine who would administer the funds. The students adamantly refused to this condition, and the Carnegie Foundation was forced, reluctantly, to withdraw its offer.

The final thrust of the "spring offensive" was directed against the Educational Opportunity Program. On February 17, EOP director Reginald Major received a directive from the President's office stating that any individual arrested in conjunction with campus disturbances would be ineligible for hiring by any college program. Major was the only program director in the entire college to receive this directive, however, and it seemed clear that Hayakawa was trying to single out certain teaching assistants in the employ of the EOP who were also active in the strike. A week later, Hayakawa ordered the program suspended pending a "high-level review" of its aims and operations. Major simply ignored both directives, and managed to keep the EOP going in the ensuing weeks despite a near-total lack of funds. Twelve third world teaching assistants, who had technically been fired, continued to work without pay for three months; eventually they were "rehired" but without receiving any back pay. As a protest against this kind of harassment, Major, together with three other black administrators (including White and Cooper), resigned at the end of the spring semester. The four cited the entrenched racism and bigotry of the college administration as reasons for their resignations, calling S. I. Hayakawa "the biggest single disaster that non-white people at San Francisco State College have ever experienced." Said Hayakawa: "I'm glad to see them go."

THE AFT STRIKE SETTLEMENT

While the Hayakawa administration was tampering with the EOP, suppressing the student newspapers, emasculating the student body government, and disciplining strike leaders, the S.F. State AFT local was privately settling its own strike. Late in January, discussions had resumed between the AFT negotiating team, headed by Art Bierman, and the representatives of the Board of Trustees, led by outgoing Trustee Louis Heilbron. A San Francisco Democrat, Heilbron had two months left to his term on the Board and knew that Governor Reagan was not likely to reappoint him (he did not); in the effort to end the teachers' strike, he worked closely with Mayor Alioto, the San Francisco Central Labor Council, and Ronald Haughton's team of mediators, all of whom were directly or indirectly involved in the discussions. The college administration also sent representatives. By mid-February, the negotiators had hammered out a slightly improved grievance procedure for state college faculty, a concession which would be billed as the highlight of the AFT settlement. In addition, there were some rather tentative provisions for the possibility of establishing a nine-unit teaching load, and a guarantee against reprisals once the AFT had returned to work. Nor unexpectedly, given the Labor Council's attitude toward the student strike, there was nothing in the agreement dealing with the TWLF demands. The stage for the official announcement of the settlement was set for late February, when the Board of Trustees voted to adopt the new grievance procedure (all the while insisting, for Governor Reagan's benefit, that the AFT had nothing to do with their decision). To help the faculty make up its mind, Labor Council stalwart, George Johns, indicated that if the AFT rank and file didn't accept the settlement the negotiators had worked out, strike sanctions would be withdrawn. Meanwhile, Hayakawa's envoy to the negotiating sessions hinted that if the teachers failed to return to work, they would all be fired.

Faced with this kind of pressure, the AFT negotiating team took their meager gains back to the general membership and urged it to accept the settlement. Most of the AFT leadership, including Art Bierman and chapter President Gary Hawkins, freely admitted off the record that nothing had been won that was very tangible; still, they hastened to point out that for the union to turn down the settlement would be suicidal. It was a bitter pill to swallow: for all the union's rhetoric, a large number of striking faculty had identified first and foremost with the students' struggle, and had struck either to show their concern for the pressing social issues the students had raised, or to try and halt the escalating level of campus violence and police repression before someone was killed. The union had attempted all along to balance the faculty's self-interest with a paternalistic allegiance to the TWLF strike; now it had to ask its members to choose consciously between the two. This dilemma led to some tortured attempts at rationalization, as Gary Hawkins revealed in announcing the AFT's eventual decision: "The action to return to work," said Hawkins, "is based on our belief that the continuing struggle must be waged on the inside, no matter how repulsive the atmosphere on campus is to us."

The faculty's decision to accept the settlement and return to work did not come easy—nor was it unanimous. A full five days after the Trustees had lent their tacit approval to the settlement, the professors had still not made up their minds to return to work. On Sunday night, February 26, a full membership meeting was held to vote on the settlement. The atmosphere at the meeting was tense and explosive, aggravated by the presence of several representatives of the Third World Liberation Front. Surprisingly, the students did not take the union to task; they were appreciative of the precarious position the individual professors found themselves in. Benny Stewart and Nesbit Crutchfield spoke quietly and at length, both alluding to their own family situations and pointing out that they, too, had been forced by the strike to overlook their personal lives and relationships. In essence, they acknowledged that the decision was one that the AFT would have to make on its own, and they would respect it no matter which way it went. The students' presentations were followed by an open debate on the proposed settlement. Most of the speakers were in favor of rejecting it, insisting that to accept it would be to violate every principle for which they had gone out on strike in the first place. Those who spoke in favor of the settlement did so apologetically; under the circumstances, they could see no other alternative but to return to work before they were all fired.

The final vote was taken by secret ballot. Each AFT member wrote out his preference on a blank piece of paper, then got in line and waited to drop it in the ballot box. The whole procedure took about fifteen minutes and was conducted solemnly and in silence. The initial count was so close that another vote had to be taken; the second time around, however, the margin for accepting the settlement widened. Having thus sealed the fate of their two-month-old strike, the professors grimly left their meeting with as little fanfare as possible.

The issue was so volatile that, even after the Sunday night vote, a rump group of about eighty professors vowed to stay out on strike until the student demands were settled. They actually did stay away from their classes on Monday, but that night they were more despondent than ever. At a hastily convened meeting, called to reassess their shaky position, the rump group was told by an AFT lawyer that if they hadn't informed their various departments of their intention to resume teaching by 5:00 P.M. Tuesday, they would be fired. Dr. Nathan Hare and Jack Alexis, representing the TWLF, were present at the meeting to urge the holdouts to return to work. Finally convinced of the futility of their gesture, the AFT rump group called an end to their one-day wildcat strike; by Wednesday, March 1, there were no longer any teachers on strike at San Francisco State College.

THE DISINTEGRATION OF THE STUDENT STRIKE

The confusion and anxiety surrounding the AFT settlement did nothing to bolster the sagging morale of the student strike. Large numbers of students who had simply stopped coming to the campus during the month of January had in effect lost contact with the TWLF leadership and had relied instead upon rumors or inaccurate newspaper reports for their information. With the advent of a new semester this situation became intolerable; registration is a highly uncertain business even under the most normal of circumstances, and the two-week moratorium on strike activity which was required for students to reestablish their enrollment came at a time when the momentum of the strike could ill afford it. The general confusion was aggravated by the state of emergency, the ban on campus gatherings, the suspension of the student newspapers, and the obvious risks of leafleting on a campus under police occupation, all of which made it next to impossible to find out what exactly was going on. Many students had complied with the AFT's request to "protect striking teachers by registering for their classes," only to have the striking teachers cave in under pressure and return to work, in violation of their own commitment to hold out until the student strike was settled. Amid reports of a total lack of consensus within the teachers' union, a number of unanswered questions rose to the fore. Was the strike over? Would students who refused to return to class be subject to academic reprisal? Which teachers could be counted on to continue to protect striking students?

The latter question betrayed another vexing problem: apart from a relative handful of faculty whose sympathies were a matter of public record, it was often difficult to know which teachers had been on strike, since some of them had tried to guard against administrative action by assiduously concealing any formal evidence that they had not been meeting their classes. This tactic had been effective throughout January, but it became a considerable nuisance to striking students in the weeks following registration. Uncertain as to their own status, the TWLF strategy, the sympathies of their professors, and the future of the strike, they found themselves forced to spend more and more time inside classroom buildings just trying to find out where things stood. Others, perceiving that the strike was no longer visibly evident, wondered if it was over or if they would be completely isolated in continuing their classroom boycott. The TWLF tried to offset this trend by sending educational teams into the classes of formerly striking teachers to explain the situation, but their efforts had a negligible effect—the third world leadership was too unsure of its own position to communicate it very convincingly to its constituents. A flurry of newspaper reports about "secret talks" between TWLF and a Select Committee appointed by Hayakawa served notice to the campus that strike leaders were seriously considering settling for something less than a total victory. The reports were not fabricated: for the first time in four months, the administration had seized the initiative, and it showed no signs of giving it back. Under the repressive situation which existed on campus, it would be difficult if not impossible to rally the student body and rebuild the momentum of the strike from scratch. Emotionally, it was hard to face up to the idea of abandoning the principle of non-negotiability, becoming pragmatic, and returning to class; still, all considerations—including the strategy TWLF had followed since November 6—seemed to indicate that it was time to "play the flea," to call off the strike for the time being at least, and to begin making preparations to resume the struggle under more favorable conditions. The TWLF Central Committee was, in any event, badly split over the issue, and striking students could do little but wait for a concrete strategy to emerge from their debate.

In the absence of viable mass action, isolated acts of terrorism continued to occur—until Tim Peebles, a 19-year-old black student in the Tutorial Program, was placed under arrest after a homemade bomb exploded in his hands in a corridor of the Creative Arts Building on the night of March 5. Peebles was almost blinded and lost three fingers on his left hand; eventually he was taken off the critical list, but for a time it looked like the strike might well have suffered its first fatality. Students were sickened by the incident, and even the usually voluble Hayakawa had little to say. The battery of felonies with which Peebles was charged (including conspiracy, possessing a destructive device, possessing

an explosive on or near a college, and maliciously placing explo-
sives with intent to destroy a building) underscored another
demoralizing problem for the strikers. A few days before Peebles
was injured, Nesbit Crutchfield had made the mistake of being
caught in the school parking lot with a handful of rags and a bot-
tle of kerosene. He said he was going to clean some paint which
had spilled in his car; police gleefully charged him with arson.
Most of the TWLF leadership had outstanding warrants against
them, and many faced felony indictments as well. The cost of
bailing out the 457 students who were arrested on January 23
had been exorbitant; worse, each of the 700-odd students arrested since November 6 faced star chamber disciplinary hearings
from the administration as well as long, arduous, and costly battles in the civil courts.

None of these problems were necessarily insurmountable.
Many had existed before the AFT went on strike. What made
them so serious was a pair of underlying difficulties, ultimately
related, that had plagued the strike since its earliest days. To
begin with, the third world students had not conceived the strike
as a localized struggle. They knew that there was not enough political muscle on the campus alone to sustain the momentum of
the strike or to force the kind of concessions which their purposes required. They had, from the outset, rejected the illusion of
instant victory in favor of the principle of "protracted struggle";
the nature of the fifteen demands—for all their programmatic
content—was such that their implementation would require not
simply some minor concessions or gestures of good will, both
largely symbolic, but an actual transfer of power and resources.
The source of power in the state college system lay with the
Trustees, not their local functionaries in the Administration
Building; the real stake in the outcome of the struggle belonged
not only to the students, but to their constituents in the ghettos
of the Bay Area, whose educational needs served as the basic rationale for the strike. As such, the innate strength of the strike,
its capacity for growth, the pressure it brought to bear upon
those against whom it was directed—all hinged upon the ability
of the strike to break out of its isolation on campus and to mobilize and involve people in the community. This demanded a good

deal of the TWLF, and for a time it was equal to the task. At the high point of the strike in the middle of December, community presence on the campus had become such a threat that Hayakawa and the Trustees were forced to abandon their "hard line" and close down the school.

When the AFT went on strike, it appeared at first that the struggle was taking on a new dimension. The faculty walkout was seen as a way of spreading the strike throughout the state, of guarding against its being quarantined to a single campus. There was speculation that if Governor Reagan and the Trustees could not "restore order" at San Francisco State, they would shut it down indefinitely rather than capitulate to the TWLF. But it would be too great a price for them to pay to have to shut down other state college campuses as well. Thus, if the AFT actions were successful, the momentum of the strike would be picked up throughout the state college system in addition to the third world ghettoes of San Francisco. This assumption was at least partly responsible for a modification in the TWLF strategy for the reopening of school on January 6. An on-campus "Third World Community Rally" had been planned for that day; in deference to the AFT, however, TWLF finally agreed to call it off in favor of a peaceful picket line around the periphery of the campus. Almost immediately there were second thoughts, and by the end of the month most of the student strikers had serious doubts about the wisdom of making accommodations in the union's behalf. The AFT was simply not strong enought to sustain a statewide strike: its constituency was too small and too easily isolated, its political perspective too narrow and self-defeating. When the AFT strike at San Jose State collapsed, the handwriting was on the wall; when Hayakawa launched his "spring offensive," the students had nothing of their own to counter with. The momentum of the student strike had been frittered away on the faculty picket lines.

THE WHITE STUDENT MOVEMENT AT THE CROSSROADS

The second problem, which was easier to recognize, had threatened to stymie the strike before it even got off the ground, and was finally revealing itself to be an enormous liability as the "protracted struggle" wore into its fourth month with no end in sight. The problem was the consistent failure of a viable mechanism of white student participation to emerge from the moment of the strike's inception. The third world students' insistence that the educational system had failed them struck a responsive chord with thousands of their white counterparts, most of whom nevertheless consciously rationalized their support for the strike with appeals to altruism or to a desire not to be caught on the wrong side in a moral crisis. In a deeper sense, however, the act of striking was, for them, a gut-level rejection of a mindless and enervating classroom routine which they had endured for too long; the strike having shattered the old educational context, white students were now left casting feverishly about for alternatives. They listened raptly during the Convocations in November, fought pitched battles with the police in December, acted as shock troops for the AFT (as long as they could stand it) in January. But nowhere were they able to develop anything more than an embryonic concept of their own grievances and their own self-interest; their political awareness lacked a sense of structure; they had none of that sense of responsibility to an off-campus constituency, and an awareness of that constituency's needs, which had so distinguished the TWLF.

To be sure, groups of individual students engaged in a number of activities highly significant in themselves. Striking drama students organized an agit-prop theatre group and performed at rallies and benefits up and down the state. Art students and faculty, whose department had been the first to throw its support to the strike, put out a superb series of silkscreen posters for propaganda and fund-raising purposes. Strike information, propaganda, and some in-depth analysis appeared in *Open Process* and the impromptu *Strike Daily* wall poster, both of which were widely distributed throughout the city and on other campuses. Clerical workers and graduate assistants organized their own AFT local. A Legal Defense Committee was set up to handle the enormous tasks of providing legal and medical aid for those arrested or injured in police confrontations, compiling evidence for court cases, and raising money for bail bonds and trial expenses. With less success, several departmental unions were formed to attack the academic hierarchy at its lower levels.

What was lacking in all of these activities was a single center of gravity to provide them with a degree of cohesion, coordination, and direction. Theoretically, this function was supposed to be served by the White Strike Support Committee; in fact, the support committee had little to do with these activities, most of which sprang up in a completely spontaneous manner. The "mass meetings" of white strike supporters rarely drew more than several hundred of the five to ten thousand students who were more than marginally committed to the strike, and those who came once or twice often found it hard to come back—it took considerable stamina and patience to put up with the turgid rhetoric and ideological hairsplitting which generally characterized the meetings.

For the most part, discussion was dominated by members of the Progressive Labor Party, whose high degree of discipline and dedication enabled them to wield influence over the amorphous and frequently chaotic Support Committee meetings in much the same way as they had wielded influence over the campus SDS chapter. In some respects, their leadership was exemplary: they never hesitated to put themselves on the line; their most prominent members earned the respect of striking students by leading huge crowds, day after day, against the police in the first weeks of December; one of their organizers took over the *Daily Gater* and was able to keep it going after Hayakawa had suspended it; after the strike, they insisted on defending themselves in the civil courts and received some of the stiffest sentences the city was capable of meting out.

Unfortunately, the Progressive Labor Party was never able to reconcile its own political philosophy with that of the TWLF. Its interpretation of Marxism-Leninism and the revolutionary role of the working class led it to conclude that "all nationalism is reactionary" and the TWLF concept of educational self-determination for third world people was reactionary as well. Though it concealed its misgivings about the fifteen demands until the waning days of the strike, Progressive Labor was reluctant—even in supporting them—to explain why the demands were necessary, how

they would work once implemented, or why they were important
to white students as well as to non-whites. In fact, the propaganda
which emanated from PL or the White Strike Support Committee
mentioned the specifics of the demands only in the most cursory
manner and focused, instead on the need of white students to
"fight racism." "Racism," of course, was a term that PL never
bothered to define, except to say that it was used to "divide
white workers from black"—a correct statement, but so abstract
and remote in its relationship to the immediate situation as to
appear vapid; it was a conclusion which stemmed more from
idealism than from functional experience. In essence, PL's ambivalent position on the strike issues rendered it incapable of appealing to students on any level other than white guilt; occasionally, for all their rhetorical militancy, its leaflets sounded
strangely like the Kerner Report, attacking racism as if it were a
malignant microbe rather than a real social condition. In three
days of Convocations the TWLF spokesmen had explained the
importance of the demands and the necessity of the strike far
more clearly and compellingly than had the Strike Support
Committee in four solid months of continual agitation. They, not
the white radicals, were the most effective organizers of the white
student body.

In early March, as the strike went into a fatal tailspin,
Progressive Labor became harshly critical of the TWLF's politics.
It denounced the demands as "petit-bourgeois" and the TWLF
Central Committee as an "anti-working class clique" whose main
concern was "getting themselves some well-paying jobs as black
faculty." This seemingly abrupt about-face succeeded in arousing
the first organized opposition to Progressive Labor's domination
of SDS at San Francisco State. A group of independent radicals
revolted, set up their own "Joe Hill Caucus," and effectively split
the SDS chapter down the middle. The split prefigured the splin-
tering in the national organization at its 1969 June convention;
there, as at S.F. State, PL was attacked for its refusal to endorse
the concept of national liberation movements for black and other
third world minorities.

To its credit, PL's "worker-student alliance" political line was
influential in giving white radicals a new perspective in their

decade-long search for a constituency. Late in December of 1968, while the AFT was courting San Francisco's labor establishment, workers at Kaiser Hospital walked off their respective jobs and were roughed up on their picket lines by the SFPD's Tactical Squad. The infuriated head of the hospital workers' local blurted to newsmen that perhaps union men should have paid more attention to S.F. State students when they complained about the conduct of the police on the campus. The white activists in the Strike Support Committee did not miss the implications of the statement, nor of the incident. Desperate for allies in the white community, where the student strike had been most hostilely received, they responded to the hospital workers' struggle by joining their picket lines. A few weeks later, workers in the Standard and Shell Oil refineries across the bay in Richmond began a long and bitter strike against the world's largest industrial juggernaut. In the weeks that followed, a near-total newspaper blackout and heavy doses of police repression were used to try to break the oil workers' strike. Indirectly, the anti-strike posture of the police and the court injunctions that were issued to prevent effective picketing of the refineries created a bond of common experience—however tenuous—between the oil workers and the S.F. State strikers.

By late January, the Strike Support Committee was sending car pools over to Richmond every morning; since strike activity on campus had gone into a lull, students showed up to help the oil workers in increasing numbers. For them, it was an unsettling and highly educational experience; the tremendous odds against which the oil workers were fighting served as a rude awakening for many students to the depth of their misconceptions about the "privileged" position of the American white working class. For its own part, the Oil, Chemical, and Atomic Workers (OCAW) local was more than happy to get some outside help. In a highly unprecedented development, it entered into a "mutual aid" pact with the AFT and the TWLF, the terms of which included a promise from each of the parties to help man the others' picket lines when deemed necessary. Close to one thousand people gathered at a rally on February 2 at the San Francisco Labor Temple to declare their solidarity with the stu-

dent-faculty struggle. Aside from the usual liberal-left labor bureaucrats, there were some glimmerings of support from the rank
and file in the appearance of the respective heads of the OCAW
local and the hospital workers' union. To be sure, the possibilities of a real and functional alliance between students and workers was still remote enough, particularly when their common
bond of sympathy went no further than a shared animosity for
the police. Still, the potentialities were for the white radicals
to savor; they forecast a totally new orientation for the student
movement in the coming years, one that would view the white
working class with a new sympathy, concern, and interest.

Early in April, 1969, the conniving of the hierarchy of their
own International forced the local oil workers to go back to work
without having secured a satisfactory contract. Two weeks earlier, the TWLF signed an agreement with Hayakawa's Select
Committee which had the effect of officially ending their
four-and-a-half-month-long strike. By and large, though it offered
some assurances for most of the fifteen demands, the agreement
was a bitter pill that the TWLF found necessary to swallow. Implementation of the more crucial programs built into the
demands—Black Studies, Ethnic Studies, open admissions—would
be piecemeal at best; they would still be plagued by a serious
shortage of resources and by an abundance of political restrictions. Implementation of the principle of self-determination
would not even receive lip-service from the college; it required
the transfer of actual power through granting the TWLF full control over their own educational programs, and this was something
that the college authorities had no intention of doing. Though it
was made to appear official on the surface, the agreement was, in
essence, a mere formality. When the strike failed to regain its
momentum after the semester break, the TWLF was left with no
real bargaining strength; hence it was inevitable that the third
world students would have to accept some sort of settlement on
terms other than their own.

The TWLF leaders were under no illusions about what they
had won for their fifteen demands. The significant gains of the
strike were not to be found in the settlement; rather, they were
implicit in the magnitude and uniqueness of the day-to-day battle

that the students had waged against those in control of the college. The strike had been an extraordinary example of the heightening of contradictions within an American social institution, a demonstration of why it would be ultimately necessary to seize power if revolutionary change was to be realized. The five months of intense conflict demonstrated that the student movement was capable of mounting a formidable and prolonged struggle against seemingly overwhelming odds, for goals it deemed imperative and just. The outpouring of third world community support for the strike attested to the importance of redefining educational issues and programs for the needs of the people most often deprived of the tools and resources available at colleges and universities. As viable outgrowths of the strike, these precedents were augmented by the principles of "self-determination" and the "seizure of power," both of which were firmly established as new theoretical foundations for a movement that had begun by seeking simple reforms within the college and the society. The strike at San Francisco State College marked the culmination of a decade of student activism on the campus and in the community. It was a transitional event, closing out the radical experimentation of the 1960's while at the same time foreshadowing a revolutionary commitment and determination that may well become the trademark of the student movement in the 1970's.

A Note on Sources

The following is a list of sources not explicitly mentioned in the body of the text; it may be considered an informal bibliography. From Chapter IV on, much of our material is drawn from personal involvement and experience. This is particularly true in regard to our description of the strike. Three sources used consistently throughout the book are the *Daily Gater*, the San Francisco State College campus newspaper, and San Francisco's two major dailies, the *Chronicle* and the *Examiner*.

CHAPTER I

For a recapitulation of the activities of the University of California Department of Agricultural Economics, see William Turner's article, "No Dice for Braceros," *Ramparts* vol. 4 no. 8 (Sept. 1965). Upton Sinclair's book was published privately in Pasadena, California, in 1923.

All material on plant facilities, cost estimates, and enrollments was taken from the various documents of the Liaison Committee of the University of California Board of Regents and the California State Board of Education; these documents are mentioned at the appropriate times in the text. Supplementary information was taken from the subcommittee reports of the Master Plan Survey Team, all of which are synopsized in the Master Plan itself. Information on the California tax structure is taken from the state budget for 1968, and from Gerhard Norman Rostvold's book, *Financing California Government* (Belmont, Calif.; Dickenson Co., 1967).

CHAPTER II

The story of the Speaker's Platform was taken from Lloyd Crisp's article, "Soapbox, Campus Style," in Vol. 3 No. 10 of *The liberal democrat*, and from interviews with Crisp and Claire Salop. Carolyn Mullen, an officer in SCOPE who helped found the S.F. State chapter of the DuBois Club, provided valuable information about both organizations; Jefferson Poland answered our queries about early student activism in the Bay Area with four long, brilliant, funny letters. Information on the Tutorial Program was taken from the Program's files, and from interviews with Guy Sandler and Donna Mikkleson. Also see David Horowitz's book, *Student* (New York; Ballantine, 1962) for a résumé of student activism in the early 1960's. Lyle Grosjean spoke with us at length about the Chessman case; Mark Linenthal, Director of the S.F. State Poetry Center, provided information about the "San Francisco Renaissance."

CHAPTER III

The history of the "SNCC Bill" came from the files of the Associated Students. Joe Persico provided us with additional information by allowing us to go through his personal files on his years at S.F. State; he also talked to us about his own experiences as a key figure in the student Programs. The files of the CIP were used extensively in tracing that organization's development. Informal talks with John Pearson, Del Sonsten, Donna Mikkleson, Chuck Crank, and Sharon Gold gave us a number of first-hand accounts of what the student activists were trying to do through the CIP. Jim Nixon and his wife Cynthia talked at length with us about the early history of the Experimental College. Ian Grand, its last director, made the EC files available to us, including the minutes of most of the staff meetings. Material on the political growth of SNCC came, in part, from SNCC activists. Julius Lester's book, *Look Out Whitey, Black Power Gonna Get Your Momma* (New York; Dial Press, 1968) served as another source. Fred Thalheimer talked to us about Jimmy Garrett and the beginning of the BSU. So did Peter Pursley, Ed Washington, and Marianna Waddy. Roger Alvarado provided us with invaluable insight into the turnover in the Tutorial Program. Early BSU literature supplied us with information on its programs and political orientation.

CHAPTER IV

Interviews with Phil Garlington and Peter Pursley helped clear up our confusion about this bewildering phase of campus history. See the marvelous exchange between Marshall Windmiller and John Gerassi ("Trouble at S.F. State") in the April 11, 1968, issue of the *New York Review of Books* (Vol 10, No. 7) for two impassioned accounts of the December 6 events and some revealing insights into both men.

CHAPTER V

Jimmy Garrett's Black Studies proposal is unpublished, as is Nathan Hare's. Both documents were supplied by the Black Studies Department at S.F. State. Elmer Cooper and Jack Alexis were helpful in explaining some of the politicking that took place around Black Studies. Nathan Hare talked to us at length about his personal background, his political beliefs, and his experiences upon coming to S.F. State. John Bunzel's article, "Black Studies at San Francisco State College" was published in *The Public Interest*, No. 13 (Fall, 1968). Hare's reply was sponsored by the BSU, which printed it for campus use and supplied us with a copy.

CHAPTER VI

The information and statistics on the problems of San Francisco's non-white minorities were taken from a report prepared in 1968 by a group of young seminarians for the San Francisco Conference on Race, Religion, and Social Concerns. The report is entitled, *San Francisco: A City in Crisis.* Juan Martinez was very helpful, providing us with information on his background and his activities at S.F. State. See the following books by Frantz Fanon for a more comprehensive understanding of his ideas: *Black Skins, White Masks* (New York; Grove Press, 1967); *The Wretched of the Earth* (New York; Grove Press, 1965); *A Dying Colonialism* (New York; Grove Press, 1967); *Toward the African Revolution* (New York; Monthly Review Press, 1967). Jesus Contreras (MASC), Pat Salavar (PACE), Roger Alvarado and Tony Miranda (LASO), and Mason Wong (ICSA) talked with us about their respective organizations. Joe Persico, Jack Alexis, Fred Thalheimer, and Jack Sheedy all helped to shed some light on the perplexing career of the Carnegie grant.

CHAPTER VII

In addition to his letter of resignation, we quoted from Robert Smith's article, "Higher Education and the Roots of Liberalism," in Vol. 4, No. 10 of *The liberal democrat* (June, 1964); see also Richard Axen, "Behind the Faculty Revolt," and Arthur Bierman, "Creon and Antigone," in the previous issue of the same journal, Vol. 4, No. 9 (May, 1964). Information on the tracking system and related subjects was supplied by the Research Organizing Cooperative in San Francisco. Other sources: *Crisis in California Higher Education* by Arthur Coons (Los Angeles: Ritchie Press, 1968); Mark Tool, *The California State Colleges under the Master Plan,* a report to the statewide Academic Senate of the California State Colleges (San Diego, Calif., 1966); *The Challenge of Achievement,* a staff report to the Joint Committee on Higher Education of the California State Legislature (March, 1969); and Frederick E. Terman, *Engineering Education in California,* a report to the Coordinating Council on Higher Education (March, 1968). Finally, information on Stanford University was furnished by David Ransom, writing in various issues of the *Midpeninsula Observer* (see especially their "Education in California" issue, February 1969), and by Art Heers. For giving some invaluable direction to our research, we are grateful to Ross Koen of the Association of California State College Professors (ACSCP).

CHAPTER VIII

A source used from time to time in this chapter and the next three, usually for purposes of quotations from principals in the strike, was *Shut it Down! A College in Crisis*, a staff report to the National Commission on the Causes and Prevention of Violence (Washington, D.C.: U.S. Government Printing Office, June, 1969). Two sources from the July, 1969, issue of *Ramparts* (Vol. 8, No. 1): Gene Marine and Art Goldberg, "I Want to Kill a Nigger," and Michael Thelwell, "From Cornell." See also the chapter on law enforcement in Jerome Skolnick's *The Politics of Protest* (New York; Ballantine, 1969), another report to the Violence Commission, and "College of San Mateo is not Ready" (interview with Aaron Manganiello), *Open Process* (Vol. 4, No. 8 (January 15, 1969).

CHAPTER IX

Bill Middleton of the BSU was an important source of information on the TWLF general meeting. Helpful in our description of the ideological direction and implications of the strike was Nathan Hare's article in *Ramparts*, Vol. 8, No. 1 (July, 1969), "From San Francisco State." The material on the Trustees' occupations and business interests comes from résumés graciously supplied by the Chancellor's office, California State Colleges.

CHAPTER X

We are indebted to the San Francisco State Legal Defense Committee, and particularly to Robert English, for providing us with material from their files on the police confrontations. The account of Hayakawa's meeting with the black community leaders is taken from our own transcript of an exclusive report by Mal LaPlace on KQED's "Newsroom" program, December 4, 1968.

CHAPTER XI

A vitally important source for our discussion of academic professionalism was Anatole Anton's article, "Sheepskin," in *Leviathan* Vol. 1, No. 9 (March 1970), on the faculty strike and its implications. Helping us to round out our account of the AFT's history and our analysis of the AFT's politics were Art Bierman, Eric Solomon, and especially Bill Stanton.

CHAPTER XII

Reginald Major cleared up some of our questions about President Hayakawa's tampering with the Educational Opportunity Program. See Robert Avakian's article on the Richmond Oil Strike, *The Movement*, Vol 4, No. 5 (April, 1969).

Appendix I: THE FIFTEEN TWLF DEMANDS

1. That all Black Studies courses being taught through various other departments be immediately part of the Black Studies Department and that all the instructors in this department receive full-time pay.
2. That Dr. Hare, Chairman of the Black Studies Department, receive a full professorship and a comparable salary according to his qualifications.
3. That there be a Department of Black Studies which will grant a Bachelor's degree in Black Studies; that the Black Studies Department, chairman, faculty, and staff have the sole power to hire faculty and control and determine the destiny of their department.
4. That all unused slots for black students from fall, 1968, under the Special Admissions program be filled in spring, 1969.
5. That all black students wishing so be admitted in fall, 1969.
6. That twenty full-time teaching positions be allocated to the Department of Black Studies.
7. That Dr. Helen Bedesem be removed from the position of Financial Aids Director; that a black person be hired to replace her; and that Third World people have the power to determine how the Financial Aids office will be administered.
8. That no disciplinary action will be administered in any way to students, workers, teachers, or administrators during and after the strike as consequence of their participation in the strike.
9. That the California State College Trustees will not be allowed to dissolve any black programs on or off San Francisco State College.

10. That George Murray maintain his teaching position on campus for the 1968–69 academic year.

11. That a School of Ethnic Studies for the ethnic groups in the Third World Liberation Front be set up with the students in each particular ethnic organization having the authority and control of the hiring and retention of any faculty member, director, and administrator, as well as the curriculum in a specific area of study.

12. That fifty faculty positions be appropriated to the School of Ethnic Studies, twenty of which would be for the Black Studies Department.

13. That in the spring semester, the College fulfill its commitment to the non-white students in admitting those who apply.

14. That in the fall of 1969 all applications of Third World students be accepted.

15. That George Murray and any other faculty person chosen by Third World people as their teacher be retained in their positions.

Appendix II: STRIKE ISSUES
OF THE SAN FRANCISCO STATE COLLEGE
AFT, LOCAL 1352

I. Strike Issues Directed to the President and Administration of San Francisco State College:
   A. Negotiation of and adoption of comprehensive rules and regulations governing:
      1. Grievance procedures related to faculty affairs.
      2. Personnel decisions (hiring, firing, tenure, promotion, demotion, suspension, lay-off).
      3. Conditions under which pay can be reduced or docked.
      4. Sick leave and other fringe benefits.
      5. Unit and class load assignments for full and part-time faculty.
      6. Stipulation of prerogatives and delineation of authority at various administrative levels.
      7. Guidelines and standards for professional prerequisites (sabbaticals, travel, research leaves).
      8. Faculty involvement in decisions on academic matters (curriculum selection, assignment of faculty and staff, grading, graduation requirements, determination of calendar, admission requirements).
      9. Faculty involvement in decisions governing all local administrative matters (office space, parking).
      10. Recovery of faculty positions bootlegged for administrative purposes.
   B. Protection of Constitutional Rights:
      1. Amnesty for all faculty, students, and staff who have been suspended or have been subjected to other disciplinary action and/or arrested, and withdrawal of outstanding warrants as a result

of activity to end racism at San Francisco State College.

  2. No disciplinary action for exercising constitutionally protected rights.

 C. Black Students' Union and Third World Liberation Front grievances must be resolved and implementation assured.

 D. All agreements on the above to be reduced to a written contract.

II. Strike Issues Directed to the Trustees of the California State Colleges:

 A. All agreements made with the local administrations under (I) above shall be binding upon and accepted by the Trustees.

 B. Sufficient funds shall be provided from current reserve and emergency funds to:

  1. Maintain the present faculty positions. (This will prevent the lay-off of 100 to 125 faculty in the spring semester, 1969.)

  2. Gain new positions to replace those given by various departments and schools to staff a Black Studies' Department and a School of Ethnic Studies.

  3. Protect the revised work loads presently scheduled in many departments for spring, 1969, and assure the same for everyone who requests it.

 C. Rescission of the ten disciplinary rules passed by the Trustees on November 26, 1968.

 D. Approval of the Student Union plan presented by the Associated Students at San Francisco State College.

 E. Cancellation of the proposed changes in Title Five that would take away student control of student body funds.

 F. Recognition of college constitution that emerges from the Constitutional Convention called by the Academic Senate at San Francisco State College.

III. Strike Issues Directed to the Governor and the Legislature:

 A. That a special joint committee of the California State Assembly and Senate be appointed to conduct negotiations with the State College Board of Trustees and the Union to agree on systematic and continuing financing for the proposals under I and II above and to provide the necessary increases in salary required to maintain a qualified faculty at San Francisco State College.

B. That when the special Legislative Committee, the Board of Trustees, and the Union have reached agreement, the Committee report to the next session of the Legislature so that necessary monies may be provided to put the agreement into effect.